Bake until Bubbly

Also by Clifford A. Wright

On Cooking

A Mediterranean Feast

Cucina Rapida

Cucina Paradiso

Italian Pure & Simple

Lasagne

Little Foods of the Mediterranean

Mediterranean Vegetables

Real Stew

Grill Italian

Some Like it Hot

On Politics and History

Facts and Fables: The Arab-Israeli Conflict

*After the Palestine-Israel War:
Limits to U.S. and Israeli Policy*
with Khalil Nakhleh

The Ultimate Casserole Cookbook

Bake until Bubbly

Clifford A. Wright

WILEY

This book is printed on acid-free paper. ♾

Published by John Wiley & Sons, Inc., Hoboken, New Jersey
Published simultaneously in Canada

For general information on our other products and services or for technical support, please contact our Customer Care Department within the United States at (800) 762-2974, outside the United States at (317) 572-3993 or fax (317) 572-4002.

Wiley also publishes its books in a variety of electronic formats. Some content that appears in print may not be available in electronic books. For more information about Wiley products, visit our web site at www.wiley.com.

Visit the author at www.cliffordawright.com

Library of Congress Cataloging-in-Publication Data

Wright, Clifford A.
    Bake until bubbly : the ultimate casserole cookbook / Clifford A. Wright.
        p.   cm.
    ISBN 978-0-471-75447-3 (pbk.)
    1. Casserole cookery.   2. One-dish meals.   I. Title.
    TX693.W73   2008
    641.8'21—dc22   2007015966

Printed in the United States of America

10 9 8 7 6 5 4 3 2 1

Contents

For Sarah K. Pillsbury,

who helped eat all these casseroles.

Acknowledgments

Making casseroles is easy. But when you're testing casserole recipes that yield six or eight servings, someone's got to eat them (I can't bring myself to throw them away). So I'd like to thank the two people who ate most of these casseroles, my youngest son Seri Kattan-Wright and my friend Sarah Pillsbury. A big thank-you goes to Gretchen Rennell Court, who casually suggested to me to write a book on casseroles after I had told her my then latest book was a stew book. I'd also like to thank my agent Angela Miller, who kept encouraging me; my former agent Doe Coover, who thought of the title; and my editor Justin Schwartz, who skillfully kept my flights of fancy in the casserole.

Introduction

E VERY HOME COOK who thinks "kids," "family," "crowd," or "party," thinks "casserole." This amazing dish is a favorite of home cooks and it requires only an oven and a casserole. Every mom knows that casseroles are the most versatile preparation for the home cook, and when dad cooks for the kids he can throw some food into a casserole, put it in the oven, and voilà, dinner! Everybody who grew up on Tuna Noodle Casserole (page 261) or Macaroni and Cheese (page 264) remembers that bubbling dish brought to the table with its top dappled golden brown, piping hot and inviting. Mom yelled "come and get it" and we did.

My passion for casseroles was born from memories of my childhood and my mother's Lasagna (page 238), thick and rich and gooey and delicious. But once I had three children of my own, casseroles were the solution to many frenzied nights. I was a single father and although I was lucky to have kids who would eat everything and anything, we all loved the simplicity, ease, and satisfaction of a well-baked casserole. It was a dish we could look forward to.

In this book, the casserole recipes range from hidden and delicious treasures from the Old World such as the marvelous Pounti (page 320), a flavorful vegetable flan of Swiss chard from the Auvergne region of France that even Francophiles don't seem to known about, to heart-healthy ones such as Casserole of New England Spring Vegetables (page 344), to some classic American ones updated for modern times such Green Bean Casserole (page 328). Others will be international favorites like Moussaka (page 90), and finally, innovative and easily put together recipes like Turkey Meatball

Casserole (page 146), which so wowed a crowd at a party I cooked for that they're still talking about it.

The casserole is a versatile preparation because it's easy to put together—often utilizing leftovers—and has something for everyone. An appealing attribute of the casserole is its ability to fulfill many purposes: as a family dinner-at-home, an elegant dish for company, a popular dish to bring to a potluck, a surprising leftover, a brunch dish, a next-day appetizer, and a dish to be made for breakfast or dessert. Waking on a Sunday morning to the aroma of coffee, and a breakfast casserole of thick slices of French toast stuffed with chopped Granny Smith apples and cream cheese served with boysenberry sauce, will knock you right out of your slippers (page 25). Many of the breakfast casseroles in the book can actually be prepared the night before and plunked into the oven in the morning.

One of my favorite dessert casseroles was the Pear Crisp (page 406) my kids and I made in late August, when our pear tree was groaning from the weight of its luscious orbs ripening and we'd try to beat the squirrels to them. We'd cut them up and arrange them in a casserole with cinnamon and then blanket them with a streusel made of flour, butter, and sugar before baking until bubbly. (Hey, what a great name for a book!)

The versatility of leftovers for casserole is so great that, when my kids were young, they actually asked me to first make a meatloaf, then grill skirt steak and chicken so that we would have leftovers in order to make a casserole (page 40). They were unimpressed when I tried to explain that you *use* leftovers, you don't make them. Oh well, I was a good dad and would make it from scratch 'cause I loved it too.

My favorite casseroles are Italian-American ones because that's what I grew up on. I fondly remember Baked Rigatoni and Sausages (page 210) emerging from the oven piping hot, filled with plump bursting Italian sausages, bubbling with tomato ragù, oozing mozzarella cheese and creamy ricotta cheese. I make this casserole often and not only is it easy, the leftovers are even better. My casseroles will make at least two meals for my family. Sometimes my oldest son, Ali, will reheat the baked rigatoni on a Sunday morning and have it with a fried egg on top. Although Americans love casseroles as we know by the ubiquitous Tuna Noodle Casserole, Macaroni and Cheese, Lasagna, or Sweet Potato Casserole, the first casseroles came from the Old World. Many of those delightful dishes are now part of the repertoire of American cooks, dishes such as Moussaka (page 90) or

Eggplant Parmesan (page 353). And don't forget that surprise guests or friends of the kids coming over for dinner are no problem at all because these casseroles are a menu for six and sometimes more.

Casseroles were invented to be economical and convenient dishes made for large groups of people. They still are. Although you could, you hardly would make a casserole for fewer than four people. In an earlier America, casseroles were called "hot dishes" and they were often associated with church suppers and barn-raisings. Women would often try to outdo each other in providing the tastiest fare, and as a result some wonderful casseroles came into being, often rich in cream and cheese. Many of us grew up on those rich casseroles of white sauce and cheese. Mothers cooked differently then, and today those casseroles based on high-sodium canned or frozen foods loaded with preservatives you can't pronounce are not as appealing. Today we're more concerned with a healthier style of feeding our families. In the olden days Chicken Divan (page 124), a classic American casserole, was made with frozen broccoli and cream of celery soup. My modern version uses fresh broccoli and natural chicken broth in a luscious dish flavored with Parmesan cheese, sherry, cream, and a touch of curry powder as the bed (*divan*) for the thinly sliced boneless organic chicken breast.

The History of the Casserole

The history of the casserole is the history of both the cooking vessel called a casserole and the name of the preparation cooked in a casserole. The history of the casserole is old, but probably not so ancient as Mesopotamia or Egypt where stews and porridges predominated. We know that casseroles existed by classical Greek times. From Aristophanes' play *The Wasps,* where a character talks about being "smothered in casserole," we know they were a good thing. The Greek author Athenaeus tells us that in the book *The Banquet,* written by Philoxenus of Leucas, he describes a seafood casserole, but says he prefers the frying pan. The special excellence of the *vulva eiectitia*, the vulva of a sow which has miscarried, is mentioned by Hipparchus, author of the Egyptian *Iliad*, in these lines: "rather, let me be cheered by a casserole or the lovely countenance of a miscarried matrix." Alexis, a Greek poet, introduces a cook in *The Lovelorn Lass* who has this to say about making salt fish: "Nevertheless, I mean to sit down here and reckon the cost of my menu, to plan what I must get first, and how I must season each dish. First comes this piece of *horaion* [a kind of smoked mackerel]; that cost a penny. I must wash it well. Then I will sprinkle seasoning in a casserole, place the slice in it, pour over it some white wine, stir it in oil and stew it until it is soft as marrow, covering it generously with a garnish of silphium." Later, Alexis describes another casserole: "first of all put some marjoram at the bottom of a large casserole, over that the liqueur, diluted with vinegar in just measure, coloring it with must and silphium; then whip it vigorously."

Where does the casserole come from? The explanation given in Alan Davidson's *Oxford Companion to Food*, who used John Ayto's *The Diner's Dictionary* (Oxford University Press, 1993), claims the word *casserole* has a complicated history. It starts with a classical Greek term for a cup (*kuáthos*), progressing to the Latin word *cattia*, which could mean both ladle and pan—then becoming the Provençal *casa* that transforms into the Old French word *casse* that gives the words today *cassolle* or *casserole*. This is indeed complicated, too complicated, and in fact, incorrect. Although my *Merriam-Webster's Collegiate Dictionary* gives the same etymology, a more convincing explanation was given by Joan Corominas (1905–1997), Professor of Romance Philology at the University of Chicago and author of the definitive four-volume *Diccionario crítico etimológico de la lengua castellana*. The English word *casserole* does indeed derive from the French word *cassolle*, which in turn derives from the medieval Occitan word *cassa*. But this word is related to the original Spanish word *cassa,* which also gives the modern Spanish word for the casserole, *cazuela*. All these words come directly from the medieval Spanish *cassa*, which is not derived from the Latin. Where does the medieval Spanish word *cassa*, meaning "a receptacle for carrying liquid," come from? Possibly, Corominas argues, it comes from *cacherulo*, a Mozarab word meaning a casserole. Mozarab was the language spoken by the Christians living in Islamic Spain in the twelfth century. *Cacherulo*, in turn, is a word derived from the Arabic *qas'at*, a large shallow earthenware bowl or pan. On the other hand, it may be derived from a proto-Hispanic word, but it doesn't derive from either Latin or Greek.

Some casseroles, such as the famous French Cassoulet (a simplified version is on page 60), have colorful apocryphal stories. One legend attributes its invention to the townspeople of Castelnaudary who in 1355 were then surrounded by the army of the Black Prince, Edward the Prince of Wales. The besieged townspeople gathered all their remaining food to cook in a huge casserole, belying the succulent tastes of this bean casserole made with duck confit, garlic sausages, lamb, and pork. And so was invented cassoulet, which simply means "casserole" in French.

In medieval times cooks would bring their uncooked casserole dishes to the town baker who would cook them according to the desires and instructions of their clients. This was before in-home ovens were common and when people toiled from dawn to dusk.

The Modern Casserole

The first mention of casseroles in English was noted in the posthumous 1706 edition of the dictionary by Edward Phillips, an English lexicographer. The English had inherited the casserole from the French, and in those days it usually meant a dish made of cooked rice that was molded to the casserole and filled with a savory and creamy stuffing, usually of either chicken or sweetbreads. As a result, the word *casserole* also came to mean the border of a dish. Early America loved casseroles too, as we can see from the "Mutton Casserolles" recipe published by Mrs. Lettice Bryan in *The Kentucky House-wife*, the first cookbook published in the state of Kentucky in 1839 (see page 98). But by the late nineteenth century the casserole was changing and starting on a long road to its position of less-than-sophisticated cooking.

In 1912 Marion Harris Neil, principal of the Philadelphia Practical School of Cookery, said in her *How to Cook in Casserole Dishes*, "there is no doubt that the fashion of cooking in casseroles . . . has come to stay in this country." She defines a casserole as "a dish, the material for which in many instances is first prepared in the sauté or frying pan and then transferred to the earthenware pan [casserole] to finish cooking by a long, slow process which develops the true flavors of the food being cooked." She goes on "when casserole cookery is thoroughly understood, many combinations of food and many inexpensive viands will be put to use and very palatable results obtained." In Fannie Farmer's classic *The Boston Cooking-School Cook Book*, her casserole is made from leftovers.

Well, not too much has changed since 1912, and you will find Mrs. Neil's words confirmed in this book as these recipes make, as she points out, "in every way for economy—economy of materials, time, and labor." We often forget that at bottom, and simply, the casserole is a labor-saving device.

Originally, a casserole was always an earthenware vessel, although today one will find ceramic and glass (Pyrex) to be used more commonly. In any case, a casserole should never be made of metal, although it can be made of enamel-glazed cast iron. That said, you will find casseroles made of cast aluminum and other metal. The non-metal casseroles were important because they are easy to clean; one never has to use elbow grease to clean a casserole.

As Russ Parsons, food columnist for the *Los Angeles Times*, wrote, "there are few names more blighted than casserole [in culinary history] . . . . But it's important to remember one thing: Casseroles don't kill palates—cooks do." The reason for the proliferation of the casserole in American cooking, as Parsons points out in his article on the history of the casserole, is that of the production by American potteries of these inexpensive cooking vessels gave it greater availability to the common people. Today's casseroles—the cooking vessels—come in many shapes ranging from oval and shallow casseroles made of enameled cast iron to round earthenware casseroles to rectangular casseroles with two handles or protuberances for lifting to small, one-person ramekins.

The poor reputation of American casseroles (the preparation) has its roots in the time before World War II, when the confluence of mass produced processed and canned foods, the availability of the casserole, and the cultural emphasis on economy and convenience produced some truly ghastly dishes—none of which are in this book. The casserole made of leftover overcooked diced chicken breast with celery, water chestnuts, overcooked broccoli covered with canned cream of mushroom soup, and a quart of Velveeta topped with crushed Fritos has had its plug pulled and is banished forever to the dustbin of culinary history.

The canned foods that became a staple of all American casseroles in the third quarter of the twentieth century gave the cook "instant leftovers," in the words of Russ Parsons. What this means is that the cook could open a couple of cans, mix their contents in the casserole, and bake. The delicate Béchamel sauce was replaced with canned cream of whatever soup, the fresh bread crumb au gratin topping was replaced with packaged cracker crumbs or crushed flakes cereal, and the delicious taste of Gruyère, Emmentaler (this is what Swiss cheese is called in Switzerland), and Parmigiano–Reggiano (the authentic and original Parmesan) cheese was replaced with processed cheeses or cheese-like food products such as Velveeta. This was indeed easy, but convenience trumped taste and produced dinners that were really not very healthy at all.

There was no doubt that the emphasis on convenience and economy rather than flavor and taste gave the American casserole its poor reputation by the 1970s. Look at the advice on the advantages of cooking in a casserole, given by *The American Women's Cook Book* published by Consolidated Book Publishers in 1940: "The casserole saves dish-washing, the casserole makes it possible to use leftovers, food cooked in this way needs little watching, a whole meal may be cooking in the oven." All this is true, but at no time do they talk about anything tasting good. In this book you're going to find flavor and taste as the Number-1 concern.

American Casseroles

Although the history of casseroles begins in Europe—and many famous casseroles come from the Old World—American cookery has truly exploited this cooking vessel to the fullest. That's probably because we were the first nation to mass-produce home ovens. And American home cooks started experimenting. But by the twentieth century the American casserole was being transformed by both modern technology and economics. The Great Depression of the 1930s meant that home cooks needed economical dishes for families, and the casserole was it. In 1934, Campbell's Soup Company made its first cream of mushroom soup and, because it was cheap, it quickly became an essential ingredient in American casseroles. In the post-World War II era, modern technology again influenced the American kitchen, offering convenience above taste. By now the American casserole, nothing more than an agglomeration of lumped together canned and processed foods, was in a sorry state.

Today, Americans have a lot of different regional names for casseroles such as stratas, scrambles, pilafs, poofs, perloos, puddings, pies, surprises, suppers, shroups, royales, stifles, supremes, bakes, gratins, cobblers, crisps, crunches, delights, dishes, hot dishes, hot pots, medleys, and melodies, but they are all casseroles. A stifle is a kind of casserole they made in Old Cape Cod (especially on the Lower Cape, where they would use haddock, cod, eels, or oysters). The word suggests that the casserole gets smothered with aromatic ingredients until it transforms during the baking process. A perloo is considered by some to be a casserole. But a perloo, a word that derives from *pilao* or *pilaf*, is a rice dish in the South. It is not necessarily cooked in a casserole or baked in an oven. A strata is simply a casserole made in layers. A hot dish is typically what they call a casserole in Minnesota and some other northern states. A gratin is simply a casserole that has a topping, usually bread crumbs, that gets browned under a broiler or in the oven. A surprise is just that, a casserole that has unexpected ingredients. I'm not sure what a shroup is, but James Villas, author of *Crazy for Casseroles*, published in 2003, says he thinks it's a combination of "shrimp" and "soup." A poof is a casserole with beaten eggs that "poofs" up. A supper is a casserole usually made for a large gathering, such as a church supper.

The Casserole

As mentioned before, the casserole is the name both of the dish prepared and the vessel in which it is cooked. In this section, I'm speaking about the vessel. Casseroles can come in many shapes and be made of a variety of materials. They can be round, square, oval, or rectangular. They can be made of glazed or unglazed earthenware, enameled cast iron, cast aluminum, anodized aluminum, aluminum-lined heavy copper, Pyrex, or ceramic. They can be deep or shallow. Typically, they have two handles for lifting (but not always) and sometimes they have lids. But all casseroles share the same unique feature that makes them casseroles: They all go into an oven to bake and they all go to the table to be served from the casserole. There are some caveats of course. Casseroles could be cooked stove-top, especially if you have flame-proof ones, but in this book all the casseroles are baked. I have all kinds of casseroles and they all get used for different foods depending on bulk and other factors (there is a list below).

In the recipes I will specify casserole size. But you will have to use what you've got, so have at least two casseroles at home. A couple of recipes call for a rather large casserole, so if you don't have one, you may need to use your roasting pan or buy an aluminum throw-away one. The ingredients should fill the casserole and still leave about an inch of space below the rim. The size of the casserole matters because if the ingredients are spread too shallow or thin they'll dry out while baking. If they are overflowing they may not get cooked and you may have a mess on your hands.

Almost all casseroles can be prepared ahead of time and refrigerated or frozen. A rule of thumb is that casseroles containing potatoes, milk, cream, sour cream, or fish don't handle freezing very well. It's also wiser to not freeze baked casseroles and to use them as leftovers instead, keeping them in the refrigerator for up to a week.

Casserole Size

Here is a basic guide to casserole capacity equivalents when using the recipes or when shopping to buy a casserole. Ideally, you should have several casseroles of different sizes, with the 2-quart (12 × 9 × 2-inch) casserole as the workhorse casserole.

	Approximate Dimensions	Approximate Liquid Capacity
rectangular	8 × 6 × 1½-inch	1-quart
oval	9 × 1½-inch	1-quart
rectangular	12 × 9 × 2-inch	2-quart
round	9 × 3-inch	2½-quart
rectangular	12 × 8½ × 2½-inch	3-quart
rectangular	13 × 10 × 2-inch	4-quart

If you're interested for shopping purposes, below is a list of casseroles that I use, arranged by capacity, which represent about ninety percent of the casseroles I own.

10-quart glazed earthenware (Italian), round (13 × 4½)

6-quart Le Creuset enameled cast-iron, oval with lid (12 × 4½)

5-quart glazed earthenware (Spanish), round (10 × 4½)

4-quart Emile Henry ceramic, rectangular (12 × 9½ × 2½)

4-quart aluminum, rectangular (14 × 9 × 2½)

3½-quart copper, round (8 × 4)

3-quart Emile Henry, ceramic, rectangular (12 × 8½ × 2½)

3-quart unglazed earthenware (Spanish), round with lid (11 × 3)

2½-quart glazed earthenware (Spanish), round (9 × 3)

2-quart Emile Henry ceramic soufflé, round (8 × 3½)

2-quart Portmeirion ceramic, rectangular (12 × 9½ × 2)

2-quart glazed earthenware (Spanish), rectangular (12½ × 9½ × 1¾)

2-quart Pyrex glass, square (8 × 8 × 2)

1½-quart glazed earthenware (Spanish), round (10 × 2)

1-quart Le Creuset enameled cast iron, oval (9 × 1½)

½-quart glazed earthenware (Spanish) (6 × 4½ × 1½)

Organization of *Bake until Bubbly*

The recipe chapters are straightforward. You start with breakfast and brunch casseroles and then move into the main-dish casserole chapters of meat, poultry, dairy, and game, seafood, pasta and noodles, rice and grains, and vegetables. But there are two vegetable chapters. They contain recipes that can be served as main courses or casseroles to be served as side dishes—it's your choice. The first of the vegetable casserole chapters is vegetable recipes that contain some meat. The second vegetable casserole chapter consists of all-vegetable recipes, that is, recipes without meat. Finally, the last chapter is desserts.

When I make casseroles I usually will cook something else, depending on the casserole itself and what it contains. Sometimes rich casseroles need only a light salad as an accompaniment. It's your choice, and I'll make recommendations in the recipes themselves.

Breakfast and Brunch Casseroles

Sausage and Egg Casserole

This casserole recipe comes from my mom who called it "make ahead breakfast" casserole. Waking up in the morning to this scrumptious casserole is a delight. When it comes out of the oven, it has an appetizing golden yellow top, and it's light tasting, yet satisfying for a day of activity. I've adapted my mom's recipe only slightly by incorporating some ideas from the breakfast sausage casserole recipe as it is done at the Summerfield Inn Bed & Breakfast in Abingdon, Virginia. It's a popular breakfast casserole in North Carolina too. • **Makes 6 to 8 servings**

1 pound pork breakfast sausages or Cajun-style sausages, casings removed
8 slices hearty white bread, cubed
1 cup (about 3 ounces) shredded mild cheddar cheese
Salt and freshly ground black pepper
8 large eggs, lightly beaten
1 teaspoon dry mustard
2⅔ cups milk

1 Lightly butter a 12 × 9 × 2-inch baking casserole.

2 In a skillet, cook the sausage meat over medium heat, stirring and breaking it up with a wooden spoon, until it loses its color, about 15 minutes.

3 Layer the bread cubes, sausage, and cheese in the baking casserole, then toss gently. Season with salt and pepper. In a bowl, combine the eggs and dry mustard, then pour in the milk to blend. Pour this egg mixture over the bread, sausage, and cheese mixture. Cover with plastic wrap and refrigerate overnight.

4 Preheat the oven to 350°F.

5 Remove the casserole from the refrigerator 30 minutes before baking it. Uncover and gently toss the bread mixture to re-coat the bread on top with the egg mixture. Season with a little salt and pepper. Bake until congealed, bubbling, and golden yellow on top, about 45 minutes. Serve hot.

Eggs and Hash Brown Casserole

Although this is an ideal casserole to make when you have leftover hash browns and breakfast sausage, it's actually good enough to whip up for any breakfast. The recipe is written assuming you're using raw potatoes. However, if you are using leftover cooked potatoes, just omit Step 2. If you don't have leftover breakfast sausages, cook the amount indicated in a lightly oiled pan over medium heat, turning frequently, for about 20 minutes.

• Makes 4 servings

1 tablespoon unsalted butter
1 tablespoon vegetable oil
5 cups (about 1½ pounds) shredded russet potatoes
1 pound pork breakfast sausages, cooked, cut in half, and drained
1½ cups (about ¼ pound) shredded Colby cheese
1½ cups (about ¼ pound) shredded Monterey Jack cheese
Salt
5 large eggs, beaten with ¼ cup whole milk

1. Preheat the oven to 350°F. Coat a 13 x 9 x 2-inch baking casserole with 1 tablespoon of butter.

2. Preheat a large cast-iron skillet over medium-high heat for 10 minutes. Add the vegetable oil and spread it over the surface and sides of the skillet. Once the oil is hot, spread the shredded potatoes over the skillet to cover the entire surface evenly. Cook until the potatoes are golden brown and crisp on the bottom, monitoring the heat so the potatoes don't burn, about 10 minutes. Using the edge of a metal spatula, cut the potatoes into four wedges. Turn each wedge over and cook until they are golden brown on the bottom, about 10 minutes.

3. In a bowl, combine the hash browns, sausages, and both cheeses. Season with salt and transfer to the baking casserole. Pour the egg mixture over. Cover the baking casserole with foil and bake for 30 minutes. Remove the foil and bake until the top is bubbling and golden, about 30 minutes more. Serve hot.

Egg Casserole

This recipe intrigued me, as it did Diana Rattray, a Mississippi-based recipe collector who writes for southernfood.about.com, and who adapted it from a 1953 newspaper clipping. This is actually an adaptation of Rattray's adapted recipe, since I've never seen the original. It has an old-timey look, and I can easily picture some society ladies eating this egg casserole for brunch at the club. • **Makes 4 servings**

1 cup fresh bread crumbs (see Note)
2 tablespoons melted unsalted butter
8 large eggs
4 medium tomatoes, sliced

For the cheese sauce

3 tablespoons unsalted butter
3 tablespoons all-purpose flour
½ teaspoon salt or more as needed
⅛ teaspoon freshly ground black pepper or white pepper
1½ cups milk
1 cup grated sharp cheddar cheese

1 Preheat the oven to 350°F. Lightly butter a 9-inch square baking casserole.

2 In a bowl, toss the bread crumbs with 2 tablespoons of melted butter and set aside. Bring a large saucepan of water to a boil over high heat, then gently lower the eggs into the boiling water and boil for 10 minutes exactly. Remove the eggs and immediately cool them in a bowl of cold water. Remove the eggshells and cut each egg in half lengthwise. Arrange the eggs, yolk side up, in the baking casserole. Arrange the sliced tomatoes over the eggs.

Bread for Breakfast

Several breakfast casseroles call for bread as a major part of the dish. Generally, you should use local artisanal or freshly baked breads that many supermarkets now make themselves. It is best to avoid any bread sold in plastic bags as these will not have the full fresh flavor needed for a superlative casserole. Look for non-sourdough fine-quality hearty wheat breads, such as French baguettes, French or Italian country breads, and similar breads usually sold without any wrapping other than an opened paper bread bag. The crusts are always used unless the recipe specifies that they are not.

③ Meanwhile, in a saucepan, melt 3 tablespoons of butter over medium heat. Stir in the flour, ½ teaspoon salt, and pepper to form a smooth roux. Cook for 1 minute, stirring constantly. Remove the saucepan from the heat and whisk in the milk. Place the saucepan over low heat and cook the sauce until it is thick and smooth, stirring frequently, about 15 minutes. Add the cheese and stir until the cheese melts and the sauce is smooth.

④ Pour the cheese sauce over the tomatoes. Sprinkle the top with the bread crumbs and season lightly with more salt, if desired. Bake until the top is light golden brown, about 20 minutes. Serve hot.

Note: A cup of bread crumbs can be made by crumbling two ½-inch-thick slices of 5¼ x 3-inch French or Italian bread in a food processor.

Cheese Strata

I really like this cheese strata, which ends up almost like a soufflé, and prefer serving it for brunch rather than breakfast. I usually serve it with some skillet-fried ham, a side of sour cream, and a few croissants. It's really quite wonderful this way and can easily tide you over until supper. A good-quality bread, such as a French country loaf, is important here. I've adapted this recipe from the one served at the Southwood Manor Bed & Breakfast in Ridge Spring, South Carolina. • **Makes 6 to 8 servings**

12 slices hearty white bread, crusts removed
1 cup (about 3 ounces) shredded Swiss cheese
1 cup (about 3 ounces) shredded mild or sharp cheddar cheese
4 large eggs
2 tablespoons very finely chopped onion
1 teaspoon salt
½ teaspoon dry mustard mixed with ¼ teaspoon water
½ teaspoon cayenne pepper
2½ cups whole milk

1. Lightly butter a 12 x 9 x 2-inch baking casserole.

2. Arrange half the bread over the bottom of the baking casserole and sprinkle with both cheeses. Cover with the remaining bread.

3. In a bowl, beat the eggs, onion, salt, mustard mixture, and cayenne pepper to blend. Stir in the milk and pour this mixture over the bread. Cover with plastic wrap and refrigerate overnight.

4. Preheat the oven to 350°F.

5. Remove the casserole from the refrigerator 30 minutes before you want to bake it. Uncover and bake until a knife inserted in the center of the strata comes out clean, 45 to 55 minutes. Serve hot.

Egg and Bacon Strata

This strata is a delight for a Sunday brunch with a few friends. The first time you make it you will immediately start dreaming up alternative fillings. No problem, it's a versatile casserole. After you make this version with bacon you can start replacing the bacon with, let's say, a cup of diced ham and a half-cup of sautéed sliced mushrooms. Or you could use Swiss cheese and diced cooked chicken, or cooked broccoli and Gruyère cheese, tomatoes and cooked pork sausage, or . . . well, you get the idea.

• Makes 6 servings

4 cups ½-inch cubes hearty white bread or French bread

2 cups (about 6 ounces) shredded mild or sharp cheddar cheese

½ cup finely chopped onion

8 large eggs

¾ cup half and half

2 teaspoons Dijon mustard

1 teaspoon salt

¼ teaspoon freshly ground black pepper

6 thick-cut bacon slices, cooked and crumbled

1 Preheat the oven to 350°F. Butter a 12 × 9 × 2-inch baking casserole.

2 In a large bowl, toss the bread cubes, cheese, and onion together, then arrange this mixture evenly in the baking casserole. In the same bowl, beat the eggs, half and half, mustard, salt, and black pepper to blend. Pour this egg mixture over the bread cubes. Sprinkle the bacon over. Bake until a knife inserted into the center of the strata comes out clean, about 25 minutes. Serve hot.

Beechwood Breakfast Strata

Although called a breakfast casserole, this dish is best had for brunch after a Sunday morning of shoveling snow. It is a substantial dish that is adapted from the one served at the Beechwood Inn Bed and Breakfast in Clayton, Georgia. Breakfast casseroles are popular at B&B's because they can be prepared the night before and baked in the morning. So, this is a perfect dish for anyone with house guests or a large family. It's even more perfect because the leftovers make a good supper. The only down side is that those house guests might stay too long if you keep serving them such good food. To make the dish lighter, leave out the ricotta cheese and a half pound of the Monterey Jack cheese. • **Makes 8 to 10 servings**

1 cup small broccoli florets
½ pound pork breakfast sausages, casings removed, crumbled
1 pound white button mushrooms, stems removed, caps thinly sliced
Freshly ground black pepper
½ pound white loaf bread or French bread, sliced ½ inch thick,
    crusts removed
1½ cups milk
½ pound ricotta cheese, at room temperature
¼ cup unbleached all-purpose flour
1 tablespoon baking powder
½ teaspoon salt
9 large eggs
1½ pounds freshly grated or shredded Monterey Jack cheese
¼ pound freshly grated or shredded sharp cheddar cheese
2 cups chopped scallions, green part only

1. Lightly butter a 15 × 10-inch baking casserole or roasting pan.

2. Bring a saucepan of water to a boil over high heat. Add the broccoli florets and cook until they are slightly tender, about 4 minutes. Drain and set aside.

3. In a skillet, cook the sausage over medium heat, breaking it up with a wooden spoon, until it is brown, about 6 minutes. Add the mushrooms to the skillet and cook, stirring frequently, until softened, about 4 minutes. Season with black pepper. Remove from the heat and cool slightly.

4. Toast the bread slices until they are golden, then sprinkle them with salt. Line the baking casserole with the toast. In a large bowl, using an electric mixer, beat the milk and ricotta cheese until well blended. Whisk in the flour, baking powder, and salt. Add the eggs, one at a time, whisking until each is fully incorporated before adding the next one. Stir in the sausage-and-mushroom mixture, the grated cheeses, the broccoli, and the scallions. Pour this mixture over the toasts in the baking casserole. Cover tightly with plastic wrap and refrigerate overnight.

5. Preheat the oven to 350°F.

6. Remove the casserole from the refrigerator 30 minutes before you want to bake it. Uncover and bake until the strata is golden brown on top and the sides are set but the center jiggles slightly when the casserole is gently shaken, about 1 hour. Cool for 5 to 10 minutes before serving.

Milk for Casseroles

You can use whatever milk you like in the recipes, but I do specify particular kinds of milk in certain recipes when I think it makes a difference. So, for example, I use whole milk when I make Béchamel (white) sauce. But you can use fat-free, one-, or two percent milk if you'd like to reduce calorie intake.

Deviled Egg and
Cream Cheese Brunch

S tuffed eggs have a long history dating back to at least Roman times. In the Middle Ages court chefs also made stuffed eggs. However, the term "deviled," meaning spicy hot food, first made its appearance in print in the eighteenth century, at which time, we can suppose, deviled eggs have their beginning as well. But it wasn't until the twentieth century when they became very popular in America. This Southern brunch dish is rich and delicious, and should be served as soon as it comes out of the oven because it cools quickly. • **Makes 6 servings**

For the deviled eggs

6 large eggs
½ cup mayonnaise
1½ tablespoons freshly squeezed lemon juice
1½ teaspoons dry mustard
½ teaspoon salt
¼ teaspoon cayenne pepper

For the mushrooms

1 tablespoon unsalted butter
¼ pound white button mushrooms, sliced

For the shrimp sauce

1¼ pounds small shrimp, peeled and deveined, shells reserved
2 cups water
2 cups heavy cream
½ pound cream cheese, cut into 1-inch cubes
½ teaspoon curry powder

1. Preheat the oven to 350°F. Lightly butter a 9 × 9 × 2-inch baking casserole.

2. Bring a large saucepan of water to a boil over high heat, then gently lower the eggs into the boiling water and boil for 10 minutes exactly. Remove the eggs, then immediately cool them in a bowl of cold water. Remove the eggshells and cut each egg in half lengthwise. Scoop out all the yolks and place them in a mixing bowl. Set the whites aside.

3. Mash the yolks well and then beat in the mayonnaise. When the yolk mixture is completely smooth, mix in the lemon juice, mustard, salt, and cayenne pepper. Taste to adjust the seasoning. Spoon this yolk mixture into the egg white halves, dividing it evenly. Place the stuffed eggs in the baking casserole.

4. In a small skillet, melt the butter over medium heat. Add the mushrooms and cook, stirring often, until they are brown and wilted, about 8 minutes. Turn the heat off and leave the mushrooms in the pan until needed.

5. Place the shrimp shells in a saucepan and pour in the water. Bring to a boil over high heat and continue to boil until the liquid is reduced by a little more than half, about 15 minutes. Strain the shrimp broth into a bowl. Discard the shells and return the shrimp broth to the same saucepan.

6. Finely chop 1/3 of the peeled shrimp in a blender. Add the cream and blend until the shrimp are and the mixture is almost smooth. Stir the cream mixture into the shrimp broth. Let the shrimp sauce cool until it is lukewarm.

7. Stir the cream cheese and curry powder into the shrimp sauce. Pour the sauce over the eggs in the baking casserole. Sprinkle with the mushrooms and remaining peeled shrimp. Bake until the top is bubbling, about 30 minutes. Serve hot.

Spinach Breakfast Casserole

One New Year's Day, my girlfriend and I found ourselves at a friend's country house where we were responsible for the potluck brunch. There were eight overnight guests and we wanted to give them something soothing and delicious for the New Year yet wouldn't take too much effort to make. So my girlfriend, Sarah Pillsbury, dreamed this up after saying, "I want something Greek." It was very well received and appreciated by the guests because eating the spinach just felt like we were doing something very healthy, especially after the party from the previous evening. I steamed the spinach before the celebrations began on New Year's Eve just in case I woke up with a hangover. Feel free to do the same. • **Makes 8 servings**

3½ pounds spinach leaves without stems, rinsed well

¼ cup extra-virgin olive oil

2 large garlic cloves, finely chopped

1 tablespoon finely chopped fresh mint or dill (optional)

Salt and freshly ground black pepper

10 to 12 large eggs

½ pound feta cheese, crumbled

2 cups plain whole yogurt

1. Preheat the oven to 350°F. Lightly oil two 12 × 9 × 2-inch baking casseroles.

2. Put the spinach into a large empty pot. The water adhering to the spinach from rinsing it will be enough liquid to help steam the spinach. Cover and cook over medium-high heat, turning the spinach a few times to ensure it cooks evenly, until it wilts, about 5 minutes. Transfer the spinach to a strainer and press out the excess water with the back of a wooden spoon. Squeeze the spinach with your hands to remove any remaining water and ensure the spinach is as dry as possible.

3. Chop the spinach and toss it in a bowl with ¼ cup of olive oil, the garlic, and mint or dill, if using. Season the spinach mixture to taste with salt and pepper. Spread the spinach mixture over the bottom of the baking casseroles, dividing equally.

4. Make 5 or 6 indentations in the spinach mixture in each baking casserole. Crack 1 egg into each indentation. Season the eggs with salt and pepper. Sprinkle the crumbled feta cheese around, but not on top, of the yolks. Bake 20 minutes for soft-cooked eggs or 35 minutes for hard-cooked eggs. Serve hot with the yogurt on the side.

Sailor's Omelet

This New England recipe is adapted from the *United States Regional Cookbook*, a fascinating book exploring American regional cuisine and first published in 1939 by the Culinary Arts Institute of Chicago. Having lived in New England for fifteen years, I was surprised never to have heard of it and was unable to find out anything about it. This old-fashioned, omelet-like casserole does have the look and taste of something a local fisherman might have whipped up in the morning before casting off. In any case, it makes a great breakfast casserole along with some fried breaded oysters on the side. • **Makes 4 servings**

6 large eggs, separated
1 teaspoon anchovy paste
1 teaspoon finely chopped fresh parsley
Salt
1 tablespoon unsalted butter
Paprika

1 Preheat the oven to 350°F.

2 In a large bowl, using an electric mixer with the whisk attached or a hand-cranked whisk, beat the whites until stiff peaks form. In another bowl, using a whisk, beat the yolks, anchovy paste, parsley, and a little salt until creamy and completely blended. Fold the whites into the yolk mixture until the whites are streaked with the yolks.

3 Place the butter in a 9 × 9 × 2-inch baking casserole or a 9-inch round baking casserole. Transfer the baking casserole to the oven until the butter melts. Remove the baking casserole from the oven and twirl the baking casserole to coat the sides with the melted butter. Pour the egg mixture into the hot baking casserole.

4 Bake until the top is brown and the eggs are set, about 20 minutes. Sprinkle with paprika and serve hot.

Stuffed French Toast Casserole

This breakfast casserole is perfect for when you have sleep-over guests. It's quite luscious and feeds a good number of people, and can even be kept warm in the oven should you decide to bake it before everyone else wakes up. It's best to make it in the baking casserole I call for, which is basically a soufflé dish, because the bread can soak better in this deep dish. This French toast is not sweet at all, so if you want it sweeter, use the suggested syrups and confectioners' sugar. • **Makes 6 servings**

Eight 1-inch-thick slices stale or fresh white loaf bread,
    crusts removed, cubed
½ pound cream cheese, cut into cubes
1 large Granny Smith apple, peeled, cored, and chopped
6 large eggs
1 cup whole milk
1½ teaspoons ground cinnamon
3 tablespoons confectioners' sugar, sifted (optional)
Maple, blueberry, boysenberry, or raspberry syrup for drizzling

1. Preheat the oven to 375°F.

2. Cover the bottom of an ungreased 8 × 3⅓-inch-deep round soufflé dish or a deep cake pan with half of the bread cubes. Scatter the cream cheese cubes evenly over the bread. Sprinkle the chopped apple over the cream cheese. Cover with the remaining bread cubes.

3. In a bowl, beat the eggs, milk, and cinnamon until well blended. Pour this egg mixture over the bread. Bake until the eggs are set and the apples are slightly crunchy, about 35 minutes. Sprinkle with confectioners' sugar, if desired, and serve with the syrup of your choice.

Baked Panettone with Ricotta and Mandarin Oranges

Panettone is a large Italian Christmas bread that's slightly sweet, rich in eggs and butter, and studded with raisins and candied citron or orange. Although it's originally from Milan, one can find panettone everywhere now, especially in Italian markets around Christmastime. This casserole is a kind of Italian version of French toast, but a lot richer as it is stuffed with ricotta cheese. In fact, the fresher the ricotta cheese, the better this casserole will turn out. It's a perfect casserole for brunch or when feeding overnight guests since you can assemble the whole casserole the night before and let it sit in the refrigerator until time to bake. • **Makes 6 servings**

1 tablespoon unsalted butter

8 ounces fresh whole-fat ricotta cheese

½ cup sugar

¼ cup heavy cream

1 tablespoon Cointreau or other orange liqueur

Six ½-inch-thick slices panettone

One 11-ounce can mandarin oranges, drained

6 large eggs

½ cup milk

½ teaspoon ground cinnamon

Orange marmalade or pure maple syrup

1. Preheat the oven to 350°F. Generously butter a 12 x 9 x 2-inch baking casserole, using all the butter.

2. In a bowl, using an electric mixer, beat the ricotta cheese, sugar, cream, and Cointreau until the mixture is very dense and smooth.

3. Arrange 3 panettone slices over the bottom of the baking casserole, covering it completely. Cover the panettone slices with the ricotta mixture and then arrange the mandarin oranges over the ricotta mixture. Cover with the remaining 3 panettone slices.

4. In another bowl, whisk the eggs, milk, and cinnamon until well blended. Pour this mixture over the panettone in the baking casserole. (At this point, the baking casserole can be covered with plastic wrap and refrigerated overnight, if desired.)

5. Bake the casserole until dark golden brown on top, about 30 minutes. If you have refrigerated it overnight, remove the casserole from the refrigerator 30 minutes before baking and uncover it. Serve with orange marmalade or maple syrup, or both.

New Orleans Baked French Toast

The most interesting thing about French toast is that it's not really French. Its roots can be traced to ancient Rome, and the method of taking stale bread and rehydrating it with liquid was common in medieval times. The contemporary American breakfast known as French toast seems to have come from New Orleans, where it was a popular breakfast dish known as *pain perdu* (lost bread). This casserole version is prepared the night before and baked in the morning. The bread you use should be a good-quality French or Italian country bread and rather dense so that it can absorb the liquid. It's so delicious that it barely needs a syrup, but I usually use maple syrup. • **Makes 4 servings**

¾ cup dark brown sugar

½ cup (1 stick) unsalted butter

2 tablespoons light corn syrup

1 round loaf French or Italian country bread (about 1 pound),
    cut into 1-inch-thick slices

5 large eggs

1½ cups whole milk

1 teaspoon vanilla extract

1. Lightly butter a 13 × 9 × 2-inch baking casserole.

2. In a saucepan, stir the brown sugar, butter, and corn syrup over medium heat until the sugar and butter melt, and the mixture is syrupy but does not caramelize, about 4 minutes.

3. Pour the melted brown sugar syrup over the surface of the baking casserole. Arrange the bread slices in the syrup. In a bowl, whisk the eggs, milk, and vanilla to blend. Pour the egg mixture over the bread slices. Cover with plastic wrap and refrigerate overnight.

4. Preheat the oven to 350°F.

5. Remove the casserole from the refrigerator 30 minutes before baking it. Uncover and bake until the bread slices puff and the liquid around the sides are bubbling, about 30 minutes. Serve hot.

"French Toast" from 1450

Around 1450, the Renaissance chef Maestro Martino wrote a recipe in his *Libro di arte coquinaria* for French toast, which he called *suppa dorata* (golden sops).

"Take some bread slices that have been trimmed of their crusts; and make them into squares, toast slightly, just enough so that they brown on all sides. Then take some eggs that have been beaten together with a generous amount of sugar and soak the bread slices in the beaten eggs; and carefully remove them and fry them quickly in a pan with a little butter or rendered lard, turning often so that they do not burn. Then arrange them on a platter and top with a little rose water that you have made yellow with a bit of saffron and a generous amount of sugar."*

*Maestro Martino of Como. *The Art of Cooking: The First Modern Cookery Book, Composed by the Eminent Maestro Martino of Como, A Most Prudent Expert in This Art, Once Cook to the Most Reverend Cardinal Trevisan, Patriarch of Aquileia*. Jeremy Parzen, trans. (Berkeley: University of California Press, 2005), 91.

Blueberry Brunch

This brunch casserole is a favorite at the Inn at Black Star Farms in Suttons Bay, Michigan, an agricultural destination in the heart of northwest Michigan's Leelanau wine country. Blueberries are a big deal in Michigan and, in fact, the Michigan Blueberry Growers Association is the single largest marketer of fresh and processed cultivated blueberries in the world. If you're serving a big crowd, this recipe can be doubled. • **Makes 6 servings**

For the breakfast casserole

4 brioche (about 14 ounces in all) or eight 1-inch-thick slices
    white loaf bread or French bread, cubed
¼ pound cream cheese, cut into cubes
¾ cup fresh or frozen blueberries
1 tablespoon freshly grated orange zest
6 large eggs
1 cup whole milk
¼ cup pure maple syrup

For the blueberry sauce

¾ cup sugar
1 tablespoon cornstarch
¾ cup water
¾ cup fresh or frozen blueberries
2 teaspoons unsalted butter
¾ teaspoon freshly squeezed lemon juice

1. Lightly butter the bottom and sides of a 12 × 9 × 2-inch baking casserole.

2. Arrange half of the brioche or bread cubes in the baking casserole. Scatter the cream cheese, ¾ cup of blueberries, and the orange zest over the brioche or bread. Top with the remaining brioche or bread cubes.

3. In a bowl, stir the eggs, milk, and maple syrup to blend. Pour this egg mixture evenly over the entire casserole. Cover with foil and refrigerate overnight.

4. Preheat the oven to 350°F.

5. Remove the casserole from the refrigerator 30 minutes before baking it. Bake covered for 40 minutes. Remove the foil and bake uncovered until puffed, golden brown, and firm, about another 25 minutes.

6. Meanwhile, prepare the blueberry sauce. In a large saucepan, blend the sugar and cornstarch, then stir in the water. Cook over medium-high heat, stirring frequently, until the mixture boils, thickens, and becomes clear, about 5 minutes. Stir in the blueberries. Reduce the heat to low and cook until the blueberries burst, about 10 minutes. Remove from the heat and stir in the butter and lemon juice and keep warm until the casserole is done.

7. Cut the baked casserole into 6 squares and transfer to plates. Pour about ¼ cup of the blueberry sauce over each portion and serve hot.

Blackberry Breakfast Casserole

Bed-and-breakfast inns around the country, known as B&B's for short, have found an ingenious way of serving a Sunday brunch without taxing their often limited kitchens. The breakfast casserole. Many of these dishes can be made ahead of time and plunked in the oven in the morning. This frankly over-the-top breakfast casserole is adapted from one that's served at the Wildflowers Farm Bed & Breakfast in Calvert City, Kentucky. At home, you'll want to serve this to a group coming over for brunch. When I first tested this recipe on a couple of 17-year-old boys they thought the phrase "French toast on steroids" was accurate.

Because the recipe is complex, although not hard, it's best to break it down into stages. I would make the blackberry syrup the day before. For real convenience, you could even assemble the entire dish and refrigerate it overnight, then take it out of the refrigerator 30 minutes before baking it. You can soften the cream cheese briefly in a microwave to make it more spreadable, or you can use whipped cream cheese which spreads easily. If blackberries are not available, use blueberries or raspberries. Finally, you will be pleased to know that you can cut the recipe in half which, theoretically, should serve six, but in reality, I'm sure four can down it without a problem outside of guilt. The cream of coconut is usually sold in the supermarket in the liquor section, as it is often used in tropical mixed drinks. Before starting the preparation, lay out your bread slices to be sure you have enough to form two layers in the baking casserole, and if necessary, trim the edges of the bread slices to fit in the baking casserole. Make sure you use evaporated milk and not regular milk to avoid curdling. • **Makes 8 servings**

For the blackberry syrup

1 pound fresh or frozen blackberries

2 cups granulated sugar

1 cup water

¼ cup cream of coconut

¼ cup (½ stick) unsalted butter

3 tablespoons pure maple syrup

1 teaspoon vanilla extract

For the bread

½ cup (1 stick) unsalted butter

1 cup plus 2 tablespoons light or dark brown sugar

½ cup molasses

1 loaf French or Italian bread, cut into 1-inch-thick slices

½ pound cream cheese, softened

8 ounces sour cream

2 Granny Smith apples, peeled, cored, and thinly sliced

1½ teaspoons ground cinnamon

1½ cups slivered almonds

For the eggs

6 large eggs

1 cup evaporated milk

½ cup light or dark brown sugar

2 tablespoons pure maple syrup

½ teaspoon vanilla extract

3 tablespoons unsalted butter, thinly sliced

For the garnish

Confectioners' sugar for dusting

① Preheat the oven to 400°F. Lightly butter a 13 × 9 × 2-inch baking casserole.

2 Prepare the blackberry syrup. Place the blackberries, sugar, water, cream of coconut, butter, maple syrup, and vanilla in a large saucepan over high heat. Bring the liquids to a boil and continue boiling, stirring often, until syrupy, about 3 minutes. Remove from the heat and let cool.

3 Prepare the bread. In a small but wide saucepan or a small skillet, melt the butter with 1 cup of brown sugar and the molasses over low heat, stirring occasionally, until everything is dissolved and the mixture is syrupy, about 5 minutes. Dunk the bread slices into this syrup to coat both sides and then arrange half of the coated bread slices in the baking casserole. Spread half the cream cheese over the bread, then spread half the sour cream over the cream cheese. Arrange all the sliced apples over the sour cream. Sprinkle with 1 tablespoon of brown sugar, half of the cinnamon, and $1/3$ of the almonds. Cover with the remaining coated bread slices. Spread the remaining cream cheese and sour cream over the bread. Sprinkle with the remaining 1 tablespoon of brown sugar, the remaining cinnamon, and $1/3$ of the almonds.

4 Prepare the eggs. In a bowl, mix the eggs, milk, brown sugar, maple syrup, and vanilla to blend. You should have about $3\frac{1}{2}$ cups of this egg mixture. If you don't, add enough water so the egg mixture equals this amount.

5 Pour the egg mixture over the bread. Dot the top with butter. Pour 1 cup of blackberry syrup over. Sprinkle with the remaining almonds.

6 Bake until the liquids bubble vigorously, about 35 minutes. Pour the remaining blackberry syrup over the casserole, sprinkle with confectioners' sugar, and serve hot.

Meat
Casseroles

Meatloaf

I often made meatloaf when my kids were little and I wanted to feed them, have them eat it, have it taste good, keep it easy, and have leftovers. This recipe, which is somewhat influenced by Italian cookbooks (written in Italian) of the 1960s, was always the perfect answer. • **Makes 4 to 6 servings**

1 bread roll, crust removed if desired, torn into pieces

1 cup whole milk

1 large egg

½ pound ground beef

½ pound ground pork

½ pound ground veal

½ cup very finely chopped onion

1 large garlic clove, very finely chopped

2 tablespoons very finely chopped fresh parsley

Salt and freshly ground black pepper

¼ pound Muenster cheese, sliced

¼ pound mozzarella cheese, sliced

3 ripe tomatoes (about 1¼ pounds), sliced

Extra-virgin olive oil for drizzling

Leftover Idea

Meatloaf leftovers make a very nice appetizer for the next day, or even a dish to bring to a potluck lunch buffet, not to mention a sandwich. For an appetizer, cut the meatloaf into neat bite-size pieces, and arrange them attractively on a platter. Place some room-temperature Gorgonzola cheese on one side of the platter, and fresh fruit, such as sliced apples, pears, or berries, on the other side and serve. For a sandwich, place the meatloaf in a soft roll and add lettuce, red onion slices, a slice of tomato, and some mayonnaise.

1 Preheat the oven to 350°F.

2 In a bowl, soak the roll in the milk. Squeeze the milk out and put the bread into a larger mixing bowl. Beat the egg into the bowl with the bread. Mix the beef, pork, veal, onion, garlic, and parsley with the bread, kneading well with both hands. Season meat mixture with salt and pepper. .

3 Spread the meat mixture in a 12 × 9 × 2-inch baking casserole until it covers the bottom evenly. Cover with the sliced cheeses and then with the tomato slices. Drizzle a little olive oil on top of the tomatoes and season with salt and pepper. Bake until cooked through and the top is dark brown, about 40 minutes. Cut the meatloaf into slices. Lift out the slices with a slotted spatula and serve hot.

Stuffed Italian Meatloaf

My mom always made a great meatloaf, and it was from her that I learned the secrets of a good meatloaf: mixed meats and not skimping on the fresh bread crumbs. Her meatloaf always had a smear of ketchup on top, too. I can't remember if she ever stuffed the meatloaf, but her Italian father certainly would have, as he was a good Neapolitan cook. Although this recipe is called *polpettone ripiene* in Italian, it really is an Italian-American favorite rather than Italian. Use the food processor only to grind the meat a little finer, not to make it pasty. Alternatively, ask the supermarket butcher to grind the meat twice for you, although he may not want to mix meats in his grinder. This is a rich dish typically made on special occasions such as Christmas Eve dinner. If you don't have a food processor, just mix the ingredients by hand. • **Makes 8 servings**

1 cup fresh bread crumbs (see Note)
½ cup whole milk
1 pound lean ground beef
1 pound ground pork
1 pound ground veal
4 large eggs (2 beaten to blend; 2 hard-boiled)
1 small onion, grated or very finely chopped
½ cup (about 1½ ounces) freshly grated Parmesan cheese
2 large garlic cloves, very finely chopped
2 tablespoons finely chopped fresh parsley
1 tablespoon finely chopped fresh basil
Freshly grated zest from 1 lemon
2 teaspoons salt
1½ teaspoons freshly ground black pepper
6 ounces provolone cheese, thinly sliced
¼ pound salami, thinly sliced

2 tablespoons unsalted butter

2 tablespoons tomato paste

2 cups beef broth

1. Preheat the oven to 350°F. Butter a 14 × 10 × 2-inch baking casserole or a large roasting pan.

2. In a bowl, soak the bread crumbs in the milk, then drain and squeeze any excess milk out with your hands. Place the bread crumbs, beef, pork, and veal in a food processor and pulse several times to mix and grind. Do this in batches, and then transfer the meat mixture to a large bowl. Using both hands, mix the meat mixture well with 2 beaten eggs, the onion, garlic, parsley, basil, lemon zest, salt, and pepper.

3. Place the meat mixture on a 12 × 14-inch piece of wax paper and form the meat into an 11 × 13-inch rectangle on top of the wax paper by patting with your palms. Slice the hard-boiled eggs and arrange them lengthwise in a row down the middle of the meat. Top the eggs with the provolone cheese and salami. Roll up the meat like a jelly-roll, using the wax paper as a guide, until you have a "log" of meat. Smooth the seam and ends using wet hands so that the meatloaf is sealed.

4. Place the meatloaf in the center of the baking casserole, seam side down. Remove the wax paper. (If desired, you can cover and refrigerate the meatloaf at this point and refrigerate it up to 8 hours.) Dissolve the tomato paste in the beef broth and pour over the meatloaf. Bake until firm when poked hard, about 50 minutes. Transfer the meatloaf to a serving platter and let rest for 10 minutes. Cut the meatloaf crosswise into slices of any thickness you desire—I think ½ inch is ideal—and serve, spooning the casserole liquid over the slices, if you like.

Note: This amount can be made from crumbling two ½-inch-thick slices of 5¼ × 3-inch French or Italian bread in a food processor.

Monday Casserole

This recipe is based on leftovers, as to make everything from scratch is a bit of work. But here's the game plan: grill the steak and chicken for your Saturday barbeque, make a meatloaf for your Sunday dinner, and then make this dish Monday evening with the leftovers. I've actually made this recipe from scratch because my kids kept asking for it when they lived at home. I give you two options for cooking the rice. The first option is for when you want to eat right away, and the second option is if you want to get everything going and then forget about it until you're ready to eat.

• Makes 4 servings

½ pound grilled skirt steak (or any leftover steak), thinly sliced

½ pound grilled boneless skinless chicken breasts, thinly sliced

½ pound baked meatloaf, cubed

2 tablespoons extra-virgin olive oil

5 scallions, trimmed, white and green parts chopped

1 teaspoon ground cinnamon

½ teaspoon sweet paprika

1 tablespoon unsalted butter

1 cup long-grain rice, rinsed and rubbed well under
    running water in a strainer or soaked in tepid water to
    cover for 30 minutes, drained

1 teaspoon salt

1½ cups water

1. Place the steak, chicken, and meatloaf in a large skillet with the olive oil, scallions, cinnamon, and paprika. Toss well and heat over medium-low heat while you prepare the rice.

2. In a large flame-proof casserole with a heavy lid, melt the butter over medium-high heat. Add the rice and cook for 2 minutes, stirring. Add the salt and water and bring to a boil. Then, if eating soon, reduce the heat to low, cover, and cook until the water is absorbed and the rice tender, without stirring or looking under the lid, about 15 minutes. If you want to cook-and-forget, turn the heat off as soon as the water comes to a boil, then cover with two sheets of paper towels and replace the lid. Let stand undisturbed until the water is absorbed, about 40 minutes. Toss the rice with the meat mixture and serve hot.

Broth

There is a wide variety of broth options for recipes calling for broth. My favorite is my homemade broth which I make two slightly different ways. I just put all the meat, either raw or roasted until it is very brown, into the stockpot with cut-up onions, carrots, celery, leeks, a bay leaf, a bouquet garni of mixed herbs, and black peppercorns. I bring the liquid to a boil, skim the surface of foam, then reduce the heat and let it simmer for 3 to 12 hours, depending on my time constraints. Then I strain the broth twice, first through a strainer and then through a cheesecloth-lined fine mesh strainer. The broth cools at room temperature and I then place it in plastic containers for freezing. But when I don't have homemade broth I have no problem using canned or carton broth, meat concentrate (paste or base), or even bouillon cubes.

Swedish Meatballs

Swedish meatballs had their first run with popularity in America at the turn of the twentieth century before sliding into old-fashionedness. They were rediscovered in the 1950s and became a great buffet favorite until they once again became old-fashioned. Now it's the early twenty-first century and Swedish meatballs are making another comeback. There just is no denying that some dishes are always good. In Swedish they're called *köttbullar,* and were a popular smorgasbord item going back at least to 1754, when the first recipe was recorded. Swedish immigrants brought them to the northern Midwest and it was here that they were turned into a casserole. And they are a very easy casserole to put together, plus they freeze perfectly. The meatballs should not be bigger than ¾ inch in diameter. You will find many lazy cooks who make the meatballs bigger and, as a result, they are heavier. Traditionally, Swedish meatballs are eaten with mashed potatoes, a cream sauce or a thin beef gravy, and lingonberry preserves. I can't emphasize it enough, but be sure to serve them with the lingonberry preserves; they're just a marvelous complement. • **Makes 100 meatballs to serve 6**

1 medium onion, quartered

1 large egg

1½ pounds ground beef (preferably chuck)

½ pound ground pork

½ cup fresh bread crumbs (see Note)

⅔ cup half and half

¼ teaspoon ground allspice

⅛ teaspoon ground cloves

1½ teaspoons salt plus more for the sauce

½ teaspoon freshly ground black pepper plus more for the sauce

2 tablespoons unsalted butter

2 tablespoons all-purpose flour
1 cup beef broth
Lingonberry preserves for serving

1. Preheat the oven to 325°F.

2. Blend the onion in a food processor until it is finely ground. Add the egg and blend for 10 seconds. Add the beef, pork, bread crumbs, ⅓ cup of the half and half, the allspice, cloves, 1½ teaspoons of salt, and ½ teaspoon of pepper. Blend until almost smooth. You may need to do this in batches if your food processor is small. Transfer to a bowl and roll 100 small meatballs, dipping your hands into a bowl of cold water to prevent the meat from sticking to them.

3. Arrange the meatballs in a 13 x 9 x 2-inch baking casserole or, preferably, a large flame-proof casserole. Bake until they have turned golden and are cooked through, about 25 minutes. Transfer the meatballs to a platter and cover to keep them warm while you make the sauce.

4. Place the flame-proof casserole on a stove-top burner over medium-high heat. If you are using a baking casserole that is not flame-proof, scrape the pan drippings into a large skillet. Add the butter to the flame-proof casserole or the skillet and stir until the butter melts. Form a roux by stirring in the flour until it has formed a thin paste, then cook for about 1 minute, stirring constantly until smooth. Remove the baking casserole or skillet from the burner and slowly whisk in the remaining half and half and beef broth until the sauce is smooth. Season the sauce to taste with salt and pepper. Bring the sauce to a simmer. Once the sauce is bubbling, remove it from the heat and spoon it over the meatballs. Serve hot with lingonberry preserves on the side.

Note: This amount can be made from crumbling one ½-inch-thick slice of 5¼ x 3-inch French or Italian bread in a food processor.

Mexican Casserole

E very American mom has a recipe for "Mexican" casserole, which of course has just about nothing to do with Mexico, as this is really a Tex-Mex casserole, probably invented in Texas in the 1940s or 1950s and originally made with a bag of tortillas chips, ground beef, canned enchilada sauce, and Velveeta. Mom probably dumped some taco seasoning mix into the ground beef. I know I'm being a snob, but personally, that's no way to eat given how good a real Mexican casserole can be with a little time, patience, and good ingredients. Some Americans call this dish "Mexican Lasagne." Yes, there is some work involved, but there's a lot here, and that means lots of dinners that also freeze well. If you decide to fry the tortillas instead of baking them (see Note), the dish will be heavier but tastier. • Makes 8 servings

Leftover Idea

S ince the Mexican Casserole on this page has a good deal of preparation it makes sense to make the whole recipe so that you can have leftovers—and you're likely to have a bit of leftovers. When you're finished with dinner and the casserole has cooled completely, cut the remainder into square single-serving portions. Wrap each separately in aluminum foil and then place all of them in a plastic freezer bag. Freeze until needed and reheat in its aluminum foil wrapper in the oven, or discard the foil and transfer to a microwave and heat. Serve the leftovers with guacamole and sour cream.

1½ pounds tomatoes

2 onions (1 medium and kept whole; 1 small and chopped)

6 large green jalapeño chiles

6 large garlic cloves (4 whole; 2 finely chopped)

6 large flour tortillas, cut in half if using a rectangular baking casserole

1½ teaspoons sugar

1½ teaspoons dried oregano

1½ teaspoons salt plus more as needed

¾ teaspoon freshly ground black pepper plus more as needed

¼ teaspoon ground cinnamon

¼ teaspoon ground cloves

3 tablespoons pork lard or vegetable oil

1 cup sour cream

2 pounds ground beef

1 teaspoon chili powder

½ teaspoon ground cumin

3 cups (about 9 ounces) mixed shredded mild cheddar and
   Monterey Jack cheese

1 Preheat the oven to 450°F.

2 Place the tomatoes, whole onion, jalapeño chiles, and whole garlic on a baking tray and bake until the garlic is soft, about 20 minutes, until the jalapeño chiles are blistered, about 30 minutes, until the tomatoes skins are splitting, about 30 minutes, and until the onion is a little softened, about 45 minutes.

3 Meanwhile, arrange the tortillas on another baking tray and bake until crisp, about 15 minutes. Break the tortillas into about 2-inch pieces.

4 Peel off the skins from the tomatoes, onion, and garlic and place the vegetables in a blender. Add the sugar, 1 teaspoon of the oregano, 1½ teaspoons of salt, ¾ teaspoon of black pepper, cinnamon, and cloves, and blend for 30 seconds.

5 Reduce the heat of the oven to 375°F.

6　In a skillet, melt 1 tablespoon of the lard or heat 1 tablespoon vegetable oil over medium-high heat. Pour in the contents of the blender and cook, stirring constantly, until bubbling and a bit thicker, 1 to 2 minutes. Add the sour cream and stir to blend. Remove the sauce from the heat.

7　In a large skillet, melt the remaining 2 tablespoons of lard or heat the remaining 2 tablespoons vegetable oil over medium heat. Add the beef, chopped onion, chopped garlic, remaining ½ teaspoon oregano, chili powder, and cumin, stirring and breaking up the meat, until it browns, about 8 minutes. Season with salt and pepper, if desired.

8　In a 12-inch round earthenware baking casserole (preferably) or a 13 × 9 × 2-inch baking casserole, arrange a third of the broken tortillas in a layer. Cover with half of the beef mixture, then spoon some sauce over the beef mixture. Finally, cover with a third of the cheese. Repeat this layering one time. Sprinkle the remaining tortillas over the casserole. Spread a thin layer of the remaining sauce over the tortillas and sprinkle with the remaining cheese. Bake until the cheese is melted and the casserole is almost bubbling, about 20 minutes. Remove from the oven, let rest 10 minutes, and serve.

Note: If you'd like to fry the tortillas instead of baking them, melt 2 cups of lard or heat 2 cups of vegetable oil in a large skillet over medium-high heat until it is almost smoking. Then fry the tortillas until they are golden brown and crisp on both sides, turning with tongs and removing to a paper towel-covered platter to drain, about 1 minute. If using lard, let it cool and congeal in the skillet; it can be used again for frying if it is clean. The vegetable oil can also be reused after cooling.

Karelian Hot Pot

This Finnish casserole from Karelia, a region that straddles Finland and Russia, is called *karjalanpaisti*. Most Karelians, a people related to the Finns and Lapps, live in Russia. Agriculture is hard in this cold northern region and that is why, in part, you find meat-rich dishes such as this casserole. After the casserole has baked, you can let it rest, covered, in the turned-off oven for another hour before serving, if you like. Serve with mashed potatoes, boiled swedes (rutabagas), and lingonberry preserves. The lingonberries provide a particularly nice counterpoint to the oniony meat.

• Makes 4 servings

¾ pound boneless beef chuck, cut into 1-inch cubes
1½ teaspoons salt
1½ teaspoons freshly ground allspice berries
¾ pound boneless pork shoulder, cut into 1-inch cubes
¾ pound boneless lamb or mutton stew meat (from the leg),
    cut into 1-inch cubes
3 medium onions, coarsely chopped
2 cups water

1. Preheat the oven to 350°F.

2. In a 9 × 9-inch square or 9 × 3-inch-deep round baking casserole, cover the bottom with the beef and season with some salt and allspice. Layer the pork on top of the beef and sprinkle it with salt and allspice. Then layer the lamb and sprinkle it too with salt and allspice. Finally, cover the meats with the chopped onions and sprinkle them with salt and allspice.

3. Pour the water over the meat until almost covered. Bake uncovered until the onions are crispy and dark brown, about 2¼ hours. Cover the casserole and bake for another 45 minutes. Serve hot.

Tomatoes Stuffed in the Style of the Sheik

One of the most popular vegetable preparations in the Arab world is stuffed vegetables, such as eggplant, grape leaves, bell peppers, or tomatoes, and many others. Stuffed eggplant are just ahead of stuffed tomatoes in popularity, but when both are stuffed with meat they are called *shaykh al-mahshi*, which means "stuffed sheik's style," meaning the vegetable contains the more elegant and expensive meat that a sheik would typically eat. In traditional Arab society, a sheik (pronounced "shake" not "sheek") was a leader of a nomadic pastoral tribe. It is also a term used for a master of the spiritual path, while today it is sometimes used as an honorific for a respected community leader, whose table would be set to reflect this status. When the tomatoes are stuffed simply with rice they are called *banadura mahshi,* stuffed tomatoes. Two Arabic words for tomato, *banadura* and *tumatim,* derive from, respectively, the Italian word for tomato, *pomodoro*, and the Nahuatl word *tomátl*, in the language of the native Americans of Mexico.

• Makes 4 servings

8 medium-size, spherical, and firm tomatoes (about 2½ pounds)

2 tablespoons extra-virgin olive oil

1 medium onion, chopped

2 tablespoons pine nuts

½ pound ground lamb

1½ teaspoons ground cinnamon

½ teaspoon ground allspice

½ teaspoon dried mint

½ teaspoon salt

½ teaspoon freshly ground black pepper

1. Preheat the oven to 350°F. Lightly oil a medium-size baking casserole.

2. Slice off the top third of the tomatoes at the stem end and set aside, saving the top. At the other end of the tomato, slice off a tiny sliver from the bottom so the tomato will stand up on it own, making sure you don't cut off so much that you create a hole. Remove the inside pulp and seeds with a spoon, being careful you don't puncture the tomato. Discard the seeds and chop the pulp and reserve.

3. In a skillet, heat 2 tablespoons of oil over medium-high heat, then cook the onion, stirring, until soft and yellow, about 6 minutes. Add the pine nuts and cook, stirring, for 2 minutes. Add the ground lamb and reserved tomato pulp. Reduce the heat to medium and cook, stirring, until the meat loses its color, about 5 minutes. Stir in the cinnamon, allspice, mint, salt, and pepper, and cook, stirring and breaking up the meat further, until the liquid from the tomato pulp evaporates, about 2 minutes.

4. Stuff the tomatoes tightly with the meat mixture. Place the tomato tops on top and arrange the stuffed tomatoes in the baking casserole. Bake until the tomatoes are soft, but not collapsing, about 30 minutes, although the time may vary depending on how firm your tomatoes are to begin with. Serve hot, warm, or at room temperature.

Tongue of the Judge

The name of this dish in Arabic is *lisan al-qadi* which literally means "tongue of the judge." You'll see why it's called "tongue" as soon as you slice the eggplant into strips. Although this kind of dish is known throughout the Fertile Crescent, this Iraqi casserole is made with strips of the long and thin eggplants known here as Japanese eggplant and are stuffed with ground beef. That's where the judge comes in. As a respected member of the community, and a better-off one as well, the judge would be expected to have his foods stuffed with meat, while the commoners or peasants would stuff theirs with rice. This casserole is also excellent at room temperature and serving it with Macaroni and Cheese (page 264) isn't a bad idea, as I discovered to my surprise. • **Makes 6 servings**

½ cup corn oil plus more as needed
6 long and thin Japanese eggplants (about 2½ pounds), peeled
Salt

For the stuffing

2 pounds lean ground beef
1 cup finely chopped onion
1 teaspoon salt
¼ teaspoon freshly ground black pepper

For the sauce

2 tablespoons corn oil
1 large onion, chopped
1 large tomato, cut in half crosswise, seeds squeezed out, and pulp grated
    against the largest holes of a box grater down to the peel
1 teaspoon turmeric
1 teaspoon salt
½ teaspoon freshly ground black pepper

One 6-ounce can tomato paste mixed with 1¼ cups water

1 cup beef broth

6 tablespoons freshly squeezed lemon juice

1. Preheat the oven to 350°F. Line baking sheets with aluminum foil and lightly oil the foil.

2. Trim off a ¼-inch-thick slice from both ends of the eggplants so they can stand up on end without tipping. Stand the eggplant up on one end and slice it into ⅛- to ¼-inch-thick vertical slices. Lay the eggplant strips on some paper towels and sprinkle with salt. Leave them to drain of their bitter juices for 30 minutes, then pat dry with paper towels.

3. Place the eggplant slices on the baking sheets and brush with oil. Bake until the slices begin turning light brown, turning once, about 25 minutes.

4. Meanwhile, for the stuffing, lightly oil a 12 × 9 × 2-inch baking casserole. In a large bowl, mix the ground beef, onion, salt, and pepper until well blended. Lay an eggplant slice in front of you and place a 1- or 2-inch sausage-shaped portion of meat stuffing on the wider end of the slice and roll up. Place the roll-ups in the baking casserole. Set aside. (The casserole can be covered and refrigerated for many hours at this point.)

5. For the sauce, in a saucepan or skillet, heat the oil over medium heat, then cook the onion, stirring, until softened, about 8 minutes. Stir in the grated tomato, turmeric powder, salt, and pepper. Then stir in the tomato paste mixture, beef broth, and lemon juice. Cover and cook over medium heat until denser and bubbling furiously, about 15 minutes. Turn the heat off.

6. Increase the oven temperature to 450°F.

7. Spoon the sauce over the rolls in the baking casserole. Cover with aluminum foil and bake until bubbling and the meat is cooked through, 55 to 60 minutes. Remove from the oven, let rest 10 minutes, and serve.

Crescent Roll Casserole

This recipe is adapted from a now defunct Web site that had a page called "history of the casserole in Minnesota" (the casserole was brought by the Finns) and is virtually the only casserole I have found that is associated exclusively with that state, or so they claim. In any case, it's a casserole that is both filling and satisfying, and which I would serve with simply prepared green beans. The crescent rolls used in this recipe are a Pillsbury Company product and can be found at the supermarket. They are basically a croissant-like dough that you roll up and bake yourself. I was curious about this dish so I contacted Lola Whalen, the kitchen manager of the Pillsbury Bake-Off Contest, who told me that the original recipe was submitted by Maeela Bathke of Wells, Minnesota, for the 1978 Pillsbury Bake-Off. It didn't win, but that doesn't mean it's not a winner. • **Makes 4 to 6 servings**

1½ pounds very lean ground beef

1 medium onion, chopped

1 pound crushed tomatoes, fresh or canned

1½ teaspoons salt plus more as needed

Freshly ground black pepper

2 cups (about 6 ounces) shredded sharp cheddar cheese

2 cups (about 6 ounces) shredded mozzarella cheese

4 Pillsbury refrigerated crescent dinner rolls (unbaked)

¼ cup sour cream

What's Lean?

In my recipes I sometimes call for just ground beef, sometimes for lean ground beef, and sometimes for very lean ground beef. What does this mean? A package of unspecified ground beef will have a fat content over 15%, while "lean beef" means a fat content of 15%, and "very lean" means a fat content of 7%. Luckily, supermarkets will specify the fat content on the packaging.

1. Preheat the oven to 375°F.

2. In a large flame-proof baking casserole, brown the beef with the onion over medium heat, stirring to break up the meat, until the beef turns color, about 12 minutes. Add the tomatoes and stir. Season with 1½ teaspoons of salt and some pepper. Cook, stirring occasionally, until the liquid evaporates, about 20 minutes. Remove the casserole from the heat.

3. Mix together the cheddar and mozzarella cheeses and sprinkle over the meat in the casserole. Unroll the crescent rolls and spread one side of each roll with 1 tablespoon of sour cream. Cover the cheese with the rolls, with the sour creamed side up. Bake the casserole until bubbly and the top of the crescent rolls are golden brown, about 35 minutes. Serve hot.

Meat and Potatoes Hot Dish

Anything called a "hot dish" is a dead giveaway that it is a casserole from some place like Wisconsin, Michigan, North Dakota, or Minnesota. They are filling and meant to feed a family. Typically they are made in the wintertime when a warm oven is a good thing and a piping hot "hot dish" can fill the house with enticing aromas. I've dispensed with the canned condensed cream of celery soup usually used in this casserole and replaced it instead with fresh celery with cream. • Makes 4 to 6 servings

4 tablespoons unsalted butter, at room temperature
2 tablespoons all-purpose flour
1 large garlic clove, finely chopped
1½ cups chopped celery
2⅔ cups heavy cream
2 pounds very lean ground beef
1 medium onion, chopped
Salt and freshly ground black pepper
1½ pounds baking potatoes, peeled and sliced ¼ inch thick
2 cups fresh or frozen peas
2 cups (about 6 ounces) shredded Muenster cheese
2 cups fresh bread crumbs (see Note)

1 Preheat the oven to 300°F.

2 In a small bowl, blend 2 tablespoons of butter with the flour, then stir in the garlic and celery. Place in a blender, add ½ cup of the cream, and blend until smooth. Add the remaining cream and blend for 5 seconds.

3 In a skillet, brown the beef with the onion over medium-high heat, stirring to break up the meat. Season with salt and pepper. Transfer half of the beef mixture to a 12 x 9 x 2-inch baking casserole and cover with the sliced potatoes. Sprinkle the peas on top of the potatoes. Season

with salt. Pour the cream mixture from the blender over the potatoes and spoon the remaining beef mixture on top. Sprinkle the cheese on top of the beef mixture.

4 In a medium-size skillet, melt the remaining 2 tablespoons of butter over medium heat, then add the bread crumbs, and cook, tossing frequently, until slightly crispy, about 4 minutes. Sprinkle the bread crumbs over the top of the casserole and bake until golden brown and crispy on top, about 2 hours. Serve hot.

Note: This amount can be made from crumbling four ½-inch-thick slices of 5 × 3-inch French or Italian bread in a food processor.

About Potatoes

It is best to buy potatoes individually rather than in bags so you can inspect each potato for quality. A potato should be firm without any soft spots. It should have smooth and even skin without any evidence of sprouting. Avoid potatoes with green skin which indicates poor handling and storage. Do not refrigerate potatoes, which will only turn their starch to sugar and make them too sweet. Potatoes will keep for two months in a cool place. Potatoes will turn color once you peel them and they are exposed to the air, so be prepared to keep them in a bowl of water if you are not cooking them right away. Different potatoes are suited to different purposes. A baking potato is starchy and turns out fluffy. A boiling potato is waxy, with low starch and high moisture content. These boiling potatoes are ideal for preparations when you want to maintain the shape of the potato rather than have it fall apart. There are more than 200 varieties of cultivated potatoes, and your supermarket will probably carry about 4 of them, including baking potatoes such as Idaho Russets, boiling potatoes such as Red Bliss, and all-purpose potatoes such as Yukon Gold or White Rose.

Reuben Casserole

The Reuben casserole is, of course, nothing but a take on the Reuben sandwich. The history of this sandwich is debated, as there are two major origination stories. Some say the sandwich was invented in 1914 by Arnold Reuben who owned Reuben's Restaurant and Delicatessen on Broadway in the theater district of Manhattan. In 1938, Arnold Reuben gave an interview for *American Life Histories: Manuscripts from the Federal Writers' Project, 1936–1940* (available for viewing at http://rs6.loc.gov/wpaintro/wpa home.html) where he says he made the sandwich for a down and out actress named Anna Selos who walked in one day asking for a sandwich, and since he was feeling good, he clowned around to slap this sandwich together. The other credible story is that the sandwich was invented in the 1920s at a late-night poker game at the Blackstone Hotel in Omaha, Nebraska, by a grocer named Reuben Kulakofsky. Its origin is still unsettled because the Reuben didn't appear on the menu of the Plush Horse, the restaurant of the Blackstone Hotel in Omaha, until the mid-1930s. In this recipe you do *not* "bake until bubbly." • **Makes 4 servings**

1 tablespoon unsalted butter
3 slices rye bread, cut into pieces
¼ cup mayonnaise
¼ cup thousand island dressing
1 pound sauerkraut, drained well
3 ounces cooked corned beef, sliced
1¼ cups (about 3½ ounces) shredded Swiss cheese
1 medium tomato, sliced

1. Preheat the oven to 350°F.

2. In a skillet, melt the butter over medium-high heat, then cook the bread pieces until light golden, about 1 minute. Set aside.

3. In a bowl, mix together the mayonnaise and thousand island dressing. In a 9 x 9 x 2-inch baking casserole, arrange the sauerkraut to cover the bottom. Lay the corned beef on top, and pour over the dressing. Sprinkle with the cheese and top with the tomato slices. Sprinkle the bread pieces on top of the tomatoes and bake until the cheese is melted but not bubbling, 20 to 25 minutes. Serve hot.

Gratin of Ground Beef and Eggplant

This casserole is a winner because the leftovers are so versatile—they can be tossed with spaghetti or combined with a leftover vegetable casserole to make yet another dish. In Provence they call it simply enough *gratin d'aubergine*, eggplant gratin. I think it would be delicious with a spinach casserole or Swiss chard casserole, or with rice on the side.

• Makes 4 servings

1¼ pounds eggplant (unpeeled), cut into ¼-inch-thick slices
Olive oil for brushing or spraying
1 tablespoon unsalted butter
1 small onion, chopped
1 pound very lean ground beef
Salt and freshly ground black pepper
2 large tomatoes, cut in half, seeds squeezed out, and
　　pulp grated against the largest holes of a box grater
　　down to the peel
4 large fresh basil leaves, finely chopped
1 large garlic clove, finely chopped
2 cups (about 6 ounces) shredded Swiss cheese

1. Preheat the oven to 425°F. Lightly oil a 9 x 9 x 2-inch baking casserole.

2. Arrange the eggplant slices on a baking tray. Brush or spray lightly the eggplant slices with olive oil and bake until golden, 20 to 25 minutes. Remove from the oven and set aside. Reduce the heat of the oven to 350°F.

3. In a skillet, melt the butter over medium-high heat, then cook the onion, stirring, until soft, about 4 minutes. Add the ground beef and cook, stirring and breaking up the meat with a wooden spoon, until it loses its color, about 5 minutes. Season with salt and pepper. Remove from the heat.

The Original Casserole?

Cassoulet is one of the classic dishes of the southern region of France known as the Languedoc. It is described as a bean stew cooked in an earthenware baking casserole, hence its name. But a cassoulet is more than a bean stew because flavors also come from sausages, pork, and the fat-preserved duck known as *confit de canard*.

The word cassoulet, as well as the English word casserole, derives from the earthenware baking casserole it is cooked in, the *cassolle* or *cassolo*, which is a special vessel made by the local potteries in the vicinity of Castelnaudary in Languedoc. The French word *cassolle* comes directly from the Spanish *cassa* which also gives the modern Spanish word for the casserole, *cazuela*. But where does the Spanish word *cassa*, meaning "a receptacle for carrying liquid," come from? Possibly it comes from *cacherulo*, a Mozarab word, which is the language spoken by the Christians living in Islamic Spain in the twelfth century. *Cacherulo*, in turn, is a word derived from the Arabic *qas'at*, a large shallow earthenware bowl or pan. On the other hand, it may be derived from a proto-Hispanic word.

4 In a bowl, stir together the tomatoes, basil, and garlic. Season with salt and pepper. Arrange half of the eggplant on the bottom of the baking casserole. Cover with half of the ground beef mixture. Sprinkle half of the cheese over the beef mixture and then spoon half of any leftover gravy from the beef mixture and the tomato mixture over the cheese. (If you don't have any leftover gravy, follow the instructions in the Note below). Cover with the remaining ingredients in the same order. Bake until bubbly, about 40 minutes. Serve hot.

Note: If you don't have any leftover gravy from Step 3, you can quickly make some by melting 2 teaspoons butter in a small skillet over medium heat and then forming a roux by stirring in 2 teaspoons flour and cooking until smooth. Then stir in ½ cup beef broth, fresh, canned, or made from a bouillon cube, and simmer 2 minutes or until it thickens.

Cassoulet

A true French cassoulet, as made in the towns of Castelnaudary, Carcassonne, or Toulouse in Languedoc, is a magnificent thing. For that recipe you will want to see my book *A Mediterranean Feast* (William Morrow, 1999). For the simpler "housewife cassoulet" (*cassoulet ménagère*) you'll want to see my book *Real Stew* (Harvard Common Press, 2002). This recipe is simpler still even though it cooks for nearly 12 hours. *Cassoulet* means "casserole" so in a sense this is the primordial casserole. This is a very doable recipe for an American home cook and doesn't call for any of the specialized ingredients needed for the authentic and true cassoulet. I recommend starting the preparation of this casserole on a Saturday evening, refrigerating it overnight, and soaking the beans overnight as well, and then cooking it on Sunday morning (preferably a cold wintery one) when the aromas emanating throughout the day make it seem like you've died and gone to heaven. You will find the marrow bones at the supermarket, where they are sometimes labeled as soup bones. • Makes 4 servings

3 tablespoons rendered duck fat (preferably), or chicken fat, or butter

1 ounce salt pork, cut into strips

1 ounce prosciutto fat (preferably) or ham fat, cut into strips

1 pound lamb shank or shoulder

1 pound sweet Italian sausages

1 medium onion, chopped

1 leek (white part only), split lengthwise, washed well, and chopped

1 carrot, chopped

1 celery stalk, chopped

4 large garlic cloves, finely chopped

¼ cup finely chopped fresh parsley

1 teaspoon freshly ground black pepper

¼ pound veal or beef marrow bones (about 2 pieces)

1½ cups dried white cannellini or navy beans, soaked overnight
    in enough water to cover

2 teaspoons salt

One 6-ounce can tomato paste

3 cups dry white wine

1 cup water

1½ teaspoons dried summer savory

1 teaspoon herbes de Provence or dried marjoram

1. Preheat the oven to 220°F.

2. In an enameled cast-iron flame-proof baking casserole or an earthen-ware baking casserole, melt the duck fat over medium-high heat, then cook the salt pork and prosciutto fat, stirring, until almost crispy, about 5 minutes. Remove from the casserole and set aside with the fat that re-mains.

3. Brown the lamb and sausages in the baking casserole on all sides, about 5 minutes. Remove the pieces of salt pork and prosciutto from the bak-ing casserole and set aside to use later. (If using earthenware you will need to use a heat diffuser and cook a little longer than described here.)

4. Cook the onion, leek, carrot, celery, and garlic in the baking casserole, stirring frequently, until softened and the onion is translucent, 8 to 10 minutes. Add the reserved salt pork and prosciutto fat, the parsley, and black pepper and stir. Add the marrow bones.

5. Drain the beans and place them on top of the vegetable mixture you've just cooked in the baking casserole. Season with salt and put the lamb shanks and sausages on top. Dissolve the tomato paste into the wine and pour the wine mixture and the water over the casserole. Sprinkle with savory and herbes de Provence. Push any beans down to submerge them completely in the liquid. Taste a little of the liquid and adjust the salt. Cover and place in the oven until the beans are tender and the meat is falling off the bone, about 12 hours.

Hamburger Casserole

A hamburger casserole is a mom's favorite because it's easy and the kids will eat it. My recipe is geared a little bit toward the adults in that I like the flavor provided by the shiitake mushrooms and the heat of the paprika. I consider it a mild taste frankly, but if you have finicky eaters you may want to leave both ingredients out. Some cooks like to add diced green bell pepper to the onions while they sauté. As far as the cheese goes, each of the suggested cheeses will provided a slightly different taste, so choose the one you like the most. • **Makes 6 servings**

2 tablespoons extra-virgin olive oil
1 large onion, chopped
3 large garlic cloves, finely chopped
1 pound very lean ground beef
½ pound white button mushrooms, sliced
1¼ pounds fresh or canned crushed tomatoes
3 tablespoons finely chopped fresh parsley
1 tablespoon sweet paprika
1 teaspoon freshly ground black pepper plus more to taste
Salt
½ pound flat egg noodles
2 tablespoons unsalted butter
2 cups (6 ounces) shredded or grated Swiss cheese,
    mild white cheddar cheese, or Muenster cheese

1 Preheat the oven to 325°F. Butter a 12 × 9 × 2-inch baking casserole.

2 In a large skillet, heat the olive oil over medium-high heat, then cook the onion and garlic, stirring, until soft, about 5 minutes. Add the ground beef and mushrooms and cook, stirring to break up the meat, until the beef loses its color, about 10 minutes. Add the tomatoes, parsley, pap-

Shipwreck

In late eighteenth century and early nineteenth century, New England taverns were regularly found on the Post Road from New York to Boston where weary travelers could find bed and board for the night. While some of these inns became quite famous for their food, others became infamous for their dreck. Some of those taverns serving poorer fare would make a casserole called a Shipwreck, Six-Layer-Dinner, or Hallelujah—usually layers of potatoes, onions, and ground beef. Doesn't sound bad, and for a contemporary family meal it isn't. But a weary traveler on the Post Road in 1798 would have preferred clam pies, clam fritters, roast partridge, pudding, pies, and plenty to drink.

rika, and 1 teaspoon of pepper. Season with salt and stir. Reduce the heat to medium-low and simmer, stirring occasionally, for about 15 minutes while you prepare the noodles.

3 Meanwhile, bring a large pot of abundantly salted water to a rolling boil. Add the noodles in handfuls and cook until al dente. Drain the noodles, then toss them in a bowl with 1 tablespoon of butter. Lay half of the noodles over the bottom of the baking casserole. Cover with the meat mixture and sprinkle with half of the cheese. Cover with the remaining noodles and sprinkle the top with the remaining cheese. Thinly slice the remaining butter and scatter it over the casserole. Bake uncovered until the cheese has melted and the top is very slightly golden yellow, about 30 minutes. Serve hot.

Beef and Stout Casserole

Here's a delightful Irish casserole that gives you the opportunity to cook with beer, in this case, a dark stout. It's also a great excuse to have a beer while you're cooking. Irish bacon is usually sold already sliced in this country and may be difficult to find, so use Canadian bacon in its place. Don't use slab bacon as it will be too fatty. Serve with lots of boiled potatoes on the side to sop up the sauce. To peel the onions quickly, plunge them in boiling water for a few minutes, drain, cut the stem end off, and pinch off the skin. • **Makes 4 servings with potatoes as a side dish**

1 teaspoon vegetable oil

1½ pounds boneless beef chuck, cut into 1-inch cubes

½ pound lean Irish bacon (preferably) or Canadian bacon, cubed

1 tablespoon unsalted butter

2 tablespoons all-purpose flour

One 12-ounce bottle stout beer (such as Guinness)

1 pound small white onions (about 14), peeled

2 tablespoons finely chopped fresh parsley

¼ teaspoon dried marjoram

Salt and freshly ground black pepper

3 large garlic cloves, finely chopped

Bouquet garni (consisting of 1 bay leaf, 4 sprigs thyme,
    3 sprigs marjoram, 6 sprigs parsley tied in cheesecloth)

1 tablespoon sugar

1 tablespoon apple cider vinegar

1. Preheat the oven to 300°F.

2. In a large skillet, heat the vegetable oil over medium-high heat, then cook the beef and bacon, stirring occasionally, until browned on all sides, about 4 minutes. Remove the meats with a slotted spoon and set aside in a bowl. Discard any accumulated fat and juices in the skillet.

3. Melt the butter in the same skillet over medium heat. Stir in the flour to make a roux and cook, stirring, for about 1 minute. Slowly whisk in the stout, stirring until the gravy is smooth.

4. Place the beef, bacon, and onions in a 12 x 9 x 2-inch baking casserole or a 10-inch round baking casserole. Sprinkle with the parsley and marjoram. Season with salt and pepper. Add the garlic and bouquet garni and stir to mix well. Sprinkle the top with the sugar and pour the gravy over the beef. Stir again to mix well. Cover and bake until the meat is very tender, about 3 hours. Remove from the oven and stir in the vinegar. Let rest for 5 minutes, then serve.

Frankfurter Casserole with Sauerkraut

When I was growing up we had frankfurter casseroles with either sauerkraut or macaroni. I liked them both, and I like the flavor the beer gave the sauerkraut before the frankfurters were added. Because this dish is so simple, the key is the quality of the sauerkraut and the frankfurters. Sure you could buy a supermarket package of eight hot dogs, but for this dish I seek out a butcher and get some handmade Frankfurter sausages, also sold as wieners in German and Hungarian delis, which are also good places to get the sauerkraut. • **Makes 4 to 6 servings**

> 2 pounds sauerkraut
> 2 cups beer (lager)
> 2 pounds frankfurters
> Hot Pommery or Dijon mustard

1. Preheat the oven to 350°F.

2. Drain the sauerkraut and place it in a 12 × 9 × 2-inch baking casserole. Pour the beer over. Cover and bake for 1½ hours. Uncover the casserole and place the frankfurters on top of the sauerkraut. Bake uncovered until the frankfurters look like they are about to split open (or are starting to split open), 25 to 30 minutes. Serve hot with the mustard on the side.

Frankfurter Casserole with Macaroni

This is one of those casseroles I remember from my childhood. It's pure comfort food, and even though it's so simple, it's a lot of bang for the buck. No, this ain't gourmet eating, but you'll like it and, as every mom knows, so will the kids. There are three basic ways of making frankfurter casserole—with sauerkraut, with macaroni, or with biscuits. I like it with sauerkraut or macaroni, and I give you both recipes (see the previous recipe for one with sauerkraut). Some cooks add cheese, but I don't think it's necessary. Half-cooked macaroni simply means cooking it half the amount of time suggested on the box. • **Makes 4 to 6 servings**

> ½ pound half-cooked macaroni (such as elbow macaroni,
>   cut ziti, or short macaroni)
> 3 tablespoons unsalted butter
> 2 cups chicken broth
> 2 pounds frankfurters
> 1 cup sour cream

1 Preheat the oven to 350°F.

2 Toss the half-cooked macaroni with the butter and place it in a 12 × 9 × 2-inch baking casserole. Pour the chicken broth over the macaroni, place the frankfurters on top. Bake uncovered until the frankfurters are nearly splitting apart, about 25 minutes. Stir in the sour cream, and bake another 5 minutes, then serve hot.

Sausage and Potato Casserole

The spiciness of this flavorful casserole comes from paprika, and to make it really special you should use spicy sausages as well. Polish delis may sell kielbasa and Hungarian sausage, both of which are properly spicy for this preparation. But if you don't have a Polish deli nearby, then use the best-quality kielbasa or Cajun sausage that your supermarket sells. This is a dish from a city called Koprivnica in northern Croatia, where the food has many similarities with the food of the old Austro-Hungarian Empire. Along the Croatian coast, on the other hand, people eat food that is closer to Italian food. Serve this casserole with a green salad. • **Makes 4 servings**

2 tablespoons vegetable oil
½ pound slab bacon, diced
1 pound spicy sausage (preferably smoked, such as kielbasa),
    thinly sliced
1 small onion, chopped
2 teaspoons sweet paprika
3 pounds baking potatoes, peeled and cubed
1 bay leaf
Salt and freshly ground black pepper
2 tablespoons all-purpose flour
1 quart water
1 to 2 tablespoons seasoned salt
6 tablespoons finely chopped fresh parsley
4 large garlic cloves, finely chopped
2 cups sour cream

① Preheat the oven to 350°F.

② In a large skillet, heat the vegetable oil over medium-high heat. Add the bacon, sausage, and onion, and cook, stirring, until the onion is soft and the meats are sticking to the pan, about 5 minutes. Don't worry if the meats stick to the bottom of the pan because you will deglaze the pan later. Season with the paprika, stir, and add the potatoes and bay leaf. Season with salt and pepper. Dust with the flour, stir well, and pour in the water, scraping the bottom of the pan with a wooden spoon to deglaze it. Taste the broth and add as much seasoned salt as you like.

3. Bring the liquid to a gentle boil over medium-high heat, then carefully transfer the contents of the skillet to a 12 × 9 × 2-inch baking casserole. Bake uncovered until the potatoes are very tender, about 1 hour. Add the parsley, garlic, and sour cream, stir to blend well, and bake until bubbling, about 15 minutes. Serve hot.

Sausages on the Net

I'm sure your local supermarket sells sausages, but for really high quality and a wide variety of sausages try the Internet. Go to www.germandeli.com for German sausages, or visit balkanbuy.com/shop for sausages from the Balkans. Go to www.donajuana.com for Spanish and Catalan sausages. A general purpose store worth visiting is www.igourmet.com for sausages and other foods. For French sausages, there's www.dartagnan.com/index.asp and the goofy site of www.3pigs.com. Terrific Polish sausages of every variety can be found at polana.com/index.aspx. Don't ignore www.amazon.com under "Gourmet Food," where you can find some amazing food products. Italian sausages are pretty easy to find at supermarkets across the country, but the quality ranges across the board. For Internet sources too, there's hundreds of choices. For starters, look at www.fortunasausage.com, www.espositosausage.com, and www.salami.com/sausage1.htm. But the best Italian sausages made in America are made at Vace Italian Deli, 3315 Connecticut Ave., Washington, D.C. 20008, Tel: 202–363–1999. They don't have a Web site, and they don't ship, but if you're ever in D.C., buy some and figure out a way to cook them. Of course you can make your own, and I tell you how at www.cliffordawright.com/recipes/salsiccia.html.

Sausage and Lentil Casserole

T his is an Italian-American casserole, which is interesting in that it doesn't contain tomatoes. That's because it's a winter casserole, and it will give you a cozy and filling dinner. The success of the dish might hinge on the quality of your sausages, so unless you make your own you will be at the mercy of your local market. The nice thing about lentils is that because they are so earthy, they can marry with anything. • **Makes 4 to 6 servings**

1 cup (½ pound) green or brown lentils, rinsed
2 teaspoons salt
1 medium onion, cut in half (1 half stuck with 2 cloves; 1 half chopped)
1 teaspoon fennel seeds
1 bay leaf
6 sweet Italian sausages (about 1½ pounds)
2 tablespoons extra-virgin olive oil
2 tablespoons unsalted butter
3 ounces slab bacon, diced
1 medium carrot, peeled and chopped
2 large garlic cloves, finely chopped
Salt and freshly ground black pepper
½ cup dry white wine

1 Preheat the oven to 350°F. Lightly oil a 9-inch round baking casserole (preferably earthenware).

2 Place the lentils in a large saucepan with the salt, the half onion with cloves stuck in it, the fennel seeds, and bay leaf. Pour in enough water to cover the lentils by 1 inch. Bring to a boil over high heat, then reduce the heat to low and simmer until the lentils are tender, 50 to 55 minutes. Turn the heat off and leave the lentils in the saucepan until needed.

3 Meanwhile, bring a large saucepan of water to a boil, then reduce the heat to low and poach the sausages for 20 minutes. Turn the heat off and leave the sausages in the saucepan.

4 In a skillet, heat the olive oil with the butter and diced bacon over medium heat, stirring occasionally, until the bacon is a little crisp, 6 to 7 minutes. Add the chopped onion, carrot, and garlic. Cook, stirring, until softened, about 6 minutes.

5 Remove the sausages from the saucepan and arrange in the baking casserole. Drain the lentils and add half to the baking casserole along with half of the sautéed onion mixture. Season with salt and pepper. Make another layer of lentils, and top with the remaining onion mixture. Pour in the wine and bake until bubbling and dark, 35 to 40 minutes. Serve hot.

Sausage, Red Bean, and Apple Casserole

My mother lives north of Tampa on Florida's west coast, and although the retirees who live there come mostly from the Northeast, the local non-sunbird food has a pronounced Cuban-Mexican flavor to it. (Sunbirds are people from the north who live in Florida only in the winter.) But there are other immigrant communities too on the west coast of Florida, such as Czechs and Greeks. I have no idea how all these people may have conspired to influence Mrs. C. S. Robinson, the cook who dreamed up this casserole and published it in *The Gasparilla Cookbook: Favorite Florida West Coast Recipes*, compiled by the Junior League of Tampa in 1961, but I have adapted it only slightly as it is a very satisfying dish. • **Makes 4 small servings**

> 1 cup (6 ounces) dried red kidney beans, soaked overnight or for 8 hours in enough water to cover, drained
> 4 teaspoons salt
> ½ pound fresh pork sausages, casings removed and meat crumbled
> 1 Granny Smith apple, peeled, cored, and cut into wedges
> 1 large onion, cut into ⅛-inch-thick slices
> ¼ cup brown sugar
> 1 large garlic clove, finely chopped
> 2 tablespoons tomato paste blended with ½ cup water
> ½ teaspoon chili powder
> ¼ teaspoon freshly ground black pepper

1 Preheat the oven to 325°F.

2 Place the drained beans in a large saucepan and add enough water to cover by several inches. Bring to a boil over high heat, then add 2 teaspoons of salt. Cook at a boil until the beans are tender but not breaking apart, about 1 to 1¼ hours. Drain.

3 In a skillet, cook the sausage over medium heat, stirring and breaking up the meat, until it has turned color, about 8 minutes. In a large bowl, toss the sausage with all the other ingredients including the remaining 2 teaspoons of salt. Arrange in a 12 × 9 × 2-inch baking casserole and bake until crispy and golden on top, about 1 hour. Serve hot.

Sausage, Celeriac, and Apple Casserole

This hearty Alsatian casserole is a spin on their famous *choucroute* and is really an ideal winter preparation. I particularly like to use a mixed variety of sausages which I think adds more flavor. The sausages can be smoked or fresh. Once cut, the celeriac will blacken just as the apple and potato will, so you need to plunk them immediately in a bowl of water acidulated with lemon juice or vinegar as you prepare the casserole. • **Makes 6 servings**

1 pound russet potatoes, peeled, cut into ⅛-inch-thick slices
1¼ pounds celeriac (celery root), peeled, cut in half, and
      each half cut into ¼-inch-thick slices
Salt
½ pound Swiss cheese, shredded
1 Granny Smith apple, peeled, cored, and cut into ¼-inch-thick slices
2 pounds mixed sausages (such as bratwurst and kielbasa),
      cut into ½-inch-thick slices
4 tablespoons (½ stick) unsalted butter, thinly sliced
½ cup beef broth

1 Preheat the oven to 350°F. Lightly butter a 13 × 9 × 2-inch baking casserole.

2 Arrange half of the potatoes and half of the celeriac on the bottom of the baking casserole. Season with salt. Cover with half of the cheese, then all of the remaining celeriac, apple, and sausages. Cover the sausages with the remaining half of the potatoes and the remaining cheese. Dot with the butter and pour the beef broth over everything. Season with salt and bake until bubbly and golden, about 1¼ hours. Let rest for 10 minutes, then serve.

Sausage and Mushroom Casserole

This casserole is a mom's favorite because the family likes it and it's easy on her. Just toss everything together and that's it, since it bakes more or less untended. But the quality of the casserole will depend on the quality of the sausages you use, so you better see the sidebar on page 69 first. You can use common white button mushrooms, but the shiitake mushrooms have such a great taste that I think they make for a better casserole. Some cooks add chopped tomatoes to this dish. • **Makes 4 servings**

1½ pounds sweet Italian sausages, cut into 1-inch pieces
1 pound large shiitake mushrooms, stems removed,
    caps quartered or halved
3 tablespoons chopped onion
2 large garlic cloves, finely chopped
½ teaspoon dried oregano
6 tablespoons extra-virgin olive oil
Salt and freshly ground black pepper

1 Preheat the oven to 325°F.

2 Toss all the ingredients in a bowl, then transfer to a 12 x 9 x 2-inch baking casserole. Bake until the sausages are browned and the mushrooms have lost half their weight, stirring once, about 1¾ hours. Serve hot.

Chorizo Sausage and Hominy Casserole

*N*ixtamal is a Mexican-style hominy, processed by mixing water and un-slaked lime with whole dry corn kernels and cooking them until the skins can be rubbed off, and then washed in water to remove all traces of the lime. It is sold fresh and in cans, but not every supermarket sells it, even in the southwestern U.S. where it is a common food, so use whatever canned whole hominy is available. On the other hand, it's not at all hard to order fresh *nixtamal* on the Internet at www.albuquerque-tortilla.com/index.html or canned *nixtamal* at www.mexgrocer.com. The chorizo sausage can be replaced with any highly spiced sausage. If using fresh *nixtamal* it should be cooked in either water or broth for about 3 hours or until it is tender. Make sure the chorizo sausages are made with pure pork and not pig parts and that they are in natural casings, otherwise they will crumble and be much too fatty. • **Makes 4 to 6 servings**

Vegetable oil or pork lard

2 ½ cups canned hominy, liquid reserved

1 tablespoon salt

1¼ pounds Mexican-style chorizo sausages, in natural casings
　　(not plastic casings)

¼ pound Monterey Jack cheese, shredded

One 5-ounce can evaporated milk

½ cup sour cream or crème fraîche

1. Preheat the oven to 350°F. Lightly coat a 12 × 9 × 2-inch baking casserole with oil or lard.

2. Place the hominy with its liquid and the salt in a large pot and cover with water. Bring to a boil over high heat, then reduce the heat to medium and cook at a gentle boil until the hominy is a little more tender, about 15 minutes. Add the sausages and cook 30 minutes with the hominy.

3. Transfer the sausages to a cutting board. Using a slotted spoon, transfer the cooked hominy to the baking casserole, saving ¼ cup of the cooking liquid. Cut the sausages in half. Arrange the sausages on top of the hominy. Sprinkle the cheese on top and then sprinkle the evaporated milk over the cheese. Sprinkle with the reserved ¼ cup of hominy cooking liquid. Bake until the cheese has completely melted and the sides are bubbling, about 30 minutes. Serve hot with sour cream or crème fraîche.

Transylvanian Cabbage Casserole

D espite its name, this casserole is a favorite in eastern Hungary, and for all its Old World flavor, it's quite easy to make because it's assembled like a lasagne. Each layer packs a wonderful amount of flavor, and although it is traditionally made with lard, you can replace the pork lard with butter if you like. This casserole is labor intensive on the front end, but once assembled you can refrigerate it until needed. If you are organized, you can do Steps 2 through 5 at the same time. • **Makes 6 servings**

Salt
1 green cabbage (about 2 pounds)
¼ pound (8 tablespoons) pork lard (preferably) or unsalted butter
1 medium-large onion, chopped
1½ pounds ground pork
2 large garlic cloves, finely chopped
1 teaspoon hot paprika
Freshly ground black pepper
¼ pound slab bacon, cut into ¼-inch dice
½ pound smoked Polish kielbasa or smoked Hungarian sausages, thinly sliced
¼ cup dry white wine or water
1 teaspoon unsalted butter
½ cup medium-grain rice
1 cup sour cream
1 green bell pepper, cored, seeded, and cut into rings
2 medium tomatoes, sliced ¼ inch thick

1 Preheat the oven to 325°F.

2 Bring a large pot of salted water to a boil. Add the whole cabbage and cook until a skewer glides easily when pushed into the core, about 20 minutes. Drain and set aside to cool slightly. When cool enough to handle, carefully separate the leaves, discarding any damaged ones, and lay them in three equal piles.

③ Meanwhile, in a large skillet, melt the lard over medium-high heat. Transfer half of the melted lard to a small bowl, keeping it warm and melted to use later. Add the onion to the skillet and cook, stirring, until translucent, about 6 minutes. Add the ground pork, garlic, and ½ teaspoon of paprika. Season with salt and pepper, mixing well and breaking up the ground meat with a wooden spoon as it cooks. Reduce the heat to medium-low and cook, stirring occasionally, until the meat turns color, about 10 minutes. Set aside until needed.

④ In a medium-size skillet, cook the bacon over medium heat until sizzling and turning color, about 4 minutes, then add the sausages and cook, stirring, for 3 minutes. Pour the wine into the skillet, scraping up any bits that have stuck to the bottom of the skillet, then set aside until needed.

⑤ Bring ½ cup of water to a boil in a small saucepan over high heat. Add ½ teaspoon of salt, the butter, and then the rice. Return to a boil, then reduce the heat to low. Cover and cook until all the water is absorbed, about 8 minutes. The rice will be half-cooked at this point. Set aside until needed.

⑥ Coat a 13 × 10 × 3-inch baking casserole with 2 tablespoons (1 ounce) of the reserved melted pork lard. Cover the bottom of the baking casserole with a third of the cabbage leaves. Cover the cabbage leaves with the bacon and sausages. Lay another third of the cabbage leaves over the bacon and sausages. Beat the sour cream with a fork until smooth, then sprinkle or spoon half of the sour cream over the cabbage leaves. Sprinkle the half-cooked rice on top of the sour cream. Season with salt and pepper. Cover with the cooked pork (from Step 3) and then cover with the remaining cabbage leaves. Arrange the green bell pepper rings and sliced tomatoes on top. Stir the remaining ½ teaspoon paprika into the remaining sour cream and cover the tomatoes and green bell pepper with the sour cream, dripping them in dollops around the top of the casserole. Sprinkle the top with the remaining 2 tablespoons (1 ounce) of melted lard and bake until the dollops of sour cream are golden brown and the bell pepper rings are withered, about 1½ hours. Serve hot.

Pork and Turnip Casserole

This Swedish-inspired casserole is perfect for fall weather, because it's luscious and the natural sweetness of the turnips complements the succulence of the pork. The juices in the casserole will flavor and thin the sour cream nicely. If you like, you can add some freshly grated or prepared horseradish to the sour cream, too. • **Makes 4 servings**

1 pound boneless pork shoulder, cut into 1-inch cubes

¼ pound slab bacon, cut into 1-inch pieces

5 turnips (about 1½ pounds), cut into 1-inch pieces

2 tablespoons unsalted butter, melted

¼ teaspoon freshly ground allspice berries

1 teaspoon salt plus more to taste

Freshly ground black pepper

2 cups sour cream

2 teaspoons prepared mustard (see Note)

3 tablespoons chopped fresh dill

1. Preheat the oven to 350°F.

2. In a 10-inch round baking casserole, toss the pork, bacon, turnips, melted butter, allspice, 1 teaspoon of salt, and some pepper together. Spread evenly in the baking casserole and bake, uncovered, until the turnips are tender, about 1¼ hours.

3. In a bowl, stir the sour cream, mustard, a little salt, and dill (saving a pinch to sprinkle over the finished casserole later) together. Pour the sour cream mixture over the pork and stir to mix well and make the sauce smooth. Continue baking until the sour cream is hot but not bubbling, about 10 minutes. Serve hot with a sprinkling of fresh dill.

Note: Prepared mustard is made by mixing dry mustard with water in equal proportions.

Pork and Cabbage Casserole

Here's a family-style casserole that is pleasing to a wide range of palates. The pork chops are seared first and then arranged in a casserole and topped with finely shredded cabbage, then cooked in wine and tomatoes. You can assemble the whole casserole a day in advance if you want and then just pop it into the oven before serving. It goes great with the Potato and Mushroom Casserole (page 333), which can be cooked at the same time in the same oven. • **Makes 6 servings**

¼ cup extra-virgin olive oil

6 pork chops (about 2½ pounds), cut ¾ inch thick

2 medium onions, thinly sliced

2 large garlic cloves, finely chopped

1 green cabbage (about 2 pounds), cored and thinly shredded (as for coleslaw)

1½ pounds ripe tomatoes, peeled, seeded, and chopped

1 cup dry white wine

½ teaspoon dried sage

½ teaspoon dried oregano

½ teaspoon dried marjoram

Salt and freshly ground black pepper

1 Preheat the oven to 350°F.

2 In a large skillet, heat the olive oil over medium-high heat, then cook the pork chops until golden brown on both sides, about 2 minutes on each side. Remove the chops and arrange them in a 12 × 9 × 2-inch baking casserole.

3 In the same skillet used for the pork chops, cook the onions and garlic, stirring constantly, until softened, about 4 minutes. Stir in the cabbage, tomatoes, wine, sage, oregano, and marjoram, and cook, stirring occasionally, until wilted, soft, and bubbling, about 20 minutes. Season with salt and pepper and stir to blend. Spread the cabbage mixture and its juices over the pork chops. Bake until the top is crispy looking, about 1 hour. Serve hot.

Pork and Black Bean Casserole

This style of pork is sometimes known as *carnitas* in Mexico and southern California. It's an earthy casserole, and very dark too, so it's nice to use the sour cream and perhaps also something red for an appetizing contrast. I usually start this recipe on a weekend day, then go about my business and return to a delicious casserole dinner. *Epazote* is a musty-smelling herb used in Mexican cooking and can sometimes be found in farmers markets in the western U.S., but if you can't find it you can try using a sprig of fresh sage instead. When it comes out of the oven after 6 hours, the casserole will look like hell, but don't worry, it tastes great . . . and that dollop of sour cream will make it look pretty too. This casserole is nice to serve hot with white rice and a lettuce and avocado salad on the side.

• Makes 4 to 6 servings

1½ tablespoons pork lard or butter
1½ pounds boneless pork shoulder, cut into ½-inch cubes
4 scallions, trimmed, white and green parts chopped
3 large garlic cloves, finely chopped
2 cups (1 pound) dried black beans
5 cups water
4 cups chicken broth
1 large sprig *epazote* (optional)
¼ cup chopped fresh cilantro
3 dried ancho chiles
4 dried whole red chiles
½ teaspoon dried oregano
2 teaspoons salt
1 teaspoon freshly ground black pepper
1 cup sour cream (optional)
Mexican hot sauce (optional)

1 Preheat the oven to 325°F. Lightly oil a 10 × 3-inch round earthenware baking casserole (preferably).

2 In a large skillet, melt 1 tablespoon of the lard over medium-high heat, then cook the pork cubes until crispy golden on all sides, 7 to 9 minutes. Add the scallions and garlic and cook, stirring, for 1 minute. Transfer the pork to the baking casserole and add the black beans, water, chicken broth, *epazote*, cilantro, ancho chiles, dried red chiles, oregano, salt, and pepper. Stir to mix well. Bake until the liquid has been absorbed, stirring once or twice, about 6 hours. Discard the *epazote* and chiles. Serve hot with the sour cream and Mexican hot sauce, if desired.

Pork and Lima Bean Casserole

It's hard to say where this hearty and filling American casserole comes from. James Beard, from whom this recipe is adapted, called it California casserole, but it was popular in the nineteenth century among the Portuguese community in Cape Cod and southeastern Massachusetts. The sausages should be fresh Portuguese-style *linguiça*, but if you can't find fresh then use smoked sausage. A nice fresh green salad dressed with oil and vinegar would go great with this dish. • **Makes 6 servings**

1 pound dried lima beans, soaked overnight or for 8 hours in
    enough water to cover, drained
1 tablespoon unsalted butter
¼ pound salt pork, diced
1 large onion, chopped
1 pound *linguiça* sausage, kielbasa, or garlic sausage,
    cut into ¾-inch-thick slices
2 large garlic cloves, finely chopped
½ teaspoon dried savory
½ teaspoon dried thyme
Salt and freshly ground black pepper
1 cup dry white wine

1. Place the beans in a large saucepan and cover with cold water by several inches. Bring to a boil over high heat, then reduce the heat to a simmer and cook until their skins start to split, about 1 to 1¼ hours. Drain and transfer the beans to a large bowl.

2. Preheat the oven to 300°F.

3. Meanwhile, melt the butter in a large skillet with the salt pork and onion, and cook over medium heat, stirring frequently, until the salt pork is crisp, about 12 minutes. Add the sausage and garlic, and cook, stirring frequently and adding a few tablespoons of water if the mixture is sticking, until the sausage browns, about 5 minutes. Stir in the reserved beans, savory, and thyme. Season with salt and pepper and mix well but carefully so you don't break the beans further.

4. Transfer the sausage and bean mixture to a 12 x 9 x 2-inch baking casserole, pour in the white wine, and stir to mix. Cover and bake until everything is very soft, about 2¼ hours. Serve hot.

Bacon and Beans Casserole

This bean casserole has some great flavors because the bacon and pears play off each other. It's a great accompaniment to a roast chicken or pork loin. This recipe from Hamburg in Germany is adapted from Mimi Sheraton's recipe called *bohnen, birnen und speck, auf Hamburger art* in her classic *German Cooking*. If you can manage to find the kind of smoked slab bacon they sell at German or any East European deli, I would use that because it has more flavor and less fat than the sliced bacon sold at regular supermarkets. • **Makes 4 servings**

2 tablespoons unsalted butter
1 pound slab bacon, cut into 1-inch cubes
1 pound dried white beans, soaked overnight or for 8 hours
    in enough water to cover, drained
4 pears, peeled, cored, and cubed
Salt and freshly ground black pepper
2 cups water
3 tablespoons finely chopped fresh parsley leaves

1 Preheat the oven to 325°F.

2 In a 9 x 4-inch oval or round flame-proof casserole, melt the butter over medium-high heat. Add the bacon and cook, stirring occasionally, until some fat is rendered, 5 to 10 minutes, depending on how crispy you want the bacon to be. Add the beans and pears. Season with salt and pepper, and stir to blend. Add the water. Cover tightly and bring to a boil over high heat. Place in the oven and bake until the beans are tender, about 2 hours. Adjust the seasoning with salt and pepper, stir in the parsley, and serve hot.

Pastitsio

This is the authentic Greek baked macaroni dish known as *pastitsio*. The traditional method of baking in Greece was to use a beehive-shaped oven called an *avli,* which was built on the side of a house. Those who couldn't afford an oven would send their food to the local baker's *fourno* (oven) for cooking. *Pastitsio* is a baked macaroni dish with meat sauce and white sauce, and an Italian-derived name, but it entails a Muslim-derived baking technique of mixing meat and pasta with spices. It is a favorite dish for the Sunday of Apokreos, the week before Lent, when meat is typically eaten. *Pastitsio* is also frequently found in tavernas and a recipe for it appears in every Greek cookbook. This recipe is based on a wonderful *pastitsio* I had years ago at a truck stop near Árta in the region of Epirus in Greece. It is not unusual to find really great and simple food at Greek truck stops. A certain kind of pasta is used for this preparation that the Greeks call "macaroni for *pastitsio,*" which is what the Italians call *ziti lunghe* or *mezzani,* long un-cut tubular macaroni, for which you can use ziti or penne if need be. *Kefalotyri* cheese is a hard, yellow grating cheese usually made of sheep's milk, though sometimes goat's milk. If you can't find *kefalotyri* cheese you can substitute pecorino Romano cheese. • **Makes 8 servings**

12 tablespoons (1½ sticks) unsalted butter
¾ cup all-purpose flour
Salt and freshly ground black pepper
4 cups hot milk
4 large egg yolks
2 large egg whites, whipped to form moist firm peaks
1 teaspoon freshly grated nutmeg plus more as needed
1½ cups (about 4½ ounces) freshly grated *kefalotyri* cheese (see headnote)
2 tablespoons extra-virgin olive oil

1 large onion, finely chopped

1 large garlic clove, finely chopped

1½ pounds ground beef

3 cups crushed or chopped fresh ripe or canned tomatoes

1 tablespoon tomato paste

1½ teaspoons ground cinnamon

½ teaspoon ground cloves

1½ teaspoons ground allspice

1 pound *ziti lunghe* or *mezzani*

1. To make a thin Béchamel (white) sauce, in a large saucepan, melt 4 table-spoons of butter over medium-high heat. Stir in ¼ cup of flour, and cook, stirring frequently, until it forms a very light brown or golden roux, 6 to 7 minutes. Lightly season with salt and pepper. Whisk 2 table-spoons of the hot milk into the egg yolks and reserve. Remove the saucepan from the heat and whisk 2 cups of the hot milk into the roux. Return the saucepan to medium-low heat and cook, stirring, for a few minutes. Remove from the burner again and stir in half of the reserved egg yolk and milk mixture. Set aside.

2. Now you'll make a thick Béchamel sauce. Follow the instructions in Step 1 using another 4 tablespoons of the remaining butter, the ½ cup remaining flour, the remaining scant 2 cups of hot milk, and the remain-ing half of the reserved egg yolk and milk mixture. Once the sauce is made, fold in the whipped egg whites, a pinch of the nutmeg, and then ½ cup of the *kefalotyri* cheese. Set aside.

3. In a large skillet, heat the olive oil over medium-high heat, then cook the onion, stirring, until translucent, 5 to 6 minutes. Stir in the garlic. Add the beef and cook, breaking it up with a wooden spoon, until browned, 3 to 4 minutes. Add the tomatoes, tomato paste, cinnamon, the remaining teaspoon of nutmeg, the cloves, and allspice. Season with salt and pepper. Stir to mix well. Reduce the heat to low, then cover and simmer, stirring occasionally, until well blended and fragrant, about 30 minutes.

4. Meanwhile, bring a large pot of water to a rolling boil, salt abundantly, and add the pasta. Cook for half the time specified on the box and drain.

5. Preheat the oven to 350°F. Butter a 12 x 9 x 3-inch baking casserole or a lasagne pan.

6. In a small skillet, melt the remaining 4 tablespoons butter over medium-high heat and once it stops bubbling and turns brown, pour over the pasta. Toss the pasta with the thin Béchamel from Step 1. (You just want the pasta coated, not soggy, with Béchamel, so you might not need to use it all.)

7. Cover the bottom of the baking casserole with half of the pasta. Sprinkle with ¼ cup of the remaining *kefalotyri* cheese. Pour the meat sauce over the pasta, spreading it evenly. Sprinkle with another ¼ cup of the *kefalotyri* cheese. Cover with the remaining pasta, and sprinkle with another ¼ cup of the cheese. Cover the pasta with the thick Béchamel sauce from Step 2. Sprinkle the remaining ¼ cup of cheese evenly on top. Bake until golden brown, 50 to 60 minutes. Let rest 10 minutes before serving.

Moussaka

Moussaka (the stress is on the last syllable) is a baked lamb and eggplant casserole covered with a layer of Béchamel sauce that becomes golden and crusty when baked. Moussaka is probably the best known Greek dish. When it is made with eggplant the dish is called *melitzanes mousaka,* eggplant moussaka, in Greek. But the lamb could be replaced by beef and the eggplant by zucchini, potatoes, or artichokes. No one knows the origin of moussaka, but I tried exploring that question in my book *A Mediterranean Feast* (William Morrow, 1999), which can also be found at www.clifforda wright.com/history/his_mousakka.html.

One potential problem with making a traditional moussaka is the amount of fat that might remain after baking. To avoid this, I've developed this recipe, which removes a lot of fat, but also retains the authentic flavor. Moussaka is an involved one-dish meal, therefore I suggest making it on the weekend and only accompanying it with a light green salad. Leftovers, though, are out of this world. • **Makes 6 servings**

For the eggplant

3 pounds eggplant, sliced ⅓ inch thick
½ to ¾ cup extra-virgin olive oil

For the meat

1½ pounds ground lamb
2 tablespoons extra-virgin olive oil
1 medium onion, chopped
2 large garlic cloves, finely chopped
½ cup dry white wine
1 large tomato (about ½ pound), peeled, seeded, and chopped
¼ cup finely chopped fresh parsley leaves

¼ teaspoon dried oregano

1 bay leaf

3 whole cloves

1 teaspoon sugar

1 small cinnamon stick

¼ teaspoon freshly ground allspice berries

1 teaspoon salt

½ teaspoon freshly ground black pepper

2 large eggs, whites beaten to form stiff peaks, yolks saved for the white sauce

2 tablespoons dry bread crumbs

For the Béchamel (white) sauce

9 tablespoons unsalted butter

9 tablespoons all-purpose flour

3 cups whole milk

½ cup (about 1½ ounces) freshly grated *kefalotyri* or *kashkaval* (preferably), or
sharp aged provolone or pecorino Romano cheese

1 teaspoon salt

Pinch of freshly grated nutmeg

To finish the moussaka

1 teaspoon unsalted butter

2 tablespoons dry bread crumbs

1. For the eggplant, lay the eggplant slices on some paper towels and sprinkle them with salt. Leave them to release their bitter juices for 30 minutes, then pat dry with paper towels.

2. Heat a lightly oiled cast-iron griddle over medium-high heat for 10 minutes. Brush each slice of eggplant on both sides with oil and cook in batches until golden brown, about 4 minutes per side. Remove and set aside on a paper towel-lined platter to absorb more of the oil.

3. For the meat, in a medium-size skillet, cook the lamb over medium heat, stirring and breaking up the meat, until it browns and loses most of its

fat, about 10 minutes. Remove the meat with a slotted spoon, pressing down each scoop with the back of a wooden spoon to squeeze out more fat. Heat the olive oil in a clean skillet over medium-high heat and cook the onion and garlic, stirring frequently so the garlic doesn't burn, until the onion is translucent, 5 to 6 minutes. Add the reserved meat and crumble it further with a wooden spoon as you stir to mix. Stir in the wine, tomato, parsley, oregano, bay leaf, cloves, sugar, cinnamon stick, allspice, salt, and pepper. Reduce the heat to medium-low, then cover and cook until the meat is soft and flavorful, about 30 minutes. Remove and discard the bay leaf and cinnamon stick. Let the mixture cool for 15 minutes, then fold in the beaten egg whites and bread crumbs and blend well.

4 For the Béchamel (white) sauce, in a saucepan melt 9 tablespoons butter over medium-high heat. Form a roux by stirring in 9 tablespoons flour and cook until very light golden, stirring, about 3 minutes. Take the saucepan pan off the heat and slowly whisk in the milk. Return to medium heat and simmer gently until the sauce is almost thick, stirring occasionally, about 10 minutes. Add the grated cheese and continue simmering until the cheese melts and the sauce is thick, about 5 minutes. Reduce the heat if the sauce is bubbling too vigorously. Stir in the salt, some grated nutmeg, and the egg yolks, then turn the heat off.

5 Preheat the oven to 400°F. Lightly butter the bottom and sides of a 12 x 9 x 2-inch baking casserole. Sprinkle 1 tablespoon of the bread crumbs over the bottom of the baking casserole, shaking and tilting the baking casserole so all sides are lightly coated.

6 Line the bottom of the baking casserole with two layers of eggplant slices, cover with the meat sauce, and layer the remaining eggplant slices on top. Cover with the Béchamel sauce and then sprinkle the remaining 1 tablespoon bread crumbs on top. Bake until the top is golden, about 30 minutes.

7 Remove from the oven. As there still may be a good deal of fat remaining, cut out a 2-inch section from the moussaka in one of the corners, then rest the casserole on a slight incline so the fat runs to that corner. After several minutes, spoon away any accumulated fat and continue to let the fat run into the corner for another 30 minutes. Place the moussaka in a warm oven until ready to serve. Alternatively, you can serve each portion with a slotted spoon or slotted spatula so some fat drains off.

Bobotee

This famous South African casserole is considered a part of Cape Malay cooking. The Cape Malays emigrated, many via India, to South Africa from the Indo-Malaysian archipelago beginning in the seventeenth century. A basic bobotee (or bobotie) begins with minced lamb or beef, a little soaked bread, eggs, butter, finely chopped onion, garlic, curry powder, and turmeric powder. All are mixed together, put in a baking casserole with meat drippings, and baked slowly. The moment the mixture begins to brown, the dish is taken from the oven and and an egg and milk mixture is poured over the top; then the dish is put back into the oven and baked very slowly to a deep brown. The pace of the cooking is important: if the oven is too hot the bobotee will be dry, and that should never happen, for an ideal bobotee is eaten moist, over rice. In her famous book *Where Is It?*, Hildagonda Duckitt, the Fannie Farmer of South Africa, says that a teaspoon of sugar should be added to the meat mixture, and an ounce of tamarind water gives the dish an

Leftover Idea

When I roast a whole leg of lamb, which I like to do at least once a year, it is an impressive dinner, and I sometimes serve it with green beans. The green beans are boiled for about 7 minutes and tossed in a pan with olive oil, garlic, and pine nuts for about 2 minutes, or until they sizzle. The awkward shape of the leg and hip bone means there will always be quite a bit of meat left over, so I use a paring and filleting knife and cut it all off the bone and into 1-inch cubes. There are often leftover green beans too. So I put the cubes of lamb meat and the green beans in a 10-inch round baking casserole, drizzle with a couple of tablespoons of olive oil, and bake it, covered, at 350°F for 30 minutes. A little salt and pepper, and it's a dinner. On the other hand, leftover lamb is perfect for the Mutton Casserolles (page 98).

exceptionally pleasant, tart flavor. But these are only a few variations, and there are almost as many variations as there are homes in South Africa. Somehow this dish also came to North Carolina where they call it hobotee. This recipe is adapted from one by Noel Mostert, a noted South African historian. I usually cook with freshly ground spices, which I grind in a coffee mill that I reserve for this purpose. Do the same and you will find the finished dish is fresher and zestier. • **Makes 6 servings**

3 tablespoons unsalted butter
3 medium onions, chopped
Seeds from 3 cardamom pods
1 teaspoon hot paprika
1 teaspoon ground cumin
1 teaspoon turmeric powder
1 teaspoon salt
½ teaspoon freshly ground black pepper
½ teaspoon ground ginger
½ teaspoon ground coriander
¼ teaspoon cayenne pepper
¼ teaspoon ground cinnamon
⅛ teaspoon ground cloves
1 tablespoon red wine vinegar
2 slices white loaf bread, crust removed
1¼ cups whole milk
2 pounds ground lamb
¼ cup chopped blanched almonds
¼ cup raisins
4 tablespoons apricot preserves
3 large eggs
2 tablespoons sliced blanched almonds
¼ teaspoon ground nutmeg

1. Preheat the oven to 325°F.

2. In a large skillet, melt the butter over medium heat, then add the onions and cook, stirring occasionally, until golden, 10 to 12 minutes. Add the cardamom, paprika, cumin, turmeric powder, salt, pepper, ginger, coriander, cayenne, cinnamon, and cloves. Add the vinegar and cook, stirring, until evaporated and well blended, about 2 minutes.

3. Soak the bread in ¼ cup of milk, then squeeze out the excess milk. Add the bread and lamb to the skillet and cook, stirring to break up the lamb, until browned, 10 to 12 minutes. Add the chopped almonds, raisins, 2 tablespoons of the apricot preserves, and 1 egg. Remove from the heat and mix thoroughly.

4. Place the meat mixture in a 12 × 9 × 3-inch baking casserole. Spread the remaining 2 tablespoons of apricot preserves over the meat. In a bowl, whisk together the remaining 2 eggs and the remaining 1 cup of milk. Pour this mixture over the layer of apricot preserves. Sprinkle the sliced almonds and a dusting of nutmeg over the top. Bake until the custard on top sets, about 1 hour. Serve hot.

Lamb Casserole from Spain

This simple lamb casserole is often made as a family meal in the Spanish province of Andalusia. Although it's called a casserole and it's cooked in a casserole, it emits so much liquid from the vegetables that it ends up being very stewy. So you can either leave it in its baking casserole with all its liquid and serve it in bowls, or you can transfer it using a slotted spoon to another serving casserole. • **Makes 6 servings**

2 pounds boneless lamb leg and/or shoulder, cut into smaller pieces
Salt and freshly ground black pepper
6 ounces Canadian bacon or cooked ham, diced
3 medium onions, chopped
3 green bell peppers, seeded and chopped
6 large garlic cloves, finely chopped
3 tablespoons finely chopped fresh parsley
1 bay leaf
1 teaspoon hot paprika
¼ cup extra-virgin olive oil
1 cup rosé wine
1 cup water

1 Preheat the oven to 350°F.

2 Season the lamb with salt and pepper. In a deep earthenware baking casserole (preferably), mix together the lamb, Canadian bacon, onions, green bell peppers, garlic, parsley, bay leaf, paprika, and some more salt and pepper. Pour the olive oil, wine, and water over the meat. Cover and bake until the lamb is falling-apart tender, about 1½ hours. Serve or let sit in the oven for 2 hours, if you like, before serving.

Mutton Casserolles

This delicious take on a shepherd's pie is not some newfangled idea, but is a preparation from old Kentucky cooking, namely from Mrs. Lettice Bryan's *The Kentucky Housewife*, published in 1839, the first cookbook published in the state of Kentucky. She instructs the cook to use two "scollop" pans to make the casseroles. These are pans shaped like scallop shells. The casserole is made with layers of mashed potatoes, tomato, shredded cooked mutton, and chopped ham, all seasoned with spices, gravy, and wine. It is served with a sauceboat on the side of melted butter mixed with wine. The original recipe called for boiled mutton, but I slowly sautéed some slices of lamb leg instead in order to get a nice brown crust that I think gives a wonderful flavor. Remember though to allow yourself the two or so hours in order to cook the lamb first, unless you've got leftover lamb. • **Makes 4 servings**

1¾ pounds boneless leg of lamb steaks or mutton steaks (leave fat on)

3 tablespoons all-purpose flour

1 cup beef broth

2 tablespoons water

1½ pounds boiling potatoes, such as Red Bliss or White Rose, peeled and quartered

4 tablespoons (½ stick) unsalted butter, plus 3 tablespoons melted

½ cup heavy cream

½ teaspoon salt, plus more as needed

¼ teaspoon freshly ground black pepper, plus more as needed

1 large ripe tomato, cut into ¼-inch-thick slices

¼ pound finely chopped cooked ham

3 tablespoons freshly squeezed lemon juice

½ teaspoon freshly grated nutmeg

¼ cup dry red wine, plus 3 tablespoons

For the side sauce

3 tablespoons melted unsalted butter

3 tablespoons dry red wine

1. Place the lamb steaks in a large skillet and turn the heat to low. Cook, uncovered, turning every 15 minutes, until crusty brown on both sides, and the meat can almost shred when pulled with a fork, about 2¼ hours. Remove the steaks and set aside to cool for 10 minutes, then cut them into thin irregular slices and pieces. Discard all but 3 tablespoons of the lamb fat in the skillet.

2. Heat the lamb fat left in the skillet over medium heat, then stir in the flour to make a roux. Add the beef broth and water and stir until blended, scraping up any crusty bits in the skillet. Cook, stirring to form a smooth gravy, 1 to 2 minutes. Turn the heat off and set aside.

3. Place the potatoes in a large saucepan and cover by several inches with water. Turn the heat to medium and bring to a very gentle boil, about 20 minutes. Cook until a skewer glides easily into the center of a piece of potato, about another 20 minutes. Drain well and mash in a bowl with 3½ tablespoons of butter, the cream, ½ teaspoon salt, and ¼ teaspoon black pepper. Set aside.

4. Preheat the oven to 400°F. Butter a 9 × 3-inch round baking casserole with the remaining ½ tablespoon butter.

5. Cover the bottom of the baking casserole with half of the seasoned mashed potatoes. Lay the sliced tomato over the mashed potatoes and then layer the lamb over the tomato. Sprinkle the ham over the lamb and season with lemon juice, pepper, and nutmeg. Pour ½ cup of the gravy on top and then sprinkle ½ cup wine over. Cover with the remaining half of the mashed potatoes and season lightly with salt. Bake until the top is a light golden brown, about 30 minutes. Serve with the sauce of melted butter mixed with 3 tablespoons wine and the leftover gravy.

Tamale Pie

You might be surprised to know that tamale pie is not a pie but rather the name of a casserole and, second, it is not a Mexican dish but a classic casserole from Texas. Although the Mexican tamale is the root of this casserole, the Mexican tamale is something else entirely. A Mexican tamale is finely ground cornmeal cooked into a mush with water that is cooled and then stuffed with seasoned and saucy meat, chicken, vegetables, or shrimp that is then rolled up in a corn husk and steamed. The American tamale pie takes this concept and puts it in a baking casserole to bake rather than steam. Some cooks stir a stick of butter into the cornmeal, and although it does enrich it wonderfully, you really don't need that much, as the tamale pie is already so flavorful. There is some work involved in this recipe, but it yields many servings and is worth the effort since it makes great leftovers and an even greater potluck supper dish. Many recipes for tamale pie don't specify what kind of cornmeal to use. There are many grades and although the fine yellow cornmeal you will find in your local supermarket works great, try to see if you can get a hold of the Mexican-style cornmeal called *masa harina*. It's not that hard to find, and it's likely your supermarket may already have it shelved with the Latino foods. If you are using Mexican chorizo sausage, as suggested in the ingredient list, make sure it's made of pure pork and not pork parts, otherwise it will be too fatty. There is one more interesting thing about this recipe that you won't find mentioned elsewhere: it is meat-rich which befits a wealthy nation, while in Mexico a tamale is really more about corn than meat. If you like, you can make another version of this tamale pie that emphasizes the cornmeal mush rather than the meat by doubling the cornmeal mush ingredients and cutting the meat filling ingredients in half.

The cooking time stays the same. It's quite rich and doesn't need any other accompaniment other than some sliced ripe avocados and tomatoes sprinkled with a touch of olive oil and fresh cilantro leaves. The cheese topping is typical of Tex-Mex cooking but you would not find it in Mexican cooking.

• **Makes 8 to 10 servings**

For the filling

4 tablespoons (½ stick) unsalted butter or pork lard

½ pound Mexican-style chorizo sausage (natural casings, not plastic), Cajun andouille sausage, garlic sausage, or sweet Italian sausage, casing removed

¼ cup chili powder

1 teaspoon ground cumin

1 large onion, finely chopped

1 green bell pepper, seeded and chopped

2 celery stalks, finely chopped

2 large garlic cloves, finely chopped

Salt and freshly ground black pepper

1½ pounds very lean ground beef

One 28-ounce can crushed peeled tomatoes

1½ cups frozen or fresh corn kernels (from 2 cobs)

1½ cups black olives, pitted and coarsely chopped

3 canned jalapeño chiles, chopped

2 tablespoons chopped pimientos

½ teaspoon dried thyme

½ teaspoon dried oregano

For the cornmeal mush

1 cup fine yellow cornmeal (preferably *masa harina*)

1 cup cold water

3½ cups boiling chicken broth or water

2 teaspoons salt

4 tablespoons (½ stick) unsalted butter or pork lard

For the garnish

1½ cups (about 4 ½ ounces) shredded sharp cheddar cheese (optional)

1. Prepare the filling. In a large skillet, melt the butter or lard over medium heat, then cook the sausage with the chili powder and cumin, stirring and breaking up the meat, until it is bubbling and aromatic, 3 to 5 minutes. Add the onion, bell pepper, celery, and garlic to the skillet and stir. Season with salt and pepper and cook, stirring occasionally, until the vegetables are slightly softened, 2 to 3 minutes. Add the ground beef and cook, stirring and breaking up the meat with a wooden spoon, until it is browned, about 5 minutes. Add the tomatoes, corn, olives, chiles, pimientos, thyme, and oregano. Reduce the heat to low and simmer until the liquid is mostly evaporated, about 45 minutes. Taste and correct the seasoning.

2. Prepare the cornmeal mush. In the top part of a double-boiler, stir the cornmeal into 1 cup of cold water to prevent lumps from forming. Add the boiling chicken broth or water and salt, stir to mix well. Fill the bottom part of the double-boiler with a few inches of water, and bring the water to a boil. Place the top part of the double boiler containing the cornmeal mixture over the boiling water. Cover and cook the cornmeal over medium heat, stirring frequently, until the water is absorbed, about 40 minutes. Stir the butter into the cornmeal until it melts and set aside, keeping it warm.

3. Meanwhile, preheat the oven to 350°F. Lightly butter a 13 x 10 x 3-inch baking casserole or any large and deep baking casserole or roasting pan.

4. In the baking casserole, spread half of the cornmeal mush to cover the bottom. Let it sit for 5 minutes to solidify. Spread the meat filling over the entire surface of the cornmeal and then cover the meat with the remaining cornmeal mush. Sprinkle the top with the cheese, if desired. Bake until the top is crusty, about 30 minutes. Serve hot.

Veal Roman Style

This a simple family casserole that you are unlikely to find on the menu of a restaurant in Rome because it's purely a home-cooked preparation. The casserole exudes a lot of juice at the end of the cooking time, so serve it with potatoes or spaghetti and a good sprinkling of cheese.

• Makes 4 servings

2 tablespoons unsalted butter
2 tablespoons extra-virgin olive oil
2 pounds boneless veal shoulder or rump, cut into 1-inch cubes
1 medium onion, finely chopped
1 celery stalk, thinly sliced
½ pound white button mushrooms, sliced
1 teaspoon chopped fresh rosemary
¾ cup dry white wine
Salt and freshly ground black pepper

1. Preheat the oven to 350°F.

2. In a flame-proof 2-quart baking casserole, melt the butter with the olive oil over medium-high heat, then cook the meat, turning frequently, until browned on all sides, about 6 minutes. Add the onion, celery, and mushrooms, and cook, stirring, until the vegetables are softened, about 5 minutes. Sprinkle on the rosemary and wine. Season with salt and pepper. Cover and place in the oven to bake, stirring occasionally, until the meat and vegetables are tender, about 1 hour. Serve hot.

Veal and Mushroom Casserole

This casserole from New England is spiced with nutmeg, which seems to draw out some wonderful flavors from the mushrooms. Much of New England cooking was well seasoned with sweet spices such as cinnamon, mace, and nutmeg. In fact, it is sometimes forgotten that Connecticut is known as the Nutmeg State. From early on, spice traders from New England were becoming rich from the spice trade with the Moluccas, in today's Indonesia. You can use the regular white button mushrooms, but I believe the final casserole will have far more flavor if you use shiitake mushrooms. If you don't have any leftover veal, follow the Note below for cooking a piece of fresh veal. • **Makes 4 servings**

2½ tablespoons unsalted butter
1 medium onion, chopped
1 tablespoon all-purpose flour
½ cup dry white wine
¼ cup beef broth (see Note)
½ teaspoon dried summer savory
¼ teaspoon freshly ground nutmeg
Salt
1 pound white button mushrooms or stemmed shiitake mushrooms, sliced
1¼ pounds leftover boneless veal roast, diced (see Note)
1 cup heavy cream

1 Preheat the oven to 350°F. Lightly butter a 10 × 2-inch round baking casserole with ½ tablespoon of butter.

2 In a skillet, melt the remaining 2 tablespoons of butter over medium heat, then add the onion and cook, stirring, until softened, about 5 minutes. Add the flour and stir until it has blended with the buttery onion, then stir in the wine, beef broth, savory, and nutmeg. Season with salt.

Cook until the sauce is smooth, about 2 minutes. Set aside. When it is time to use the sauce, if it is too thick, stir in a few tablespoons of water to thin it to a consistency that is more like a gravy.

③ Arrange half of the mushrooms on the bottom of the baking casserole. Cover with half of the veal. Spoon half of the sauce over the veal, then cover with the remaining mushrooms, the remaining veal, and the remaining sauce. Pour the cream over everything and bake until bubbly, about 1 hour.

Note: A veal broth makes a terrific alternative to the beef broth. To make a quick veal broth, preheat a cast-iron skillet or other heavy skillet over medium-high heat. Add a 1½-pound veal shoulder chop and cook until medium rare and golden brown on both sides, about 15 minutes total. Let cool a bit, then dice the meat, discarding any gristle and bones. Pour ½ cup of water into the skillet and cook, scraping up any bits, over high heat for about 2 minutes or until the liquid is reduced by half.

Leftover Idea

The Veal and Mushroom Casserole has a pretty hearty taste, but when you mix those leftovers with leftover Simple Spinach Casserole (page 372), you've really invented something greater than its parts. Make a Mornay sauce (a Béchamel sauce, page 88, made with Swiss cheese) and spread it over the mixed casseroles in an appropriately sized casserole and bake at 350°F until very hot, about 30 minutes.

Veal Saltimbocca

This famous preparation called *saltimbocca alla Romana* probably had its origins in a nineteenth-century Roman restaurant. *Saltimbocca* means "jump in the mouth," referring to the fact that it's so appetizing that the morsels of scallopini jump right into your mouth. In the U.S., during the 1970s and 80s, veal saltimbocca was a very popular Italian restaurant menu item. It went out of fashion, not because it wasn't good, but simply because restaurant-goers always want something new. But the tried and true is nothing to scoff at, as we know from meatloaf or lasagne. This recipe is the classic one with prosciutto, sage, and mozzarella cheese. Scallopini are usually cut from veal rump (although the name now applies to pork and turkey too) and are then pounded until not more than $1/16$ inch thick. Typically, they are cooked very briefly because they are so thin and delicate. Saltimbocca can be served with roasted potatoes, and with carrots and broccoli that are sautéed in butter. • **Makes 4 servings**

2 tablespoons unsalted butter
2 tablespoons extra-virgin olive oil
8 veal scallopini (about 1 pound total)
8 large fresh sage leaves
Salt and freshly ground black pepper
8 thin slices prosciutto (about ¼ pound)
8 slices fresh mozzarella cheese (about ½ pound)
¼ cup dry white wine
1 tablespoon finely chopped fresh parsley

1. Preheat the oven to 375°F. Lightly oil a 12 x 9 x 2-inch baking casserole.

2. In a large skillet, melt the butter with the olive oil over medium heat until the butter stops bubbling. Cook the scallopini until they lose their pinkness, turning only once, about 1 minute in all. Transfer the scallopini to the baking casserole. Reserve the skillet.

3. Place a sage leaf on each scallopini and season with salt and pepper. Place a slice of prosciutto on top of each scallopini, folding the prosciutto over upon itself, if necessary, to fit, and then top each prosciutto slice with a slice of mozzarella. Bake until the cheese melts, about 10 minutes. Turn the oven off. Transfer the scallopini to a warm serving platter, cheese side up. Cover with aluminum foil and keep warm in the turned-off oven.

4. Pour the accumulated juices from the baking casserole into the reserved skillet. Turn the heat to high, and once it starts to bubble, pour in the wine. Cook, scraping and stirring with a wooden spoon to loosen the bits and deglaze the skillet, until the liquid is reduced by half, 3 to 4 minutes. Pour this sauce over the saltimbocca, sprinkle with parsley, and serve hot.

Leftover Idea

Frankly, these days I rarely have leftovers, as my three ravenous young adult children take no prisoners when it comes to dinner. But when they were little, someone would always leave a piece of veal saltimbocca behind—I would stick it in a soft roll with some lettuce leaves, a slice of tomato, and a drop or two of olive oil, and enjoy it for lunch the next day.

Ham and Broccoli Casserole

The little golden and dark brown flecks that dot the top of this casserole as it comes out of the oven are a sure sign that everyone will gobble it down. The important thing to remember in this recipe is not to cook the broccoli too long the first time, as it will continue cooking while it bakes in the oven. A high-quality sliced ham is worth using here too. This family casserole is adapted from Judith and Evan Jones's *The L.L. Bean Book of New New England Cookery*. • **Makes 4 servings**

1¾ pounds broccoli, stems removed and peeled, then cut
    into 1-inch pieces, florets left whole
Salt
4 tablespoons (½ stick) unsalted butter plus more as needed
¼ cup all-purpose flour
1 tablespoon Dijon mustard
2 cups whole milk
8 fresh sage leaves
Freshly ground black pepper
8 slices cooked ham (about ½ pound)
½ cup fresh bread crumbs (see Note)
¼ cup (less than 1 ounce) freshly grated cheddar cheese
    (preferably aged 15 months or more)

1. Preheat the oven to 350°F. Lightly butter a 12 × 9 × 2-inch baking casserole.

2. Bring a large saucepan of lightly salted water to a boil, then cook the broccoli stems until al dente, about 4 minutes. Add the florets and cook until bright green and tender, 6 minutes. Do not cook the broccoli more than this. Drain stems and florets together and well. Break up the florets into smaller pieces. Arrange the florets and stems in the baking casserole. Salt the broccoli.

Mustard

In the many recipes calling for mustard, I sometimes specify Dijon mustard and other times prepared mustard, which consists of mixing mustard powder with enough water to form a consistency a little looser than that which comes out of a squeeze bottle, usually in equal proportions. Using this prepared mustard will give a sharper taste because it contains no other ingredients, as does Dijon mustard. The mustard found in squeeze bottles for hot dogs should not be used in my recipes that call for prepared mustard.

3 In a saucepan, melt 4 tablespoons of butter over medium-high heat, then stir in the flour to form a roux and cook, stirring, for 1 minute. Stir in the mustard and remove the saucepan from the heat. Slowly stir in the milk and sage, whisking well as you do. Return the saucepan to the heat and cook over low heat, stirring frequently, until the sauce thickens, about 12 minutes. Season with salt and pepper.

4 Cover the broccoli with the slices of ham and spread the sauce on top. Sprinkle the top with the bread crumbs and cheese. Bake until light golden, about 25 minutes. Increase the heat to "broil" or turn the broiler on and broil until the bread crumb topping is spotted with golden and black flecks, about 3 minutes. Serve hot.

Note: This amount can be made from crumbling one ½-inch-thick slice of 5¼ × 3-inch French or Italian bread in a food processor.

Ham Melody

This recipe is adapted from one posted at cooks.com. The recipe doesn't say anything about its provenance or who created it. But I immediately liked the chicken, ham, and Swiss cheese combination, and thought it would make a great family casserole. When I made it for my family it indeed disappeared quickly, but someone asked "Why 'ham' melody? Seems it should be chicken melody!" The one tricky thing here—and this was not mentioned in the recipe posted at the Web site—you need to be careful that you do not poach the chicken at a boil otherwise it will be tough. Instead, poach the chicken in barely simmering water so that it stays very tender and will melt in your mouth. • **Makes 4 servings**

3 chicken breast halves on the bone (about 2½ pounds)
Water as needed
6 tablespoons (¾ stick) unsalted butter
1 cup fresh bread crumbs (see Note)
2 tablespoons chopped onion
¼ cup all-purpose flour
2 cups whole milk
Salt and freshly ground black pepper
1 large egg, beaten to blend
¼ cup heavy cream
6 slices (about ¼ pound) cooked ham
6 slices (about ¼ pound) Swiss cheese

① Preheat the oven to 350°F. Generously butter a 12 x 9 x 2-inch baking casserole.

② Place the chicken breasts in a large saucepan and cover with water. Bring to just below a boil, making sure the water never boils and is only shimmering at the most or else the chicken will be tough. Cook gently until the meat is white and firm, about 20 minutes in all. Remove the chicken breasts from the broth and cool. Once they are cool, carefully remove the meat from the bone and cut it into large chunks.

③ In a saucepan, melt the butter over medium-high heat. Remove 2 table-spoons of melted butter and toss it with the bread crumbs in a small bowl. Set the breads crumbs aside. Cook the onion in the remaining butter, stirring, until translucent, about 3 minutes. Add the flour and stir to form a roux. Cook for 1 minute, then remove from the heat and slowly whisk in the milk. Season with salt and pepper. Return the sauce-pan to the heat and simmer over medium-low heat, stirring frequently, until the sauce thickens, about 12 minutes. Add the egg and cream and continue stirring continuously for another minute.

④ Arrange the chicken in a layer over the baking casserole. Cover with the ham and then the cheese. Pour the sauce over the casserole. Sprinkle the reserved bread crumbs over the entire top of the casserole. Bake until golden brown on top, about 30 minutes.

Note: This amount can be made from crumbling two ½-inch-thick slices of 5¼ x 3-inch French or Italian bread in a food processor.

Cheesy Ham Poof

It was only after I first made this casserole that I realized it was a Nebraska frittata! How else to describe this light and airy casserole than as a poof stuffed with ham and cheeses? I've adapted the recipe from Nebraska home-maker and author Beverly Nye's recipe in her cookbook, *Everyone's a Home-maker*, published in 1982. It is best made with an electric mixer, but you can use a whisk and a little muscle instead. It's a good casserole for brunch, and little squares of it can also be served as an appetizer. • **Makes 6 servings**

6 large eggs
½ cup all-purpose flour
1½ teaspoons baking powder
1 cup whole milk
1 cup (about ¼ pound) finely chopped cooked ham
3 ounces (about ½ cup) cream cheese
2 cups (about 6 ounces) shredded mild cheddar cheese
1 cup (8 ounces) cottage cheese
2 tablespoons unsalted butter plus more as needed
3 scallions, white and green parts chopped
1 tablespoon finely chopped fresh parsley
¼ teaspoon sweet paprika
1 teaspoon salt
½ teaspoon freshly ground black pepper

① Preheat the oven to 350°F. Lightly butter a 9 × 9 × 2-inch baking casserole.

② In an electric mixer bowl, beat the eggs for 1 minute, then stir in the flour and baking powder. Slowly beat in the milk. Add the ham, cream cheese, cheddar cheese, cottage cheese, 2 tablespoons of butter, scallions, parsley, paprika, salt, and pepper. Continue mixing until well blended, about 3 minutes at medium speed. Transfer to the casserole and bake until a knife inserted into the middle of the casserole comes out clean and the top is golden brown, 50 to 60 minutes. Serve hot.

Leftover Idea

If you're making the Cheesy Ham Poof, which I also like to call a Nebraska frittata, you just may have leftovers that you can turn the next day into a delightful little appetizer. A frittata is actually called a tortilla in Spain (having nothing to do with the flatbread), and Spaniards often serve little squares of this dish as a tapa. You can do the same with your Nebraska frittata. Cut it up into half-inch squares and serve with mayonnaise or some hot sauce to dip them in.

Ham Crêpes Casserole

This luscious recipe, called *les crêpes au jambon* in French, is a well-known dish in the region of Auvergne in France. The crêpes are made with and cooked in *beurre noisette*, clarified butter that is heated until golden brown in color. They're stuffed with strips of cooked ham and rolled up and arranged in a row in the casserole. This recipe is said to come from the little town of Ambert in the heart of the mountains of Livradois. The famous cheese, *fourme d'Ambert*, also comes from this town. This recipe is adapted from Gaston Joyeux, who bought the Hôtel du Livradois in 1946 and became its chef. The recipe can be doubled, but if you do, use two baking casseroles. The best ham to use is Bayonne ham, a cured ham, which some fancy gourmet shops might have. Otherwise, Black Forest ham or Virginia Smithfield ham is best. • **Makes 4 servings**

4 tablespoons clarified unsalted butter
Salt and freshly ground black pepper
½ recipe Crêpes (page 392, 8 to 9 cooked crêpes made with
  beurre noisette in Step 1 of that recipe)
½ pound cooked ham, thinly sliced
1 cup heavy cream
½ cup (about 1½ ounces) shredded Gruyère cheese
1 tablespoon unsalted butter

1. Preheat the oven to 325°F.

2. In a small saucepan, make the *beurre noisette* by cooking the clarified butter over medium heat until it melts and turns golden brown, about 2 minutes; watch it all the time so it doesn't become too brown. Season with salt and pepper and set aside.

3. Butter a 12 × 9 × 2-inch baking casserole, using about 1 teaspoon of the *beurre noisette*. Following the instructions in Step 1 on page 392, make 8 or 9 crêpes using the remaining *beurre noisette*.

4. Stuff each crêpe with the strips of ham. Roll the crêpes up and arrange in the baking casserole. Pour the cream over the stuffed crêpes, sprinkle the cheese on top, and dot with 1 tablespoon of unsalted butter. Bake until the top is browned, 15 to 20 minutes.

Poultry, Dairy, and Game

Casseroles

Chicken Casserole

Be aware before you start this recipe that it needs to sit for the whole day in the refrigerator before baking, so you need to begin the preparation in the morning. There are a million recipes for chicken casserole and the only thing that links them is that they all have chicken. This recipe is rather typical of an all-American chicken casserole. It comes out of the oven bubbling from the cheddar cheese, and as soon as you plunge your spoon into it, you can tell it will be delicious. It has a bread pudding-like taste and consistency and, despite the ingredients, actually tastes light. The dish hinges on the quality of your bread in the first place, so use an artisanal type of French country bread, but not sourdough. If you don't have leftover chicken, pan-sear two boneless skinless chicken breast halves over medium-high heat until golden brown and firm when poked, about 12 minutes. If using leftover chicken, taste it first. If it tastes dry, don't use it; instead, pan-sear two fresh chicken breasts. • **Makes 6 servings**

> 8 slices French country bread, crusts removed and cut into squares,
>   white part diced separately
> ½ teaspoon ground sage
> 2 cups (about 1 pound) diced cooked chicken breast
> ½ cup chopped celery
> ½ cup mayonnaise
> ¼ cup chopped onion
> ½ teaspoon salt plus more as needed
> ⅛ teaspoon freshly ground black pepper plus more as needed
> 2 large eggs
> 1½ cups whole milk

For the Béchamel (white) sauce

3 tablespoons unsalted butter

3 tablespoons all-purpose flour

1 cup chicken broth

¾ cup whole milk

½ cup heavy cream

Salt and freshly ground pepper

2 cups (about 6 ounces) shredded mild cheddar cheese

1. At least 8 hours before you plan to serve the casserole, spread the crust squares on the bottom of a lightly buttered 12 x 9 x 2-inch baking casserole and sprinkle with the sage.

2. In a bowl, combine the chicken, celery, mayonnaise, onion, ½ teaspoon of salt, and ⅛ teaspoon of black pepper. Spread this mixture over the bread crusts. Arrange the diced white part of the bread over the chicken mixture. In a bowl, beat the eggs with the milk, then pour over the bread. Cover and refrigerate all day or overnight.

3. Preheat the oven to 350°F.

4. To make the Béchamel sauce, in a saucepan, melt the butter over medium heat. Add the flour and stir to form a roux. Continue to cook, stirring, for about 1 minute. Remove the saucepan from the heat and slowly whisk in the chicken broth, milk, and cream. Season with salt and pepper. Return the saucepan to the heat and simmer, stirring occasionally, over low heat until dense, about 12 minutes.

5. Pour the sauce over the chicken casserole and bake until bubbly and golden, about 45 minutes. Remove the casserole from the oven, sprinkle the cheese on top, then return to the oven and bake until the cheese melts, 8 to 10 minutes. Serve hot.

Chicken Broccoli Casserole

This is a most inviting casserole, as the final dish is completely encrusted with a golden brown bread crumb topping. As you plunge the serving spoon into the crust it releases a perfume of flavorful poached chicken. There are literally thousands of recipes for this popular American family dish, but frankly, most of them will remind you of nothing but canned food from the fifties. This casserole starts with the basics, and the basics, in this case, is a gently poached free-range organic chicken. This is an excellent way to use up leftover chicken or turkey too. Some cooks add sliced mushrooms or cream of mushroom soup, but I think you will be a lot happier with this recipe. There are two critical steps you must pay attention to in this recipe, otherwise you will not be eating what I've described. First, poach the chicken whole and never let the liquid come to a boil, otherwise the chicken will be tough. Make sure the water is never more than a shimmer on the surface. Second, never cook broccoli too much, otherwise it will release, as do all cruciferous vegetables, sulfurous compounds such as ammonia and hydrogen sulfide, which interact with the chlorophyll in the broccoli, causing it to turn an unappetizing gray and giving off an unpleasant smell. This means, never cook broccoli more than 6 or 7 minutes at a boil, then drain it immediately and plunge it into cold water to stop it from cooking. • **Makes 6 servings**

One 4-pound chicken
1 ½ teaspoons salt plus more as needed
10 black peppercorns
1 celery stalk, cut up
1 carrot, cut into rounds
1 onion, quartered
6 tablespoons (¾ stick) unsalted butter

Poaching a Whole Chicken

The star of many casserole recipes is chicken, and some recipes call for poaching a whole chicken or for cooked diced chicken, which comes from a poached chicken. You will want to exercise some care when doing this, because chicken flesh will toughen when boiled. So, first, never boil chicken. Always poach chicken in liquid that remains just under a boil throughout the cooking time. The surface of the water should only be shimmering while the chicken cooks. Choose a good-tasting chicken and don't settle for any supermarket chicken. Look for a free-range organic chicken. It will cost more, but you can penny-pinch on other less-important items. Finally, I often wrap the whole chicken in cheesecloth and tie it off with kitchen twine to make retrieving it from the pot easier and to keep parts of the chicken from falling back into the broth and then having to fish them out.

¾ cup fresh bread crumbs (see Note)

¼ cup all-purpose flour

1 cup whole milk

¼ teaspoon freshly ground black pepper plus more as needed

1 cup mayonnaise

1 teaspoon freshly squeezed lemon juice

1 pound broccoli florets

1. Place the chicken in a large pot and add just enough water to cover, along with 1 teaspoon of salt, peppercorns, celery, carrot, and onion. Bring to just below a boil over high heat, then reduce the heat to low and simmer until the chicken is almost falling off the bone, about 1¼ hours; make sure the liquid never comes to a boil, otherwise the chicken will be tough. Remove the chicken from the broth and let cool. Strain the broth and reserve 2 cups for this recipe and freeze the rest for another recipe, such as Baked Rice with Garlic (page 308). Remove the meat from the bones and dice the meat. Discard the bones and skin.

2. In a small saucepan, melt the butter over medium-high heat. Transfer 2 tablespoons of the butter to a bowl and toss with the bread crumbs. Set the bread crumbs aside.

3 Heat the remaining 4 tablespoons of melted butter over medium heat, then add the flour and stir to form a roux. Continue to cook, stirring, for about 1 minute. Remove the saucepan from the heat, then slowly whisk in the milk and the 2 cups of reserved chicken broth. Return to the heat, reduce the heat to medium-low, and continue to cook, stirring frequently, until smooth and dense, about 15 minutes. Remove from the heat and season with $\frac{1}{2}$ teaspoon of salt and $\frac{1}{4}$ teaspoon of black pepper. Add the mayonnaise and lemon juice, and whisk until smooth.

4 Preheat the oven to 350°F. Butter a 12 × 9 × 2-inch baking casserole.

5 Bring a large saucepan of water to a boil, then cook the broccoli until bright green and tender, 6 to 7 minutes and not more. Drain in a colander and cool immediately under cold running water to stop it from cooking, then let drain again. Arrange the broccoli on the bottom of the baking casserole. Place the chicken on top of the broccoli, season with salt and pepper, then cover with the white sauce. Sprinkle the bread crumbs over the white sauce. Bake until golden brown, about 45 minutes. Remove from the oven and let rest 15 minutes before serving.

Note: This amount can be made from crumbling two $\frac{1}{2}$-inch-thick slices of $5\frac{1}{4}$ × 3-inch French or Italian bread in a food processor.

Chicken and Mushroom Casserole

This delicious casserole turns a gorgeous golden brown on top while it is in the oven. It's ideal when accompanied by a casserole of roasted carrots. You can also serve it with some noodles or orzo with peas and butter.

• Makes 4 servings

1¾ pounds (about 4) chicken thighs on the bones, skin removed
1 teaspoon sweet paprika
Salt and freshly ground black pepper
4 tablespoons (½ stick) unsalted butter
½ pound white button mushrooms, thinly sliced
4 scallions, white and green parts thinly sliced
¼ cup all-purpose flour
¾ cup chicken broth
3 tablespoons dry sherry
1 sprig fresh rosemary

1 Preheat the oven to 350°F.

2 Sprinkle the chicken with paprika, salt, and pepper. In a large skillet, melt 2 tablespoons of butter over medium heat, then cook the chicken, turning occasionally, until light golden brown, about 12 minutes. Arrange the chicken in a single layer in a 9-inch round baking casserole.

3 Add the remaining 2 tablespoons of butter to the skillet, then cook the mushrooms and scallions, stirring occasionally, until softened and lightly browned and the liquid has evaporated, about 5 minutes. Sprinkle the flour over the mushroom mixture and stir a few times, then pour in the chicken broth and sherry and add the rosemary sprig. Cook, stirring, until the sauce becomes denser and smooth, about 1 minute. Pour the mushroom sauce over the chicken. (The casserole can be refrigerated at this point, if desired. If refrigerating the casserole, remove it from the refrigerator 30 minutes before you bake it.)

4 Bake until dark golden brown and bubbling, with little liquid remaining, and without turning the chicken, about 1 hour. Discard the rosemary sprig and serve hot.

Chicken Divan

It's hard to believe that this classic American casserole made by moms across the country had its origins in a New York restaurant. Patricia Bunning Stevens, in her book *Rare Bits: Unusual Origins of Popular Recipes* (Ohio University Press, 1998), tells us that chicken divan, a chicken casserole with broccoli and Mornay or hollandaise sauce, was the signature dish of a 1950s New York restaurant, the Divan Parisienne, in midtown Manhattan. The restaurant was around in the 1940s and the dish seems to have been invented there. The restaurant was given what was thought to be an elegant French name in the then competitive restaurant world where elegance meant Frenchness conveyed by the idea of "continental cuisine." Although *divan* came to mean "sofa" in English and French, the word derives from the Turkish word *diwan*, meaning the chambers of an administrative bureau or the privy council of the Ottoman Empire, itself derived from the Persian word for an account book. The owners of the Divan Parisienne thought that this name conveyed the idea of a continental restaurant. The dish quickly entered the home kitchen where it was always made with frozen broccoli and cream of celery soup. My modern version uses thinly sliced boneless chicken breast and natural chicken broth in a luscious sauce flavored with Parmesan cheese, sherry, cream, and a touch of curry powder as the cushion (divan) for the fresh broccoli. The recipe is ideal for leftover chicken breast, but if you are going to cook the chicken breast for this preparation, it is best to sear it quickly in a cast-iron skillet until golden brown. • **Makes 4 servings**

1½ pounds broccoli, stems removed and saved for another purpose,
    florets left whole
4 tablespoons (½ stick) unsalted butter
¼ cup all-purpose flour
2 cups chicken broth
½ cup heavy cream
¼ cup dry sherry
½ teaspoon freshly squeezed lemon juice
½ teaspoon salt
¼ teaspoon freshly ground black pepper
¼ teaspoon curry powder
4 cooked boneless skinless chicken breast halves
    (about 1¾ pounds total), thinly sliced
½ cup (about 1½ ounces) freshly grated Parmesan cheese

1. Preheat the oven to 350°F. Lightly butter a 12 × 9 × 2-inch baking casserole.

2. Bring a saucepan of water to a rolling boil, salt lightly, and cook the broccoli until al dente but still bright green, 6 or 7 minutes. Drain in a colander and cool immediately under cold running water to stop it from cooking. Separate the florets into smaller pieces by breaking them off the central stem.

3. In a saucepan, melt the butter over medium-high heat, then add the flour and stir to form a roux. Continue to cook, stirring, for 1 minute. Remove the saucepan from the heat, then slowly whisk in the chicken broth, cream, sherry, and lemon juice. Whisk in the salt, pepper, and curry powder. Return to low heat and continue to cook, stirring occasionally, until the sauce is denser, about 12 minutes.

4. Arrange the chicken in the baking casserole and spoon half of the sauce over it. Put the broccoli on top of the sauce in the baking casserole. Stir ¼ cup of cheese into the remaining half of the sauce, and then cover the broccoli with the sauce. Sprinkle the top with the remaining cheese and bake until the top is light golden, about 30 minutes. Serve hot.

Chicken Dried Beef Casserole

I had never heard of this old-fashioned casserole before writing this book. Subsequently, I learned that it's a casserole made in the South, although it's not too common. I'm including it in this book for a very simple reason—it's good and worth keeping out of the recipe heavens. Some cooks sprinkle Ritz crackers on top for an au gratin finish. It's excellent with egg noodles. When serving, remember to dig deep to get some of the beef jerky on the bottom. • **Makes 6 servings**

4 tablespoons (½ stick) unsalted butter
3 ounces white button mushrooms (about 6), finely chopped
2 tablespoons finely chopped onion
¼ cup all-purpose flour
½ cup whole milk
½ cup heavy cream
1 cup chicken broth
Salt and freshly ground black pepper
8 boneless skinless chicken breast halves (about 3½ pounds total)
8 bacon slices
5 ounces dried plain beef jerky pieces
2 cups sour cream

1 Preheat the oven to 300°F.

2 In a saucepan, melt the butter over medium heat, then cook the mushrooms and onion, stirring, until softened and brown, about 4 minutes. Add the flour to form a roux, stirring for about 1 minute. Remove the saucepan from the heat, then slowly whisk in the milk, cream, and chicken broth. Return to the heat, season the mushroom sauce with salt and pepper, and simmer over low heat, stirring occasionally, until dense, about 10 minutes.

Free-range Chicken

Some years ago this became the catchphrase for a good-tasting chicken. It meant a chicken that wasn't cooped up in a tiny box, but allowed to peck around for its food in an open enclosure. The only problem was that this better-tasting chicken was mis-named and should have been called a semi free-range chicken. A truly free-range chicken would be one heck of a tough bird that you would chew for quite some time be-cause all that physical activity means tough muscles, not tender eating. Although I don't specify what kind of chicken to use in the chicken casseroles, I believe you'll find the best-tasting ones to be free-range organically raised chickens available in natural food stores and, increasingly, in many supermarkets.

3 Place each of the chicken breast halves between 2 pieces of wax paper and pound a little thinner with a mallet or the side of a heavy cleaver. Roll each breast up lengthwise. Wrap each chicken roll-up with a slice of bacon.

4 Arrange the beef jerky on the bottom of a 12 × 9 × 2-inch baking casse-role. Place the chicken roll-ups, seam side down, on top of the jerky. In a bowl, stir the sour cream and mushroom sauce together. Pour the sauce over the chicken. Bake until the sauce is bubbling and the bacon is crisp, about 2 hours. Serve hot.

Chicken and Sausage Casserole

This inviting casserole comes out of the oven looking pretty with the skin of the chicken a golden color and scrumptious eat-me-now sausage morsels. The quality of the dish will rest on the quality of your chicken and sausage. So for the chicken, you should consider free-range organic chickens or even poussin (very young chickens) or Cornish game hens. Buy the best Italian sausages you can find, preferably ones without preservatives. For more on chicken and sausages see pages 127 and 69. • **Makes 4 servings**

3 medium russet potatoes (about 1½ pounds total),
   peeled and each cut into sixths
1 large garlic clove, very finely chopped
1 teaspoon sweet paprika
1 teaspoon dried oregano
½ teaspoon salt
¼ teaspoon freshly ground black pepper
One 1½- to 2-pound frying chicken, cut into serving pieces
½ pound sweet Italian sausage, cut into 1-inch pieces
3 tablespoons extra-virgin olive oil

1 Preheat the oven to 425°F.

2 In a 10-inch round baking casserole, arrange the potatoes to cover the bottom. In a small bowl, mix the garlic, paprika, oregano, salt, and pepper. Sprinkle half of the seasoning over the potatoes. Lay the chicken and sausages pieces on top of the potatoes. Pour the olive oil over the ingredients and sprinkle with the remaining seasoning. Cover with aluminum foil and bake for 30 minutes. Reduce the heat to 375°F, remove the foil, and bake until the chicken becomes golden brown and the sausage browns, about 45 minutes. Serve hot.

Cranberry Chicken Casserole

My mom told me that this casserole was "out of this world." She passed on a recipe from her friend and next-door neighbor Trudy Snyder. But I wasn't keen on using the can of cranberries, the Lipton onion soup mix, and the Catalina salad dressing (whatever that was) called for in Trudy's recipe. But it did sound good and my mom vouched for it. The first project was to see what was contained in a Catalina salad dressing besides the potassium sorbate and red food color #2. Well, it was basically a tomato vinegar sauce and the rest was easy. And it will be easy for you too. A nice accompaniment is white rice. Notice too that no fat is used in the recipe.

• Makes 4 servings

One 3-pound chicken, cut into 8 or 10 pieces
1 small onion, chopped
One ¾-pound package fresh cranberries
¾ cup water
¼ cup tomato paste
2 tablespoons red wine vinegar
2 teaspoons onion powder
½ teaspoon sugar
½ teaspoon salt
¼ teaspoon freshly ground black pepper

1. Preheat the oven to 350°F.

2. Arrange the pieces of chicken in a 12-inch round baking casserole or a 12 × 9 × 2-inch baking casserole. Sprinkle the chopped onion on top, then the cranberries.

3. In a bowl, stir together the water, tomato paste, vinegar, onion powder, sugar, salt, and pepper until blended well. Pour the sauce over the cranberries and chicken. Bake until the chicken is firm when poked and the cranberries are bubbling and about to burst, about 1 hour. Serve hot.

Chicken Scallopini with Fontina Cheese and Mushrooms

This old classic of Italian-American restaurants in New York is one I remember fondly. It's also fun having this recipe in the book, because I don't make it anymore, now that my kids are grown. When they were little they loved it and would ask for it often, made with chicken, pork, veal, and even turkey scallopini. You can prepare this recipe in manageable steps. For instance, when I used to make this a lot, I would flatten and flour the chicken breasts and then freeze them individually and pull them out of the freezer when I needed them, cutting down prep time significantly. You can even make the whole thing and freeze it. The fontina cheese called for in the ingredient list can be any fontina cheese, but I prefer the best, fontina Val d'Aosta cheese, usually found in Italian markets and gourmet cheese stores.

• Makes 4 to 6 servings

4 boneless skinless chicken breast halves (about 1¾ pounds total)
8 tablespoons (1 stick) unsalted butter
½ cup olive oil
½ cup all-purpose flour
3 tablespoons freshly and finely grated Parmesan cheese
½ teaspoon salt
⅛ teaspoon freshly ground black pepper
2 large eggs
½ pound white button or cremini mushrooms, thinly sliced
½ pound diced cooked ham (about 1 cup)
¼ pound shredded fontina cheese

Olive Oil

In the Mediterranean, there are codified meanings to the terms "extra-virgin" or "olive oil." But not in the U.S. When I use the term "olive oil" I mean the lower grade olive oil that is sometimes called pure olive oil or virgin olive oil. It is an oil that is not as complex in taste as an extra-virgin olive oil, and that has utilized heat in its processing, which is not the case with the best extra-virgin olive oils. It is also cheaper. The reason I call for these lesser kinds of olive oils, including olive pomace oil, an oil made from olive by-products, is that some recipes call for deep-frying and you don't need to use an expensive oil when cooking in that manner. An extra-virgin olive oil is too fine to take the roughness of high deep-frying heat and is better suited to sautéing. An estate-bottled cold-pressed extra-virgin olive oil is finer still and usually reserved for salads and drizzling on foods that are cooked.

1. Preheat the oven to 350°F.

2. Place each chicken breast half between two sheets of wax paper and pound them with a mallet or the side of a heavy cleaver until they are thin scallopini and about 9 x 6 inches.

3. In a large 12-inch skillet, melt the butter with the olive oil over medium heat. On a sheet of wax paper, mix together the flour, grated Parmesan cheese, salt, and pepper. In a bowl, beat the eggs. Dredge the chicken scallopini in the flour mixture, tapping off the excess flour, and then dip them in the egg. Working in batches, place the chicken breasts in the skillet and cook until golden, turning once, about 5 minutes a side.

4. Remove the chicken breasts from the skillet and arrange in a 12 x 9 x 2-inch baking casserole. In the same skillet, cook the mushrooms, stirring, until softened, about 5 minutes. One minute before the mushrooms are tender, add the ham. Spoon the mushroom and ham mixture over the scallopini. Sprinkle the fontina cheese over the mushrooms and bake until bubbly, 20 to 25 minutes. Serve immediately.

Chicken Scallopini with Three Cheeses

This is a simple family-style casserole that you can make after a busy day, as it doesn't take much effort. You could use any three cheeses, but the ones I suggest here will give the dish a real Italian flavor. There's nothing fancy about this dish, but it tastes good and looks appetizing.

• Makes 4 servings

2 teaspoons extra-virgin olive oil
4 boneless skinless chicken breast halves (about 1¾ pounds total)
Salt and freshly ground black pepper
2 ounces pecorino or provolone cheese, freshly grated
1 ounce fontina or Swiss cheese, thinly sliced
6 ounces fresh mozzarella cheese, sliced
1 ripe tomato, peeled, seeded, and chopped
½ teaspoon dried oregano
1 tablespoon finely chopped fresh basil or parsley

1. Preheat the oven to 350°F. Lightly oil a 13 × 9 × 2-inch baking casserole with ½ teaspoon of oil.

2. Place each chicken breast half between two sheets of wax paper and pound them with a mallet or the side of a cleaver until they are thin scallopini and about 9 × 6 inches.

3. Arrange the chicken to cover the bottom of the baking casserole. Season the chicken with salt and pepper. Sprinkle the cheeses and tomato on top. Sprinkle with the oregano and season with a little more salt and pepper. Drizzle the remaining olive oil over the casserole. Bake until bubbling, about 25 minutes. Sprinkle the basil on top and serve.

Chicken en Casserole

This is an old-time chicken pudding recipe from the Midwest, perhaps made by a farm wife in the Mississippi Valley of Missouri, southern Illinois, or Iowa, and typical of the cooking in the mid-twentieth century. It has its roots in the medieval blancmange, a kind of chicken-based or sweet white pudding, and is rarely made anymore. Sadly, nowadays, a chicken casserole is more likely to come from a TV dinner, but this recipe is how a good chicken puddin' should taste. Serve it with a green salad. • **Makes 4 servings**

4 tablespoons (½ stick) unsalted butter
6 tablespoons all-purpose flour
1 cup canned evaporated milk
1 cup chicken broth
1 teaspoon salt
¼ teaspoon paprika
3 large eggs, slightly beaten
1½ cups diced cooked chicken breast
3 tablespoons chopped pimiento
3 tablespoons diced green bell pepper

1 Preheat the oven to 300°F. Lightly butter a 9 x 3-inch round baking casserole.

2 Add water to the bottom of a double boiler and bring to a boil. Place the top of the double boiler on and melt the butter, then blend in the flour. Add the milk and chicken broth and cook, stirring almost constantly, until thick, about 10 minutes. Mix in the salt and paprika.

3 Pour the beaten eggs into the milk mixture, stirring constantly. Add the chicken, pimiento, and bell pepper, and stir to mix well. Pour the mixture into the casserole. Bake until the pudding has set and a knife inserted in the center comes out clean, about 20 minutes. Serve hot.

Widower's Casserole

The first time I ever heard of a "widower's casserole" was when my then 87-year-old mother, who lives in a golfing retirement community north of Tampa, Florida, mentioned it when I told her I was writing this book. In her village, this is what they call the casserole brought to the newly widowed man, usually made and brought to him by other widows. I don't know if this has any history outside of where my mom lives, but she tells me, laughing, that the widows figure the poor guy probably isn't eating very well, and after all, he is single now, too. In any case, my mom says that they try not to be too quick or obvious in bringing their casseroles over, but when they do, their ulterior motive is in play. This recipe is also called chicken casserole deluxe and is one I've modernized from my mom's friend Trudy Snyder, and is typical of these casseroles that always have meat, as most Great Depression-era men love their meat. • **Makes 4 servings**

4 boneless skinless chicken breast halves (about 1¾ pounds total)
Salt and freshly ground black pepper
12 ounces white button mushrooms, sliced
1 cup heavy cream
3 tablespoons all-purpose flour
1 cup sour cream
¼ cup dry white wine

1. Preheat the oven to 325°F. Lightly butter a 9 x 9 x 2-inch baking casserole.

2. Arrange the chicken in the baking casserole. Season the chicken with salt and pepper. Scatter 10 ounces of the mushrooms over the chicken, and season again with salt and pepper.

3. Place the remaining 2 ounces of mushrooms in a blender with the cream and blend until puréed. In a bowl, stir the flour into the sour cream, then stir in the puréed mushroom mixture and white wine, mixing well. Pour over the chicken and bake until the top is browned, the sauce has reduced, and the chicken is springy to a poke with a fork, about 1¼ hours. Serve hot.

Chicken Supreme

This American casserole is based on the famous *suprême de volaille* of French cuisine, which is made with only the breasts of young spring chickens, floured and sautéed in clarified butter. The classic American chicken supreme was a casserole that saw the chicken breasts being dipped in canned condensed cream of mushroom soup and coated with crushed Rice Krispies or corn flakes. I've update this classic by using Japanese bread crumbs, called panko flakes, that are available in Asian markets and in most supermarkets in the international foods aisle. I think my recipe is a simpler way of doing it and much nicer tasting. Some cooks add chopped mushrooms and brandy to the white sauce. Chicken supreme was also once the name for chicken Kiev, a breaded and deep-fried chicken breast stuffed with herbed butter. • **Makes 4 servings**

4 tablespoons (½ stick) unsalted butter, melted
2 cups panko flakes (Japanese bread crumbs)
1 teaspoon paprika
1 large egg
¾ cup whole milk
¾ cup all-purpose flour
1½ teaspoons salt
¼ teaspoon freshly ground black pepper
1½ pounds boneless skinless chicken breast halves,
    cut in half horizontally into flatter fillets,
    patted dry with paper towels

1. Preheat the oven to 350°F. Butter a 13 x 9 x 2-inch baking casserole with 1 tablespoon of melted butter.

2. In a shallow dish or pan, combine the panko with the paprika and spread out in the dish. In a second dish, such as a Pyrex baking dish or cake pan, beat the egg and milk slightly, then add the flour, salt, and pepper and stir until smooth.

3. Dip the chicken breast pieces in the egg batter, then dredge them in the panko to coat both sides. Place the chicken breasts in the baking casserole in one layer. Drizzle the breaded chicken breasts with the remaining melted butter and bake, without turning the chicken while baking, until golden and tender, about 1 hour.

Chicken Strata

Not your grandmother's strata. This chicken strata is a light, airy, and delicious casserole that is rich with the taste of butter-sautéed shiitake mushrooms. As with all stratas, the ingredients are layered. This popular casserole is usually made with leftover chicken, but follow the instructions carefully for poaching the chicken if you are making it from scratch. The traditional recipes for chicken strata usually call for canned cream of mushroom soup and regular white button mushrooms. I know you will find this casserole with its earthy shiitake mushrooms and cognac cream sauce far more pleasant to eat. Turkey stratas are also popular, and you can use turkey breast instead of chicken in this recipe if you like. • **Makes 6 servings**

6 tablespoons (3/4 stick) unsalted butter

1 pound shiitake mushrooms, stems removed and
    caps thinly sliced

Salt and freshly ground black pepper

8 slices stale white Italian country bread,
    crusts removed and bread cubed

½ cup chopped onion

½ cup chopped celery

½ cup chopped green bell pepper

½ cup chicken broth

½ cup heavy cream

2 tablespoons Cognac or brandy

1 pound uncooked boneless skinless chicken breasts or
    2 cups diced cooked chicken

½ cup mayonnaise

2 large eggs, lightly beaten

1½ cups whole milk

1½ cups (about 4 ½ ounces) shredded sharp
    white cheddar cheese

1. Lightly butter a 9 × 9 × 3-inch baking casserole or cake pan or a 10 × 4-inch round baking casserole.

2. In a medium-size skillet, melt the butter over medium-high heat, then cook the mushrooms, stirring, until softened, about 5 minutes. Season with salt and pepper and set aside.

3. Layer the bottom of the baking casserole with half of the bread cubes. Spoon half of the mushrooms, and all of the onion, celery, and green bell pepper over the bread cubes. Place the remaining mushrooms in a blender and blend with the chicken broth, cream, and Cognac until smooth. Remove the mushroom sauce from the blender, then cover and refrigerate until needed.

4. If using raw chicken, place the chicken breast in a saucepan or nonstick skillet and cover with water. Bring the water to just under a boil over medium-high heat, then reduce the heat to low and poach the chicken until the meat is white and firm, about 25 minutes. Make sure the water at no time comes to a boil, otherwise your chicken will be tough. Remove the chicken, let cool, then dice.

5. In a bowl, mix the cooled diced chicken with the mayonnaise and season with salt and pepper. Spread this mixture over the vegetables. Whisk the eggs and milk in a bowl to blend and pour the egg mixture over the chicken. Add the remaining half of the bread cubes. Cover with plastic wrap and refrigerate for 1 hour or overnight.

6. Preheat the oven to 350°F.

7. Pour the reserved mushroom sauce over the casserole and sprinkle the cheese on top. Bake until the cheese melts, is dappled light brown, and is bubbly, about 35 minutes. Serve hot.

Chicken Cordon Bleu

This Southern U.S. take on the famous veal cordon bleu of classic French cooking is succulent and much less expensive and time consuming than the original dish that's made of pounded veal scallops sandwiching ham and Swiss cheese and fried in plenty of clarified butter. Many dishes are called "cordon bleu" and all that means is that it is a first-rate dish. And this dish is first rate. It makes a nice company dinner and, although it requires only a salad to accompany it, you can serve it for a special occasion with a pasta casserole or some spaghetti with butter and parsley.

• Makes 4 to 6 servings

1 large egg
1½ cups whole milk
2 pounds boneless skinless chicken breasts, cut into bite-size pieces
1½ cups dry bread crumbs
4 tablespoons (½ stick) unsalted butter
¼ cup all-purpose flour
1 cup chicken broth
Salt and freshly ground black pepper
½ cup clarified butter (see facing page)
½ pound Swiss cheese, cubed small
½ pound cooked ham, cubed small

Leftover Idea

As long as you're cooking a casserole as luscious as Chicken Cordon Bleu (this page) you might as well go all the way and combine the leftovers with the leftovers of Le Gratin Dauphinois (page 332) to have an over-the-top extravaganza. Or go lighter with some Broccoli and Fennel Gratinate (page 394) leftovers, which will be just as good.

Clarified Butter

Clarification of butter is the process of removing the milk solids from butter so it can be used at higher-cooking heats without burning. To clarify butter, place the butter in a small butter warmer or saucepan and melt over low heat. The milk solids will settle to the bottom, and some may float on top. Remove the foam on top with a spoon, and then slowly and carefully pour the clarified butter into a bowl, leaving the milk solids at the bottom of the saucepan. Alternatively you can pass the butter through a cheese-cloth-lined strainer to strain out the milk solids.

1. In a medium-size bowl, whisk together the egg and ½ cup of the milk. Dunk the chunks of chicken in the egg-milk mixture, then drain through a strainer. Place the bread crumbs in another bowl, add the chicken pieces, and toss well so all pieces are covered with bread crumbs. Remove the chicken pieces, tapping them to knock off excess crumbs, and set aside on a large platter or tray, and refrigerate for 30 minutes.

2. Meanwhile, prepare the white sauce. In a saucepan, melt the butter over medium-high heat. Add the flour and stir to make a smooth roux. Continue to cook, stirring constantly, until it turns pale golden, about 2 minutes. Remove the saucepan from the heat, then slowly whisk in the chicken broth and the remaining 1 cup of milk until blended and smooth. Return the saucepan to the burner and continue to simmer over medium-low heat, stirring occasionally, until dense, 10 to 12 minutes. Season with salt and pepper. Set aside, keeping the sauce warm.

3. Preheat the oven to 350°F.

4. In a large skillet, heat the clarified butter until very hot over medium-high heat, then cook the chicken pieces in 2 or 3 batches, without overcrowding them, until golden brown, about 2 minutes for each batch. Transfer the chicken pieces to a 13 x 9 x 2-inch baking casserole.

5. Scatter the Swiss cheese and ham cubes in the baking casserole and on top of the chicken pieces. Spoon the reserved white sauce over the contents of the casserole. Season with a little salt and pepper. Bake until bubbly, about 30 minutes. Serve hot.

Chicken and Oyster Casserole

The traditional way to cook this old New England casserole is with cut-up broiler chickens, on the bone and with their skin. Although that is a delicious way to make it, the method I use here creates a wonderful casserole where the chicken and the oysters taste like they've come from the same fruit tree—both melt in your mouth. Your results will vary because there's no way to calculate the amount of water the chickens release or the amount of juice in the oysters. So your final dish might be saucy or it might be soupy. In either case you'll have one very desirable casserole.

• Makes 4 servings

2 tablespoons unsalted butter
All-purpose flour for dredging
Pinch of freshly grated nutmeg
Salt and freshly ground black pepper
1½ pounds boneless skinless chicken breast halves
½ cup boiling water
½ cup heavy cream
1½ cups shucked oysters and their juice (20 to 24 oysters)

1. Preheat the oven to 350°F. Butter a 12 × 9 × 2-inch baking casserole with 1 tablespoon of butter.

2. Season the flour with nutmeg, salt, and pepper. Dredge the chicken halves in the seasoned flour. Do not pat off the excess flour. Lay the chicken halves in the baking casserole. Season the chicken with more salt and pepper. Pour the boiling water over the chicken. Cover with aluminum foil and bake until slightly springy to a poke with your finger, about 30 minutes.

3. Remove the chicken from the oven, uncover, and add the cream, remaining 1 tablespoon of butter, and the oysters. Cover, return to the oven, and continue baking until the edges of the oysters curl, about 10 minutes. Serve hot.

Chicken Cacciatore

Many Italian Americans grew up on this dish. I certainly remember it well from when I lived on Long Island as a teenager. It starts with chicken, but after that, all kinds of things can go into a chicken cacciatore depending on the cook. But they shouldn't. The dish is meant to be simple, as indicated by its name which means "hunter-style." I've seen cacciatore with green bell peppers, celery, mushrooms, or bacon in it, and while there's nothing wrong with adding them, I prefer the version here. Remember, the better your chicken, the better the cacciatore. Also, there is no need to stir or turn; just let it bake. • **Makes 4 servings**

¼ cup extra-virgin olive oil plus more as needed
One 3- to 3 ½-pound chicken, cut into 10 pieces
1 large onion, cut into eighths
1 bay leaf
2 sprigs fresh rosemary
2 tablespoons unsalted butter, cut into thin slivers
1 pound ripe plum tomatoes (about 8), peeled and cut in half
Salt and freshly ground black pepper

1 Preheat the oven to 400°F. Lightly oil a 13 × 9 × 2-inch baking casserole.

2 In the baking casserole, arrange the chicken pieces and onion. Push the bay leaf and rosemary between the chicken and onion. Dot the casserole with the slivers of butter. Arrange the cut tomatoes, cut side down, attractively around the chicken . Pour ¼ cup of olive oil over everything, then finally, season with salt and pepper. Bake until the chicken is golden brown, the edges of the onion are blackening, and the sauce is bubbling, about 1½ hours. Discard the bay leaf and rosemary sprigs if you can find them easily, and serve hot.

Chicken and Potato Pizzaiola

This casserole is exceedingly simple and surprising, given how much flavor it has. Just put everything in the casserole and then into the oven. The name of the dish refers to a final sauce that is reminiscent of a pizza sauce. In Sicily, this dish (without the chicken) has a vulgar name involving the priest and his mistress. • **Makes 4 servings**

¾ pound boneless skinless chicken or turkey breast,
    cut into 1-inch cubes
1 pound baking potatoes, peeled and cut into ¾-inch cubes
2 pounds ripe tomatoes, peeled and cut into ¾-inch-thick slices
6 tablespoons extra-virgin olive oil
2 tablespoons dried oregano
Salt and freshly ground black pepper
Freshly grated Parmesan cheese for sprinkling

1. Preheat the oven to 400°F.

2. Place the chicken, potatoes, tomatoes, olive oil, and oregano in a 12 x 9 x 2-inch baking casserole. Season with salt and pepper, and toss a few times to mix well. Bake until the chicken is cooked through and the potatoes are tender, about 45 minutes. Remove and serve hot with the Parmesan cheese.

Leftover Idea

It seemed that whenever my mother made chicken cacciatore, which we pronounced "catch-a-tory," she would have a bit of leftovers. The leftovers always got tossed with some leftover macaroni, then layered with mozzarella cheese, and into the oven it went. Umm, it was good.

Turkey Meatball Casserole

B ecause everyone loves turkey, this casserole is always popular, especially during the holidays. This casserole has some resemblance to Swedish meatballs, except for the fact that the balls are bigger and the taste is milder. I once made five huge turkey meatball casseroles for fifty people and they finished everything, meaning they ate nearly 6 meatballs each! Damn, because I was hoping to use the leftovers in my hero sandwich (see box). Leftovers go great, too, with any of the leftover potato casseroles. • **Makes 6 servings**

1 teaspoon vegetable oil
2 cups fresh bread crumbs (see Note)
⅔ cup half and half
2 pounds ground turkey
1 medium onion, finely chopped
½ bunch fresh parsley, leaves only, finely chopped
2 large eggs
1½ teaspoons salt plus more for the sauce
½ teaspoon freshly ground black pepper plus more for the sauce
¼ teaspoon ground cinnamon
3 tablespoons unsalted butter
3 tablespoons all-purpose flour
¾ cup beef broth
¼ cup dry red wine
¼ cup heavy cream

1 Preheat the oven to 350°F. Lightly oil a 13 × 9 × 2-inch baking casserole or, preferably, a large flame-proof casserole.

2 Soak the bread crumbs in the half and half for a minute, then squeeze out the excess liquid.

3 In a large bowl, mix together the bread crumbs, turkey, onion, all of the chopped parsley leaves except for 2 tablespoons, the eggs, 1½ teaspoons of salt, ½ teaspoon of pepper, and the cinnamon until very well blended.

I'm just crazy about hero sandwiches and I put all kinds of leftovers in them. But the leftover turkey meatballs from the Turkey Meatball Casserole (page 146) are just too good to pass up any other way. Place the meatballs in French rolls with a little Tomato Sauce (page 243), a few slices of mozzarella cheese, and a sprinkle of grated Parmesan cheese, then place the sandwiches on a baking tray and bake at 400°F until the bread is getting crispy. You'll love it.

Roll into 50 to 60 small meatballs (a wee bit larger than a golf ball), dipping your hands into a bowl of cold water to prevent the meat from sticking to them.

④ Arrange the meatballs in the baking casserole. Bake until they have browned and are cooked through, 25 to 30 minutes. Leave them in the turned-off oven until needed, while you make the sauce.

⑤ If you have used a flame-proof casserole to cook the meatballs, transfer the meatballs to a baking sheet and set them aside, and use the baking casserole to make the sauce. Otherwise, use a large saucepan to make the sauce. Melt the butter in the baking casserole or saucepan over medium-high heat, then stir in the flour until it has formed a roux. Continue to cook, stirring constantly, until smooth, about 1 minute. Remove the saucepan or baking casserole from the heat, then slowly whisk in the beef broth, wine, and cream until smooth (scraping up the browned bits on the bottom of the baking casserole if you have used one). Season with salt and pepper,. Reduce the heat to low and return the saucepan or baking casserole to the heat and simmer, stirring occasionally, until dense, about 12 minutes. Add the meatballs to the gravy in the flame-proof casserole, turning to coat, or pour the gravy over the meatballs in a standard baking casserole and sprinkle with the reserved 2 tablespoons of parsley. Serve hot.

Note: This amount can be made from crumbling four ½-inch-thick slices of 5¼ × 3-inch French or Italian bread in a food processor.

Turkey Fatta

*F*atta refers to a family of Arab culinary preparations popular in the eastern Mediterranean in which pieces of stale, toasted, or fried flatbread are crumbled and used as a foundation for a casserole. These preparations developed quite naturally in the Arab world because much of the bread that is consumed there is flatbread, a bread that dries out quickly, so this casserole became a practical way for using stale bread. There are many varieties of these kind of dishes, all based on a foundation of flatbread. If you fry the bread in sunflower or grapeseed oil the taste will be lighter and less rich.

• Makes 4 servings

1 cup sunflower seed, corn, grapeseed, or olive oil
1 large Arabic flatbread (pita or pocket bread) or
    2 to 4 smaller ones, split into two leaves and
    each cut into quarters
3 tablespoons extra-virgin olive oil
1 medium onion, chopped
2 large garlic cloves, finely chopped
1 pound boneless cooked turkey breast,
    cut into ½-inch cubes
1½ teaspoons *baharat* (see Note)
¼ teaspoon ground cinnamon
Salt and freshly ground black pepper
2 cups whole plain yogurt, beaten with a fork
¼ cup crushed walnuts

1. Preheat the oven to 350°F.

2. In a large skillet, heat the 1 cup of oil over medium-high heat, until nearly smoking, then fry the bread until golden, about 10 seconds a side. Set the fried bread aside to drain on paper towels. Let the oil cool, then discard the oil and wipe the skillet clean with a paper towel, or use another skillet for the next step.

3. In a large skillet, heat the extra-virgin olive oil over medium-high heat, then add the onion and garlic, and cook, stirring constantly so the garlic doesn't burn, until the onion is translucent, about 5 minutes. Add the turkey, *baharat*, and cinnamon, season with salt and pepper, and cook, stirring occasionally, until the turkey is heated through, 3 to 4 minutes. Set aside.

4. Arrange the fried bread on the bottom of a 12 × 9 × 2-inch baking casserole. Cover with the turkey mixture and spread the yogurt over that. Sprinkle the walnuts on top. Bake until the yogurt is hot but not bubbling, 15 to 20 minutes. Serve hot.

Note: This Lebanese spice mix can be made by mixing together ½ teaspoon ground black pepper, ½ teaspoon ground allspice, ⅛ teaspoon ground cinnamon, pinch of nutmeg, and a pinch of ground coriander seed. It is preferable to grind these spices freshly.

Mexican Turkey Hash Casserole

The whole family will like this casserole which has a little kick to it. It's rich in vegetables so you don't really need to serve anything on the side. If you like, you can spoon it into a tortilla and eat it wrapped up. One of its ingredients, chayote, is a kind of small pear-shaped squash with ridges. If you can't find it, replace it with any kind of summer squash. Although fresh corn will be best in this dish, use frozen corn kernels if you must. The chorizo sausage should be made of pork meat and not inner parts, stuffed in natural casing not plastic, so examine the label when you're in the supermarket. You can replace it with hot Italian turkey sausage if you want. The casserole can be prepared ahead of time and kept in the refrigerator until you want to bake it. • **Makes 6 servings**

3 tablespoons corn or vegetable oil
1 medium onion, chopped
2 poblano chiles, seeded and chopped
½ pound Mexican-style chorizo sausage,
    casing removed and meat crumbled
2 chayote squash (about 1 pound), peeled,
    pitted, and diced small
2 corn cobs, husked and kernels removed (about 2 cups)
4 plum tomatoes, peeled, seeded, and chopped
1 habanero chile, finely chopped
1 teaspoon dried *epazote* (optional)
1 teaspoon chili powder
1 teaspoon dried oregano
½ teaspoon ground cumin
3 whole cloves
1¼ pounds ground turkey
3 tablespoons finely chopped cilantro
¾ pound *queso asadero* or Monterey Jack cheese, sliced

1 teaspoon Mexican-style hot sauce (such as Cholula)

6 corn tortillas, warmed

1 cup sour cream

1. Preheat the oven to 325°F.

2. In a large skillet, or a flame-proof 13 x 9 x 2-inch baking casserole, heat the oil over medium-high heat, then add the onion and poblano chiles and cook, stirring, until softened a bit, about 5 minutes. Add the chorizo sausage, chayote squash, corn, tomatoes, habanero chile, *epazote*, if using, chili powder, oregano, cumin, and cloves. Cook, stirring, until all mixed together, about 5 minutes. Add the ground turkey and cilantro, and cook, stirring and mixing, until the corn and chayote are al dente, about 15 minutes.

3. Transfer the mixture to a 13 x 9 x 2-inch baking casserole if you've cooked the mixture in a skillet. Cover the casserole with the cheese slices, overlapping slices slightly. Drizzle with the hot sauce and bake until the cheese has melted, is dappled brown, and bubbling, about 45 minutes. Serve hot with corn tortillas and sour cream.

Kentucky Hot Brown Casserole

The original Kentucky Hot Brown was actually an open-faced sandwich created by Chef Fred K. Schmidt of the Brown Hotel in Louisville, Kentucky, in 1926 for the late-night dancing crowd in the hotel's ballroom. Even today, some people call it a hot brown sandwich, but it's basically a casserole. They seem to know this casserole only in Kentucky, as I can't find anyone outside of Kentucky who has heard of it. It's a great casserole to make on the Saturday after Thanksgiving with leftover turkey. This utterly rich recipe with its Mornay sauce is adapted from one published in the *Louisville Courier-Journal* by Chef Patrick Dale of Chester's Tavern in Louisville. The better your ingredients, the better the casserole, so use a high-quality artisanal bakery-style bread. Because it's so rich you will want to accompany it with only a green salad. If you don't have any leftover turkey, then cook some fresh diced turkey breast in a skillet over medium-high heat, stirring, until golden brown, 6 to 7 minutes. • **Makes 8 servings**

3 cups ½-inch cubes toasted bread
3 cups (about 2 pounds) diced cooked boneless turkey breast

For the sauce

1 cup (2 sticks) butter
⅔ cup all-purpose flour
Salt and freshly ground black pepper
1½ cups half and half
1½ cups heavy cream
1 cup whole milk
1¼ cups (about 4 ounces) freshly grated Parmesan cheese
1¼ cups (about 4 ounces) freshly shredded mild or
    sharp white cheddar cheese

For the topping

½ cup chopped cooked bacon (but not crispy)
½ cup diced tomato
½ cup (about 1½ ounces) freshly grated Parmesan cheese

1. Preheat the oven to 350°F. Lightly butter a 12 × 9 × 2-inch baking casserole.

2. Place the bread cubes in the bottom of the baking casserole. Arrange the diced turkey on top. Set aside while you make the sauce.

3. In a large saucepan, melt the butter over medium-low heat. Increase the heat to medium, then add the flour and stir to make a smooth roux. Season with salt and pepper. Continue to cook, stirring, until the flour barely begins to brown, about 5 minutes. Remove the saucepan from the heat, then slowly whisk in the half and half. Next, slowly whisk in the heavy cream. Finally, whisk in the milk. Return to the heat and continue to cook, stirring, until the mixture bubbles, about 8 minutes. Add the cheeses, remove from the heat, and stir until melted and the mixture is smooth.

4. Pour the cheese sauce over the bread and turkey. Sprinkle the bacon and tomato on top of the sauce. Sprinkle the Parmesan cheese on top of the bacon and tomato and bake until bubbly, about 35 minutes.

Turkey Mole and Hominy Casserole

A Mexican mole is a sauce based on a fine grinding of nuts and seeds that is cooked and puréed with vegetables and chiles. Many people think of a mole as containing chocolate, and at least one mole does. But in the Mexican state of Oaxaca, the home of mole, there are many moles, and the most famous one you already know of, namely, guacamole. This casserole is labor intensive; that's why I prepare it beforehand and keep it refrigerated until time to bake. But the reward is well worth the effort. *Nixtamal* is a Mexican-style hominy—corn that has been processed by mixing the whole dry corn kernels with water and unslaked lime, and cooking them until the skins can be rubbed off, and then washing them in water to remove all traces of the lime. Many supermarkets sell it, and you can order it from the Internet (page 76), but use whatever whole hominy is available. • **Makes 6 servings**

2½ cups canned hominy, drained

1 tablespoon salt plus more to taste

¼ cup sesame seeds

2 ounces (½ cup) unsalted pumpkin seeds

3 whole cloves

8 black peppercorns

¼ teaspoon cumin seeds

4 tablespoons pork lard or butter

2 cups chicken broth

4 green bell peppers

8 Boston lettuce leaves, sliced

5 Swiss chard stalks (leaves only), sliced

1 bunch cilantro (leaves only), chopped

1 small bunch fresh parsley (leaves only), chopped

1 large green tomato, chopped

2 large garlic cloves, finely chopped

2 poblano chiles, seeded and chopped

8 serrano chiles, seeded and chopped

1¼ pounds uncooked boneless turkey breast,
    cut into 6 or 7 slices

½ pound *queso fresco*

1 cup sour cream

6 corn tortillas, warmed

① Place the hominy in a large saucepan and cover with water by several inches. Bring to a boil, add 1 tablespoon of salt, then reduce the heat to medium and let cook, stirring once in a while, until the hominy is softer, about 30 minutes.

② Meanwhile, put the sesame seeds in a cast-iron skillet with no liquid and toast them over medium heat, shaking the pan frequently, until light brown, about 7 minutes. Remove the sesame seeds. Add the pumpkin seeds to the skillet and toast them too for about 5 minutes. Cool the seeds. In an electric spice grinder (preferably) or mortar, finely grind the sesame seeds and pumpkin seeds with the cloves, black peppercorns, and cumin; set aside.

③ In a large 12-inch skillet, melt 2 tablespoons of lard over medium-high heat, then add the spice mixture, stirring, until fragrant, about 1 minute. Add 1½ cups of chicken broth to the skillet, along with the bell peppers, lettuce, Swiss chard, cilantro, parsley, green tomato, garlic, poblano chiles, and serrano chiles, adding them in batches if necessary until the previous batch wilts. Cook until wilted and softened, about 20 minutes. Transfer this sauce to a blender with the remaining ½ cup of chicken broth. Blend until smooth, stopping the blender and pushing down chunks when necessary. Remove the purée from the blender and pass through a food mill. Clean the skillet, as you will need it in the next step.

④ In the same large skillet, melt the remaining 2 tablespoons of lard over medium-high heat. Add the purée of vegetables, reduce the heat to low, and simmer, stirring frequently, until the sauce is dense, about 30 minutes. Season with salt. The sauce should have a nutty, toasted flavor with a little spike from the chiles. Add the turkey slices to the sauce and flip a few times to coat them with the sauce.

5. Preheat the oven to 350°F.

6. Pour the cooked hominy into a 12 × 9 × 2-inch baking casserole, spreading to cover the bottom. Lay the sauced turkey slices over the hominy and spoon the remaining sauce over the turkey. Bake until the top looks very dense and it is very slightly blackened on the edges, about 45 minutes. Crumble the cheese over the casserole and let it sit 5 minutes for the cheese to melt slightly. Serve hot with the sour cream and tortillas.

Quail Casserole

I n this recipe the quail are *spatchcocked*, an old English word that means split down the back and pulled open and flattened slightly, which allows more of the surface of the meat to brown while cooking. This recipe is adapted from the Minnesota-based *Bird Dog and Retriever News Cookbook*, which includes all kinds of game recipes. It leaped out at me because I love quail and because it's so simple. The original recipe calls for canned mushrooms, but when made with fresh mushrooms it packs a lot more flavor.

• Makes 4 servings

1 cup all-purpose flour

½ teaspoon salt

6 quail, split down back and flattened slightly

6 tablespoons (¾ stick) unsalted butter

12 ounces white button mushrooms, sliced

2 tablespoons chopped fresh parsley

1 cup (about) dry white wine

1 Preheat the oven to 350°F.

2 Toss the flour and salt together on a plate, then dredge the quail through the flour to coat on all sides, tapping off any excess flour.

3 In a large skillet (you may need to use 2 skillets, in which case divide the butter between them), melt the butter over medium heat, then cook the quail on both sides until golden brown, turning once, 10 to 12 minutes. Transfer the quail to a 12 × 9 × 2-inch baking casserole and pour all the pan drippings from the skillet over them. Scatter the mushrooms and parsley over and around the quail. Pour in enough wine to half-cover the quail. Cover and bake until the mushrooms are soft and the quail is cooked through and tender, about 1 hour. Serve hot.

Duck and Bean Casserole

This casserole is best made with duck legs and thighs, but they are not always sold this way, so you may have to use a whole duck. This delicious dish depends on rendering much duck fat so that it doesn't go into the casserole. That's not hard to do because you will be sautéing the duck pieces first. The final dish is quite nice and the beans will be saturated with flavor. A side dish of Swiss chard, spinach, turnip greens, or mustard greens would complete the meal. • **Makes 4 servings**

1 cup dried red kidney beans (about ½ pound),
    soaked overnight or for 8 hours in enough water to
    cover, drained
1 teaspoon salt plus more as needed
1 small onion, finely chopped
1 tablespoon finely chopped fresh basil
½ teaspoon freshly ground black pepper
1 ounce salt pork, diced small
4 duck legs and thighs (about 3 pounds total),
    or one 5-pound duck, separated into 2 leg and
    thighs pieces and 2 breasts (remaining pieces saved
    for another purpose), fat removed
All-purpose flour for dredging

1. Place the beans in a large saucepan and cover with fresh water by several inches. Turn the heat to high and bring the water to a boil. Once it boils, reduce the heat to medium-high, season with a little salt, and cook until the beans are tender, 1 to 1½ hours. Drain the beans, reserving the cooking liquid. Toss the beans in a bowl with the onion, basil, 1 teaspoon of salt, and ½ teaspoon of pepper. Place the beans in a 10 x 3-inch round baking casserole

2. Preheat the oven to 350°F.

3. In a large skillet, cook the salt pork over low heat, stirring, until it is crispy, about 10 minutes. Using a slotted spoon, remove the bits of salt pork from the skillet and stir them into the beans; reserve the pork fat in the skillet.

4. Dredge the duck pieces in the flour, tapping off any excess flour, then cook them in the same skillet with the reserved pork fat over low heat until much fat is rendered and the duck is golden on both sides, 45 to 50 minutes. Transfer the duck pieces to the baking casserole, laying them on top of the beans. Pour 1 cup of the reserved bean cooking liquid over the duck. Cover the baking casserole and bake until the duck and beans are fully tender, about 1½ hours. Serve hot with a slotted spoon to leave duck fat behind.

Escargot Crêpes with Escargot Butter

I first had this dish called *galette escargot au beurre d'escargot* at a delightful outdoor crêperie called Au Blé Noir on the Place Terrisse in the French seaside resort of Cap d'Agde on the Mediterranean. It was a beautiful and warm summer night. They offered a wide variety of crêpes to sample, and we ate all night. In southwestern France, crêpes are also known as *galettes*. This snail butter crêpe was slightly crispy and very buttery, which was good.

• Makes 4 appetizer servings

6 tablespoons (¾ stick) unsalted butter
3 tablespoons finely chopped shallot
1 large garlic clove, finely chopped
One 7-ounce can snails, drained, ¾ sliced, ¼ finely chopped
2 tablespoons finely chopped fresh parsley
Salt and freshly ground black pepper
4 Crêpes (page 392)
4 tablespoons (less than 1 ounce) shredded Gruyère cheese

1 Preheat the oven to 375°F. Using ½ tablespoon of butter, butter a small baking casserole that can hold the 4 crêpes relatively snugly, such as one 8 x 6 x 1½ inches.

2 In a small skillet, melt 5 tablespoons of butter over medium heat, then add the shallot and garlic and cook, stirring constantly so the garlic doesn't burn, until softened, about 3 minutes. Add the snails and parsley, and season with salt and pepper. Cook, stirring, only until the snails are heated through, about 2 to 3 minutes. Remove from the heat and set aside.

3 Arrange about a quarter of the snail mixture in a row on each crêpe. Roll them up away from you and line them up in the baking casserole. Spread the remaining ½ tablespoon butter over all the crêpes and sprinkle each with 1 tablespoon of Gruyère cheese. Bake until the cheese is melted and dappled golden, about 20 minutes. Serve hot.

Escargots en Casserole

This recipe is adapted only slightly from Chef Tommy DiGiovanni of the famous Arnaud's restaurant in New Orleans. The snails are cooked in individual ramekins in lots of herbed butter and capped with flaky pastry. The dish is typically served as an appetizer at Arnaud's. Although you could make it in one large casserole, it is far more elegant and not that much more difficult to make them in small 2-inch ramekins. • **Makes 6 servings**

For the garlic butter

1 cup (2 sticks) plus 2 tablespoons unsalted butter, softened
1 cup finely chopped fresh parsley
¼ cup Herbsaint or any anise-flavored liqueur, such as Pernod or ouzo
6 large garlic cloves, finely chopped
Salt and freshly ground black pepper

For the casserole

Three 7-ounce cans snails, rinsed and drained
6 ounces frozen puff pastry, defrosted
1 large egg, beaten

1. Preheat the oven to 425°F.

2. To prepare the garlic butter, in a bowl, stir together the butter, parsley, Herbsaint, and garlic with a fork until well blended. Season with salt and pepper. Alternatively, beat the ingredients at low speed in an electric mixer for 5 minutes.

3. Place 6 or 7 snails in each of six 2-inch ramekins. Cover each with the garlic butter, divided evenly among the 6 ramekins.

4. Roll the puff pastry to ⅛-inch thickness. Using a 2-inch pastry cutter, cut out 6 rounds. Cover each ramekin with a puff pastry round, pressing the edges lightly to seal. Brush the pastry with the beaten egg. Bake until the pastry turns golden brown, about 20 minutes. Serve hot.

Fromage

In Louisiana, they call this late-night Creole favorite simply "cheese" (*fromage*). You'll be hard-pressed not to eat this cross between a quiche and fondue all by yourself. If not for late night, it is also a great appetizer. Eat it with pieces of French bread. • **Makes 6 servings**

2 large eggs
4½ cups (about 1 pound) shredded Swiss cheese
1 cup half and half
½ teaspoon cayenne pepper
½ teaspoon salt
¼ teaspoon sweet paprika

1. Preheat the oven to 350°F.

2. In a bowl, beat the eggs, then stir in the cheese, half and half, cayenne, salt, and paprika. Pour into an 8 × 3½-inch baking casserole or soufflé dish and bake until it has set and is slightly golden on top, about 20 minutes. Serve hot.

Seafood
Casseroles

Red Snapper and Tomato Casserole

This casserole can be made in a jiffy because you just layer and bake. If you serve it with a potato casserole or zucchini casserole, everyone will be satisfied. Leftovers are also good at room temperature as an appetizer, dressed with a little more olive oil and a drizzle of some good-quality vinegar.

• Makes 4 servings

1 tablespoon extra-virgin olive oil
4 red snapper fillets (about 1½ pounds total)
Salt and freshly ground black pepper
3 tablespoons chopped fresh dill
2 ripe but firm medium tomatoes, sliced
¼ cup very thin red onion slices

1 Preheat the oven to 450°F. Lightly coat a 12 x 9 x 2-inch baking casserole with some of the olive oil.

2 Lay the fish fillets in the baking casserole, overlapping them slightly if necessary, and season with salt and pepper. Sprinkle half of the dill over the fish and cover with the sliced tomatoes. Scatter the onion slices over the top and sprinkle with the remaining dill. Drizzle with the remaining olive oil and season lightly with salt and pepper. Bake until bubbling on the sides and the fish is cooked through, about 20 minutes. Serve hot.

Leftover Tip

Don't freeze leftover fish casseroles. Simply refrigerate them and eat within three days. Your best bet is to have them as an appetizer the next day, served at room temperature.

Blue Cheese Halibut Bake

This Canadian way of baking fish is utterly simple. Don't be tempted to cut corners and pour some bottled salad dressing on top instead of making it from scratch. There's a difference. The recipe can easily be cut in half or quartered to feed fewer people, although this is a nice company dish because it's easy. Remember to use good-quality blue cheese, preferably Roquefort, and very fresh fish, and you can't go wrong. • **Makes 6 servings**

6 ounces blue cheese, crumbled
2 cups buttermilk
1½ cups mayonnaise
½ teaspoon freshly ground black pepper
½ teaspoon freshly ground white pepper
1 large garlic clove, mashed in a mortar with
    ½ teaspoon salt until mushy
2 pounds halibut steak or fillet, cut into 6 pieces
1 small red onion, thinly sliced

1. In a bowl, mix 4 ounces of blue cheese with the buttermilk, mayonnaise, black pepper, white pepper, and mashed garlic. Chill the blue cheese dressing for 2 hours.

2. Preheat the oven to 350°F.

3. In a 12 × 9 × 2-inch baking casserole, spoon some of the blue cheese dressing to form a thin layer on the bottom. Arrange the fish on top of the dressing, then cover with the remaining dressing. Layer the red onion and remaining crumbled blue cheese on top. Bake until the fish flakes, about 20 minutes. Serve hot.

Flounder and Spinach Pie

The only thing you need to pay extra attention to when making this flavorful dish is that no white pith from the lemon gets into it, otherwise it will taste bitter. You can use any white-fleshed fillets from flatfish, such as fluke or flounder, or small fillets of red snapper or a similar fish. The seasoning of this dish is, believe it or not, typically Sicilian, and you will find that the final golden-crusted puff pastry on top makes for an inviting casserole.

• Makes 4 to 6 servings

2 tablespoons extra-virgin olive oil plus more as needed
¾ pound spinach leaves without stems
2 tablespoons finely chopped fresh parsley
1 large garlic clove, finely chopped
1½ teaspoons fennel seeds
¼ teaspoon red chile flakes
1 lemon, peeled, all white pith removed, flesh very thinly sliced
    into rounds and seeds discarded
Salt and freshly ground black pepper
1 pound flounder or other flatfish fillets
5 ounces frozen puff pastry, defrosted (follow instructions
    on package for defrosting)
1 large egg, beaten to blend

1. Preheat the oven to 350°F. Oil a 12 × 9 × 2-inch baking casserole.

2. In a large skillet, heat 1 tablespoon of olive oil over medium heat. Add a large handful of spinach leaves and stir until they begin to wilt, continuing to add handfuls of spinach as soon as there is enough room in the skillet to hold more. Continue cooking until they are all barely wilted, turning and folding them as they wilt, about 5 minutes.

3. In a small bowl, toss the parsley, garlic, fennel seeds, red chile flakes, and lemon slices together. Season with salt and pepper. Lay the fish fillets in

Mayonnaise

Mayonnaise is such an important ingredient in casseroles that it's a shame we have to use commercially made mayonnaise from the supermarket. Homemade mayonnaise is an amazing food and not hard to make —it's all about emulsifying egg and oil. The kind of oil you use will effect the taste of the final mayonnaise. I like to make my own mayonnaise and use a combination of light-tasting oils in it. When I do use supermarket mayonnaise there's only one brand I buy, Hellmann's mayonnaise (sold as Best Foods west of the Rockies).

¾ cup olive oil
¾ cup vegetable oil
1 large egg
1 large egg yolk
1 tablespoon freshly squeezed lemon juice or good-quality white wine vinegar
½ teaspoon very fine salt
½ teaspoon very finely ground white pepper

Mix the oils together in a measuring cup. Put the egg and egg yolk in a food processor and blend for 30 seconds. Slowly pour in the oil in a very thin stream with the processor running, about 5 to 6 minutes of pouring. Blend in the lemon juice or vinegar for 30 seconds. Add the salt and pepper and continue blending for 30 seconds. Refrigerate for 1 hour before using. • Makes 2 cups

the baking casserole. Salt and pepper the fish. Sprinkle the parsley–fennel mixture over the fish, making sure the lemon slices are evenly dispersed. Arrange the spinach atop. Drizzle lightly with the remaining olive oil. Roll the puff pastry out so it is large enough to cover the casserole. Set the pastry atop the casserole and pinch the sides of the puff pastry against the edge of the casserole to adhere. Score the pastry in 8 places with a knife. Brush the surface with the egg. Bake until golden brown, about 35 minutes. Serve hot.

Halibut Cheeks and Shrimp Casserole

Y ou might be wondering . . . cheeks, are you serious? Well, they are nothing new to anyone from New England where they have enjoyed cod cheeks for decades. Restaurant chefs have also fallen in love with cod and halibut cheeks, so you'll see them on the menus of trendy restaurants. What do you do with them? You could bread them and fry them of course, but this casserole is a nice alternative and delicious too. The availability of fish cheeks is both seasonal and regional, so if your local fish market doesn't have them, use skate wings, and failing that, a piece of halibut fillet.

• Makes 6 servings

1¾ pounds ripe plum tomatoes, cut in half, seeds
    squeezed out, and flesh grated against the largest holes
    of a box grater down to the peel, or one 28-ounce can
    whole plum tomatoes, drained
2 tablespoons extra-virgin olive oil
1 tablespoon finely chopped fresh basil
Salt and freshly ground black pepper
1½ pounds halibut or cod cheeks
12 jumbo shrimp (21 to 25 count per pound), peeled

1. Preheat the oven to 350°F.

2. Place the tomatoes and olive oil in a large skillet and cook over medium heat, stirring occasionally, until dense, 20 to 25 minutes, depending on how juicy the tomatoes are. Mix in the basil. Season with salt and pepper. Spread half of the sauce over the bottom of a 12 × 9 × 2-inch baking casserole.

3. Arrange the halibut cheeks and shrimp in the baking casserole and spread the remaining tomato sauce over the top. Bake until the shrimp have turned orange-red and the fish flakes, about 35 minutes. Serve hot.

Swordfish, Tomato, and Mint Casserole

With its Greek inspiration, this casserole tastes flavorful and light, and makes the perfect dinner at the end of the summer when fresh tomatoes are still ripe. I sometimes make this casserole with mixed fish cubes because it tends to be cheaper than buying only swordfish. If you do the same, make sure the fish you buy are more or less all firm-fleshed, otherwise some of the fish will dry out before other pieces finish cooking. This recipe will provide you with some leftovers which will go great on top of some cooked pasta like penne or macaroni. Even nicer, serve the leftovers cool or at room temperature for an appetizer the next day • **Makes 4 servings**

2 pounds ripe, but firm tomatoes, peeled, seeded, and
   cut into large chunks
1½ pounds swordfish or mixed firm-fleshed fish,
   cut into 1½-inch cubes
6 tablespoons extra-virgin olive oil
6 tablespoons finely chopped fresh mint leaves
3 large garlic cloves, finely chopped
2 ½ tablespoons freshly squeezed lemon juice
Salt and freshly ground black pepper

1 Preheat the oven to 350°F.

2 In a 10-inch-wide baking casserole (preferably earthenware), toss together the tomatoes, fish, olive oil, mint, garlic, and lemon juice until mixed well. Season with salt and pepper, and toss again. Bake until the edges are bubbling, about 20 minutes. Serve hot.

Brazilian Fish Casserole

This casserole is called *moqueca de peixe* in Portuguese and is a variation of a stew made with shrimp. The unique *dendê* oil used in Brazil, also called red palm oil, is what makes the dish unique, so I recommend you get some. It is sold in South American and African markets, but since those markets are not as common as other ethnic grocers, you may need to order it over the Internet which you can do easily at safarimkt.com or notinmylocal shop.com or jbafricanmarket.com. If you just can't get this oil, then use walnut oil mixed with a little paprika. This recipe can also be made with shrimp, in which case you will need to peel 1¾ pounds of medium-size shrimp. The canned coconut milk called for in the ingredient list will be found in your supermarket's international/ethnic foods aisle, shelved in the Asian or Thai section. Serve with white rice. • **Makes 4 servings**

2 tablespoons red palm oil (*dendê* oil) or walnut oil mixed
  with ⅛ teaspoon paprika
1 large onion, finely chopped
4 large tomatoes (about 1½ pounds), cut in half, seeds
  squeezed out, and flesh grated against the largest holes
  of a box grater down to the peel, or one 28-ounce can
  whole plum tomatoes, drained
1¼ pounds yellowtail, mahimahi, or sea bass, cut into 1½-inch cubes
One 14-ounce can unsweetened coconut milk
2 tablespoons freshly squeezed lemon juice
2 tablespoons finely chopped fresh parsley leaves
3 garlic cloves, crushed
1 fresh red jalapeño or serrano chile, finely chopped
1 teaspoon freshly ground black pepper
½ teaspoon salt

① Preheat the oven to 350°F.

② In a skillet or shallow flame- and oven-proof casserole, heat the red palm oil over medium heat, then cook the onion, stirring, until golden, about 5 minutes. Stir in the tomatoes, fish, coconut milk, lemon juice, parsley, garlic, chile, black pepper, and salt. Immediately transfer the mixture to a 12 × 9 × 2-inch baking casserole. Bake until the fish begins to flake, about 15 minutes. Serve hot.

Baked Swordfish with Feta Cheese

In Greece, a popular taverna dish called *garides me feta* is a casserole of baked fresh shrimp and feta cheese. Since fresh shrimp are so hard to find, this recipe replaces the shrimp with swordfish, which has a perfect texture for this casserole. It is usually cooked in an earthenware baking casserole called a *youvetsi* (or *giouvetsi*), derived from the Turkish. Any earthenware baking casserole will do, and lacking that, any ceramic or glass baking dish is fine. If swordfish is too expensive, shark, opah, monkfish, yellowtail, and mahimahi all work as good substitutes. I like to use Greek or Bulgarian feta cheese which is usually sold in Middle Eastern markets, but use whatever you find available. Serve with a simple green vegetable or green salad, and French fries, plain white rice, or garlic bread. • **Makes 6 servings**

2 pounds swordfish, cut into 1 1/2-inch cubes
2 tablespoons freshly squeezed lemon juice
6 tablespoons extra-virgin olive oil
1 medium onion or 3 shallots, finely chopped
5 scallions, white and light green parts only, finely chopped
3 pounds ripe tomatoes, cut in half, seeds squeezed out,
    and flesh grated against the largest holes of a box grater
    down to the peel, or three 15-ounce cans whole plum
    tomatoes, drained
1/3 cup dry white wine
2 large garlic cloves, finely chopped
3 tablespoons finely chopped cilantro leaves
1 tablespoon fresh basil leaves
Salt and freshly ground black pepper
1/2 pound feta cheese, crumbled into large 1-inch chunks
Fresh parsley leaves for garnish

1. Place the swordfish in a large bowl and pour the lemon juice over it. Toss and set aside in the refrigerator.

2. In a large skillet, heat the olive oil over high heat, then cook the onion or shallots and scallions, stirring occasionally, until translucent, about 5 to 6 minutes. Add the tomatoes, wine, garlic, cilantro, and basil, and season with salt and pepper. Stir well, reduce the heat to low and simmer, stirring occasionally, until dense, about 1½ hours.

3. Preheat the oven to 450°F.

4. Spoon some sauce into a 12 x 9 x 2-inch baking casserole or a large round earthenware baking casserole. Arrange the fish in the baking casserole and cover with the remaining sauce. Spread the feta cheese around the fish, pushing the chunks of cheese into the sauce. Bake until the swordfish cubes are cooked and the cheese melted, 20 to 25 minutes. Garnish with parsley leaves and serve hot.

Monkfish Casserole

Basques are famed throughout Spain as being great cooks, and a taste of this rich but delicate casserole will give you an idea why. Although I think monkfish works best in this Basque-inspired casserole, you can substitute any white firm-fleshed fish. You can hard-boil the eggs and cook the asparagus at the same time in the same saucepan. As an accompaniment, rice or noodles are nice, as is any non-cream-based vegetable casserole.

• Makes 4 servings

4 large thick asparagus spears, scraped and trimmed

3 large eggs

¾ cup extra-virgin olive oil

1 medium onion, chopped

5 large garlic cloves, finely chopped

1½ pounds monkfish fillets, cut into 1-inch pieces

Salt and freshly ground black pepper

8 littleneck clams, scrubbed

6 ounces fresh or frozen peas

6 tablespoons finely chopped fresh parsley leaves

Leftover Idea

A good casserole to make at the same time as the Monkfish Casserole (this page) is the Cabbage Casserole #1 (page 308). If you have leftovers from both, you can place the Swiss chard in a small 1-quart baking casserole and top it with the leftover monkfish casserole, then stick it into the oven until hot. It's quite nice.

1. Preheat the oven to 350°F.

2. Bring a saucepan of lightly salted water to a boil over high heat, then add the asparagus and eggs. Cook until the asparagus is soft, about 10 minutes. Drain and set aside the asparagus spears, keeping them warm. Cool the eggs immediately in cold water, then remove their shells when they are cool enough to handle. Cut the eggs into wedges and set aside.

3. Meanwhile, set an 8- to 10-inch round earthenware baking casserole on a heat diffuser. Heat the olive oil in the baking casserole over medium-high heat, then add the onion and garlic, and cook, stirring frequently so the garlic doesn't burn, until the onion is softened, about 6 minutes. (If your earthenware baking casserole is flame-proof, less time may be needed, and if you are using a non-earthenware flame-proof casserole, you will not need the heat diffuser and even less time will be needed.)

4. Remove the casserole from the heat. Season the fish with salt and pepper and add it to the casserole. Add the clams, peas, and parsley, and stir gently to mix. Bake until the clams open wide and the fish is firm and white, about 40 minutes. Garnish with the asparagus and eggs, and serve hot.

Turkish Fish Casserole

This simple recipe called *balik güveç* in Turkish, which means "fish casserole," is concocted from a description given by the nineteenth-century Turkish cookbook author Turabi Efendi. It is a casserole quite common in the Turkish home, and when you make it you'll see why—it is both delicious and easy. You may not be able to find whole blue mackerel, although it is preferable to have a whole fish on the bone that is cut into steaks, in which case, you should simply get whatever the fishmonger has that is whole, dark-fleshed, and fresh and have it cleaned and cut into ½-inch-thick steaks. Some alternative fish to use are whole gray mullet or bluefish or yellowtail or mahimahi steaks. • **Makes 6 servings**

½ cup extra-virgin olive oil
4 medium onions, sliced ¼ inch thick
½ cup finely chopped fresh parsley
2 whole blue mackerel (about 3 pounds total),
    cleaned and gutted (see headnote for alternatives)
Salt and freshly ground black pepper
¼ cup white wine vinegar
¼ cup water
4 ripe tomatoes (about 1¾ pounds total),
    sliced crosswise into quarters

① Preheat the oven to 350°F.

② In a large skillet, heat the olive oil over medium-high heat, then add the onions and cook, stirring, until softened and golden, about 12 minutes. Add the parsley and cook until wilted, about 1 minute.

③ Arrange half of the onion mixture on the bottom of a 10-inch round baking casserole (preferably earthenware, otherwise use what you have). Place the fish steaks on top of the onions, season with salt and pepper, and cover the fish with the remaining onions and oil left in the skillet. Pour the vinegar and water over the fish, then arrange the tomato slices over the top. Bake until the fish separates when poked, 45 to 50 minutes. Serve hot.

Fish Florentine Casserole

Today, any dish called Florentine means it contains spinach, an appellation adopted from the French and still used in French cooking. In Italian, a dish described as Florentine simply means it's from Florence and doesn't necessarily contain spinach. In England, a Florentine was traditionally a meat pie often made with veal kidney and a pastry crust. The Italians played a role in the introduction and popularization of spinach in Europe in the thirteenth and fourteenth centuries and may have been responsible for this "Florentine" idea. This casserole begins with fish fillets that cover the bottom of the baking casserole, then creamed spinach goes on top, and finally it's completed with thinly sliced potatoes and cheese. If you want, you can use plain steamed spinach instead of making it creamed, but either way you make it, remember to chop it. • **Makes 4 servings**

1 pound spinach leaves without stems, rinsed well
2 tablespoons unsalted butter plus more as needed
¼ cup finely chopped onion
1 large garlic clove, finely chopped
2 tablespoons all-purpose flour
1 cup whole milk
Salt and freshly ground white or black pepper
1 pound fish fillets, such as sole, flounder, or red snapper
1 large baking potato (russet), peeled and cut into ¹⁄₁₆-inch-thick slices
6 ounces Bel Paese or Muenster cheese, sliced

1. Preheat the oven to 375°F. Lightly butter a 12 × 9 × 2-inch baking casserole.

2. Place the spinach in a medium saucepan with only the water adhering to it from its last rinsing. Turn the heat to high, cover, and steam, tossing a bit, until the spinach wilts, 3 to 5 minutes. Drain well by squeezing the water out of the spinach, then chop the spinach. Set aside until needed.

3. In a small saucepan, melt the butter over medium-high heat, then add the onion and garlic and cook, stirring until softened, about 3 minutes. Add the flour and stir to form a roux, about 1 minute. Remove the saucepan from the heat and slowly whisk in the milk. Return the saucepan to the heat, reduce the heat to low, and simmer, stirring occasionally, until thickened, about 12 minutes. Add the chopped spinach, season with salt and pepper, and cook over low heat for 5 minutes.

4. Cover the bottom of the baking casserole with the fish fillets. Season with salt and pepper. Spoon the spinach mixture evenly over the fish. Lay the sliced potatoes over the spinach in one layer. Season with a little salt. Lay the cheese over the potatoes. Bake uncovered until the casserole is bubbling and the top is dappled a light golden, about 25 minutes. Serve hot.

Catfish Casserole with Horseradish Sauce

Although catfish is well known in most of the U.S. now, before 1985 the only people who ate it regularly were Southerners and people living along the Mississippi River. Today, "blackened catfish" is a cliché. Catfish has long been associated with the Cajun and Creole cooking of Louisiana, but its widespread popularity probably resides in the fact that it is a firm-fleshed fish that slices into nicely sized fillets, which allows it to be used in many ways. In this recipe, the egg white topping goes over the fish and becomes like a meringue, making the fish look quite inviting. Because the horseradish sauce is white too, your final dish will be very white, so you'll definitely want to use the parsley and cayenne to provide some color and bite.

• Makes 4 servings

2 tablespoons unsalted butter plus more as needed
1½ pounds catfish fillets
1 tablespoon freshly squeezed lemon juice
2 large egg whites
2 tablespoons sour cream
1 tablespoon grated onion
1 large garlic clove
¼ teaspoon dry mustard
¼ teaspoon ground white pepper
2 tablespoons all-purpose flour
1 cup whole milk
4 teaspoons prepared horseradish
2 tablespoons finely chopped fresh parsley
Cayenne pepper

1. Preheat the oven to 375°F. Lightly butter a 12 × 9 × 2-inch baking casserole.

2. In the baking casserole, arrange the fish fillets and sprinkle with lemon juice.

3. In a small bowl, beat the egg whites until they form soft peaks. Fold in the sour cream, onion, garlic, mustard, and ⅛ teaspoon of white pepper. Spoon some of the mixture on top of each fillet.

4. Bake until the fish is opaque or a skewer glides easily through the flesh and the top is dappled golden brown, about 20 minutes.

5. Meanwhile, in small saucepan, melt the 2 tablespoons of butter over medium heat, then add the flour, stirring constantly to form a smooth roux. Remove the saucepan from the heat and stir in the milk, horseradish, and the remaining ⅛ teaspoon of white pepper. Return to the heat and continue to cook over medium-low heat, stirring until the mixture is bubbly and slightly thickened, about 5 minutes. Once the fish is done, spoon the horseradish sauce over the fish, sprinkle with parsley and a dusting of cayenne pepper, and serve hot.

Kedgeree

This is an old Cape Cod dish that was once a family supper dish, and is how one would use leftover rice and fish. In the late eighteenth and early nineteenth centuries, as Yankee traders were sailing to India and the Spice Islands making their fortunes, they brought back spices, as well as Persian rugs and Chinese porcelain and recipes. This is the reason Connecticut is known as the Nutmeg State and why curry powder is found in New England cooking. It's quite amazing to think about the transformation of the Indian dish called *khichri*, made of rice and pulses that became, first, the Anglo-Indian and eventually the New England preparation called kedgeree. Yes, they are related, and the story is a long and fascinating one that I partially tell in my *A Mediterranean Feast* (William Morrow, 1999). The macaroni, lentil, and rice dish known as *kushary* in Egypt is on the same family tree. The first American kedgerees seem to have been made around 1800 and they contained fish. The dish is also known in England where it is eaten for breakfast. Traditionally, salt cod or finnan haddie, which is smoked haddock, was used in this dish. One seasons the dish at the table with salt and pepper, and some cooks add parsley and thyme. In earlier times, curry powder was also once used in kedgeree. If you do use curry powder, keep it in moderation, say, half a teaspoon in this recipe. • **Makes 6 servings**

2 cups cooked and flaked white-fleshed fish, such as sole,
    fluke, cod, haddock, halibut, flounder, salt cod, or
    finnan haddie (from about 1 pound of raw fish)

2 cups cooked long-grain rice (made from ⅔ cup raw rice)

4 hard-boiled eggs, shelled and chopped

4 tablespoons (½ stick) unsalted butter, melted

½ teaspoon curry powder

1 cup heavy cream

Salt

1. Preheat the oven to 375°F.

2. In a bowl, toss all the ingredients, seasoning with salt as needed and mixing well. Transfer the mixture to a 12 x 9 x 2-inch baking casserole. Bake until heated through, about 20 minutes. Serve hot.

Leftover Idea

Once the Kedgeree (this page) is cool, form the rice into balls the size of a small lemon, then flatten the balls in your palm. Place a ½-inch cube of Muenster, mozzarella, or mild white cheddar cheese in the middle of each rice patty and reform the rice into a ball enclosing the cheese. Don't press together firmly like a snowball, but squeeze gently simply to form balls without cracks. Dip the rice balls into some beaten egg and then dredge in dry bread crumbs. In a deep fryer or an 8-inch saucepan fitted with a wire fry basket, preheat some vegetable oil to 360°F. Deep-fry the rice balls without crowding them in the frying oil, until golden, about 4 minutes. Serve warm as an appetizer.

Fish and Cheese Casserole

This old New England casserole was always made with haddock and mild cheddar cheese. The pairing of fish and cheese is considered a no-no in many cuisines, but apparently those old New England day-boat captains weren't informed. Some cooks layer the fish on top of each other with a layer of white sauce between them, but this recipe keeps the fish in one layer. The dish is best accompanied by plain white rice and green beans.

• **Makes 4 servings**

2 tablespoons unsalted butter plus more as needed
2 tablespoons all-purpose flour
1½ cups whole milk
Salt and freshly ground black pepper
¾ cup (about 2½ ounces) shredded mild white cheddar cheese
1 pound fish fillets, such as haddock, sole, red snapper,
    flounder, or fluke
Freshly grated nutmeg

1 Preheat the oven to 450°F. Lightly butter a 12 × 9 × 2-inch baking casserole.

2 In a saucepan, melt the butter over medium heat, then add the flour and stir to form a roux. Reduce the heat to medium-low and continue to cook, stirring, for 2 minutes. Remove the saucepan from the heat, then slowly whisk in the milk. Return the saucepan to medium heat and continue to cook, stirring, until it is smooth and a little denser, about 7 minutes. Season with salt and pepper. Stir in the cheese until it melts, 4 to 5 minutes.

3 Arrange the fish fillets in the baking casserole. Spread the white sauce over the fillets and sprinkle with nutmeg. Bake until bubbling and dappled golden brown, 20 to 25 minutes. Serve hot.

Salmon and Potato Casserole

The secret to this simple casserole is to make sure the layer of scalloped potatoes on the bottom of the baking casserole first bakes until the potatoes are slightly crispy, so that when you put the salmon on top of this bed of potatoes they finish cooking by slowly absorbing the juice from the fish, and end up aromatic and savory but not soggy. • **Makes 4 servings**

6 tablespoons (¾ stick) unsalted butter
2 medium baking potatoes (about 1 pound total), peeled and
      cut into ¼-inch-thick slices
3 large garlic cloves, finely chopped
Salt and freshly ground black pepper
1½ pounds salmon steaks or boneless skinless salmon fillets,
      cut into cubes or strips

1 Preheat the oven to 350°F.

2 Place the butter in a 10- to 12-inch round baking casserole and melt in the oven. Remove the baking casserole from the oven.

3 In a bowl, toss the potatoes and garlic together, then arrange the potato slices over the bottom of the baking casserole in concentric circles. Season with salt and pepper. Bake until firm and slightly browned on the edges, about 45 minutes.

4 Place the salmon on top of the potatoes and season with salt and pepper. Bake until the salmon flakes and is pale orange, about 12 minutes. Serve hot.

Salmon Avocado Casserole

Although you might think this is the simplest casserole in the world, the tastes are stunningly delicious and give a lot more bang for the buck than you'd expect. As with all fish dishes, the quality depends entirely on the freshness of the fish. Arrange the salmon and avocado attractively in the baking casserole and then pop it into the oven. It's visually pleasing too with the orange and green contrast from the salmon and avocado, and the crispy golden topping of the bread crumbs. The recipe can be doubled to feed 4, in which case, use a larger baking casserole. • **Makes 2 servings**

½ pound boneless skinless salmon fillets, or salmon steaks,
    cubed into 1-inch pieces
1 small ripe avocado, cut in half, stone removed, flesh scooped
    out whole with a spoon and cut into ½-inch-thick slices
Salt and freshly ground black pepper
½ cup heavy cream
1 cup fresh bread crumbs (see Note)
2 lemon wedges (optional)

1. Preheat the oven to 400°F. Lightly butter a 10 × 8-inch baking casserole.

2. Arrange the salmon and avocado in the baking casserole. Season with salt and pepper. Pour the cream over the salmon and sprinkle the bread crumbs on top. Bake until bubbling and the salmon is cooked, about 20 minutes. Serve with lemon wedges, if desired.

Note: This amount can be made from crumbling two ½-inch-thick slices of 5¼ × 3-inch French or Italian bread in a food processor.

Crab Casserole

The crab casserole is a favorite brunch dish on the eastern U.S. seaboard. It's typically a rich casserole that is ideal served accompanied only by a tossed green salad. An even richer casserole can be made by adding several chopped hard-boiled eggs into the crab mixture along with a Béchamel sauce. The top can also be sprinkled with bread crumbs to make it a gratin. Some cooks don't use cheese and call the dish a crab meat hot dish.

• Makes 4 to 6 servings

3 cups ½-inch cubes toasted French or Italian bread
1½ cups lump crab meat (about 6 ounces), picked over
½ cup (about 1½ ounces) shredded sharp cheddar cheese
2 tablespoons chopped pimientos
2 tablespoons finely chopped onion
3 cups whole milk
6 large eggs
1½ teaspoons dry mustard
½ teaspoon salt
½ teaspoon Tabasco sauce
5 slices bacon, cooked until crispy and crumbled

1 Preheat the oven to 325°F. Lightly butter a 12 × 9 × 2-inch baking casserole.

2 Spread the cubes of toasted bread on the bottom of the baking casserole. Sprinkle the crab, cheese, pimientos, and onion over the bread. In a bowl, beat the milk, eggs, dry mustard, salt, and Tabasco sauce together. Pour the milk mixture over the crab. Bake until a knife comes out clean when inserted into the center of the casserole, 45 to 50 minutes. About 10 minutes before the casserole is done, sprinkle the crumbled bacon on top. Serve hot.

Crab Meat and Shrimp Casserole

This incredible casserole has been described as a quick entrée and a family favorite in Mississippi and Louisiana. But its taste is rich, luscious, and complex, and I find it is a great casserole to serve to shrimp and crab lovers. Some cooks add the old-fashioned cream of mushroom soup, but I prefer this recipe, which I adapted after looking at the recipes of Martha Yost, executive chef of the University Club of Jackson in Mississippi, and Judy Howle, a Mississippian home cook who posted her recipe on the Internet.

• Makes 6 to 8 servings

6 tablespoons (¾ stick) unsalted butter

1 medium onion, finely chopped

3 celery stalks, finely chopped

1 medium green bell pepper, cored and finely chopped

1 pound cooked small shrimp (51 to 60 count per pound), peeled

1 pound lump crab meat, picked over

1½ cups fresh bread crumbs (see Note)

1 cup (about 3 ounces) shredded mild white cheddar cheese

½ cup heavy cream

½ cup mayonnaise

1 large egg

1 tablespoon Worcestershire sauce

2 teaspoons dry mustard

1 teaspoon Louisiana-style hot sauce
   (such as Crystal Hot Sauce or Tabasco sauce)

1 teaspoon salt plus more to taste

¼ teaspoon ground coriander

¼ teaspoon ground cumin

¼ teaspoon ground nutmeg

¼ teaspoon ground star anise

1½ cups crushed plain water crackers

½ teaspoon hot paprika

1. Preheat the oven to 400°F. Butter a 12 × 9 × 2-inch baking casserole.

2. In a skillet, melt the butter over medium-high heat, then transfer 3 table-spoons of the melted butter to a medium bowl and set aside, keeping it warm and melted. Add the onion, celery, and bell pepper to the skillet, then cook, stirring, until the onion is translucent, about 8 minutes. Transfer to a large bowl and let cool a bit. Add the shrimp, crab meat, bread crumbs, half of the cheddar cheese, the heavy cream, mayon-naise, egg, Worcestershire sauce, dry mustard, hot sauce, 1 teaspoon of salt, coriander, cumin, nutmeg, and star anise to the onion mixture and toss gently but thoroughly to mix the ingredients.

3. Put the crab and shrimp mixture into the baking casserole, spreading it evenly to cover the bottom of the baking casserole. Top with the crum-bled crackers and remaining cheddar cheese, and sprinkle with paprika. Drizzle the reserved 3 tablespoons of melted butter over. Bake until golden brown and the melted cheese looks like lace (you'll see what I mean when it's baked), about 25 minutes. Serve hot.

Note: This amount can be made from crumbling four ½-inch-thick slices of 5¼ × 3-inch French or Italian bread in a food processor.

Lobster and Mushroom Casserole

Lobsters were cheap seventy years ago on Cape Cod, and that's probably why this casserole could be whipped up anytime, as opposed to today when it is warranted only on special occasions due to its high price. This great recipe is adapted from an old Cape Cod cookbook called *From Cape Cod Kitchens,* published by the Harwich Port Library Association in 1934. It's quite rich, and because of that, it will feed four people when served with another dish on the side. To give you an idea of what old Cape Cod was like in 1930, the telephone number of the Eldridge Stores Groceries and Provisions, where you might have picked up your eggs, milk, and cream for this casserole, was 58. • **Makes 4 servings**

> Two 1½-pound live lobsters
> 6 tablespoons (¾ stick) unsalted butter
> 1 pound white button mushrooms, sliced
> 3 tablespoons all-purpose flour
> 1 teaspoon salt
> ⅛ teaspoon hot paprika
> 1 cup whole milk
> ½ cup heavy cream
> 2 large egg yolks, beaten to blend
> ½ cup fresh bread crumbs (see Note)

1. In a very large pot, steam the lobsters with 1 cup of water for 25 minutes. Remove the lobsters from the pot and let cool a bit, then crack all the shells and remove all the meat. Dice the meat and set it aside. Return the shells to the pot and cover with water. Bring to a boil, then reduce the heat and simmer for 1 hour. After an hour, reserve ½ cup of the lobster broth to use in this recipe and save the remaining broth for another purpose.

2. Preheat the oven to 475°F. Butter a 9 × 9 × 2-inch baking casserole with 1 tablespoon of butter.

3. In a skillet, melt 4 tablespoons of butter over medium-high heat, then add the mushrooms and cook, stirring occasionally, until they have softened and their liquid has evaporated, about 7 minutes. Add the flour, salt, and paprika, and cook, stirring constantly, for 5 minutes. Remove the skillet from the heat and slowly whisk in the milk and reserved lobster broth, stirring constantly and scrapping the bottom of the skillet. Once it is blended, cook for 3 minutes, then whisk in the cream, egg yolks, and reserved lobster meat. Pour into the baking casserole. Cover the top with the bread crumbs and dot with the remaining 1 tablespoon of butter. Bake until the top is golden and the sides bubbling, about 15 minutes. Serve hot.

Note: This amount can be made from crumbling one ½-inch-thick slice of 5¼ × 3-inch French or Italian bread in a food processor.

Alabama-Style Shrimp Bake

This recipe is adapted from one found on the Internet, which I eventually tracked down with some difficulty because no one posting the recipes over and over acknowledged the source as being the *Bubba Gump Shrimp Company Cookbook*. Although I found the movie *Forrest Gump,* which inspired this faux-Bayou restaurant chain, unappealing, and was very suspect of this dish, as I am suspect of national chain restaurants, it's actually quite good—made all the better with fresh shrimp, if you can find any. If you do, double the amount of shrimp below and keep their heads on, but remove the shells. You do need to be careful not to overcook the shrimp, as they will taste dry and rubbery the instant you do. The amount of Worcestershire sauce called for is not an error. • **Makes 4 to 6 servings**

1 cup (2 sticks) unsalted butter, melted

¾ cup freshly squeezed lemon juice

¾ cup Worcestershire sauce

1 tablespoon freshly and coarsely ground black pepper

1 tablespoon Louisiana-style hot sauce
    (such as Crystal Hot Sauce or Tabasco sauce)

1 tablespoon salt

3 large garlic cloves, finely chopped

1 teaspoon dried rosemary

⅛ teaspoon cayenne pepper

1 medium onion, thinly sliced

2½ pounds jumbo shrimp (21 to 25 count per pound), peeled

2 lemons, thinly sliced

Fresh rosemary sprigs for garnish (optional)

1. Preheat the oven to 425°F.

2. In a small bowl, mix the butter, lemon juice, Worcestershire sauce, pepper, hot sauce, salt, garlic, rosemary, and cayenne.

3. In an ungreased 12 × 9 × 2-inch baking casserole, cover the bottom with the onion, then attractively layer the shrimp on top. Cover the shrimp with the lemon slices and pour the butter mixture over the shrimp. Bake uncovered until the shrimp turn pink-orange, basting occasionally with pan juices, about 20 minutes (but check for doneness by tasting a shrimp after the first 15 minutes). Garnish with fresh rosemary sprigs and serve hot.

Eggplant with Shrimp Casserole

This fantastic Creole casserole begs for fresh shrimp, but you will be just as happy using frozen shrimp. If you do use frozen shrimp, make sure you defrost them slowly in the refrigerator, which will keep the texture and taste of the flesh closer to that of fresh shrimp. This casserole is known as baked eggplant Radosta in Mary Land's *Louisiana Cookery,* published in 1954. Radosta is the name of a restaurant in Metairie, and is also a family name. Since Ms. Land doesn't provide any information about the origin of her recipe, I'm guessing it may in some way be connected to the Radosta family. But this particular recipe is adapted from the one served at the well-known Cajun-French restaurant, Prejean's, in North Lafayette, Louisiana. Some cooks boil the eggplant and use bread crumbs on top, but I much prefer this recipe. • Makes 6 to 8 servings

2 eggplants (about 3 pounds total), peeled and cut into 1-inch cubes
Salt
2 cups vegetable oil
3 slices bacon
2 pounds large shrimp (31 to 40 count per pound), peeled
2 medium onions, chopped
1 cup diced crustless French bread, soaked in
    milk or water, then squeezed
½ cup chopped celery
½ cup freshly grated pecorino Romano cheese
1 medium green bell pepper, cored and chopped
2 large eggs
¼ cup finely chopped fresh parsley leaves
4 large garlic cloves, finely chopped
1 tablespoon finely chopped fresh basil
1 teaspoon freshly squeezed lemon juice
1 teaspoon ground sage

1 teaspoon fresh or dried rosemary
¼ teaspoon cayenne pepper
⅛ teaspoon Tabasco sauce
Freshly ground black pepper
Freshly ground white pepper

1. Preheat the oven to 350°F. Butter a 13 x 9 x 2-inch baking casserole.

2. Lay the eggplant on some paper towels and sprinkle with salt. Leave them to drain of their bitter juices for 30 minutes, then pat dry with clean paper towels.

3. In a large skillet, heat the vegetable oil over medium-high heat for 10 minutes, then cook the eggplant until golden brown, turning when necessary, about 4 minutes total. Transfer the fried eggplant cubes to a large bowl, with a slotted spoon. (You will need to cook the eggplant cubes in batches so they are not crowded.) Discard the oil.

4. In the same large skillet, cook the bacon over medium heat until it is almost crispy, about 5 minutes. Remove the bacon, reserving the fat in the skillet. Crumble the bacon and add it to the bowl with the fried eggplant. Increase the heat to high, then add the shrimp to the skillet with the bacon fat and cook until orange-red and firm, about 3 minutes. Transfer the shrimp to the bowl of eggplant.

5. Add the onions, bread, celery, half of the cheese, the bell pepper, eggs, parsley, garlic, basil, lemon juice, sage, rosemary, cayenne pepper, and Tabasco sauce to the bowl of eggplant and toss well. Season the eggplant mixture with black pepper and white pepper. Transfer to the baking casserole. Sprinkle the remaining cheese on top. Bake until bubbly and crusty-looking on top, about 45 minutes. Serve hot.

Shrimp Scampi

This classic Italian-American dish from the 1960s is a real favorite of many families in New York and New Jersey where the dish was originally popularized. *Scampi* is the Italian plural for "prawn," a relative of the shrimp, so it's a nonsensically named dish since it means "shrimp prawn." In a New York-style shrimp scampi there are two stars—the shrimp and the garlic. Although the shrimp could be sautéed, I like to make this preparation the way I remember having it at those festive Italian-American restaurants of my youth—you know, the ones with their red-checked tablecloths, basket-wrapped Chianti bottle used as a candle holder, garlic bread galore, and oregano dispensers on the table. The shrimp came out in individual baking casseroles and we would dip the bread into the garlic-flavored olive oil. The whole dried piquin chiles (also called bird chiles) used in this recipe are only about $1/4$ inch long and perfect for this dish. They can be ordered from friedas.com or penderys.com, otherwise you can use whatever red chile flakes you have, if you decide to use chiles at all. • **Makes 4 servings**

1½ pounds medium shrimp
    (41 to 50 count per pound), peeled
½ cup extra-virgin olive oil
8 large garlic cloves, very finely chopped
1 large shallot, finely chopped
1 teaspoon dried piquin chiles or
    ½ teaspoon red chile flakes (optional)
1 teaspoon salt plus more if desired
Freshly ground black pepper

1 Preheat the oven to 425°F.

2 In a bowl, toss the shrimp with the olive oil, garlic, shallot, chiles, if using, and 1 teaspoon of salt. Season with black pepper. Transfer to a 10-inch round baking casserole, or use individual baking casseroles, and bake until the shrimp are pink-orange and firm, 13 to 15 minutes. Serve hot.

Seafood Crêpe Casserole

S ave the shrimp shells to make the broth that provides so much flavor in the sauce for this casserole. I became fascinated with savory crêpes as a child when I lived in France in the 1950s. Even so, this casserole is an all-American dish that I adapted from Marion Cunningham's *The Fannie Farmer Cookbook*, inspired after having been an overnight guest at her house and treated to these crêpes' cousin, the yeasted waffles Marion had prepared for us. • Makes 6 servings

½ pound medium shrimp (41 to 50 count per pound),
    peeled and chopped, shells saved for making broth
4 tablespoons (½ stick) unsalted butter
1 large shallot, finely chopped
¼ cup all-purpose flour
½ cup half and half
3 tablespoons dry sherry
¼ pound white fish fillet, such as cod, sand dab,
    or halibut, chopped
½ teaspoon Tabasco sauce
Salt
12 Crêpes (page 392)

1. Preheat the oven to 350°F.

2. Place the shrimp shells in a small saucepan and cover with 1½ cups of water. Bring to a boil, then reduce the heat to low and simmer until the liquid is reduced to 1 cup. Strain the broth and set aside until needed.

3. In a skillet, melt the butter over medium-high heat. Remove about ½ tablespoon of melted butter and use it to coat a 15 × 9 × 2-inch baking casserole (or 2 smaller casseroles). Add the shallot to the remaining melted butter in the skillet and cook, stirring, until softened, about 2 minutes. Sprinkle the flour over the butter mixture and stir. Continue to cook until a roux is formed, about 2 minutes. Remove the skillet from the heat and slowly add the reserved 1 cup of the strained shrimp broth, whisking as you do, and stirring until smooth. Pour in the half and half and sherry and cook, stirring constantly, until smooth, about 5 minutes. Add the shrimp and fish; season with Tabasco sauce and salt. Stir 1 minute, then remove from the heat.

4. Fill a crêpe with about 3 tablespoons of the shrimp mixture, then roll up and place in the baking casserole, seam side down. Repeat with the remaining crêpes and shrimp mixture, saving at least a few tablespoons of the sauce from the shrimp mixture to spread on top of the crêpes later. Place the crêpes next to each other until the baking casserole is filled. Spoon the extra sauce over the top, and bake until bubbly, about 25 minutes. Serve hot.

Scalloped Clams

This old Cape Cod casserole probably has its origins in the nineteenth century. It's quite nice given how simple it is. There are many varieties of this dish in Cape Cod and it ranges in how it is made toward the north into maritime Canada and south to Long Island. South of there, even more variations come into play. Sometimes the dish is called escalloped clams, and is made with clams as well as scallops, oysters, lobster, or some combination of these seafoods. Cracker crumbs are also traditionally used instead of bread crumbs, and when you see celery, garlic, or other ingredients in the recipe, it means it's "modern," whatever that means. The whole business of a dish cooked "scalloped" means that it was originally cooked in either a baking casserole that was shaped like a scallop shell or the scallop shell itself. But later it came to mean a dish with sauce that was baked with a bread or cracker crumb topping. The clams are best when freshly shucked, but you can also use canned or frozen. • **Makes 4 servings**

2½ cups chopped quahogs, cherrystone clams,
   or surf clams, liquid saved
2 cups fresh bread crumbs (see Note)
3 tablespoons thinly sliced unsalted butter
   plus 1 tablespoon melted
¼ cup half and half
Salt

1. Preheat the oven to 350°F. Butter an 8 × 8-inch baking casserole.

2. Layer a third of the chopped clams on the bottom of the baking casserole. Sprinkle with a third of the bread crumbs. Dot with 1½ tablespoons of the thinly sliced butter. Repeat layering another third of the clams and bread crumbs, and the remaining 1½ tablespoons of sliced butter. Cover with the remaining third of the clams. Toss the remaining third of the bread crumbs in a bowl with the remaining 1 tablespoon of melted butter. Sprinkle the buttered bread crumbs over the casserole. Drizzle the top with the half and half, season with salt, and add 2 tablespoons of the reserved clam juice. Bake until golden, about 40 minutes. Serve hot.

Note: This amount can be made from crumbling four ½-inch thick-slices of 5¼ × 3-inch French or Italian bread in a food processor.

Eating Seafood on Cape Cod

For nearly fifteen years, I would take my children to Wellfleet on Cape Cod, where we would rent a house and live by the sea for a couple of weeks in the summer. We always had a great time and we ate lots of seafood, never tiring of it. Interestingly, although we ate everything, native Cape Codders don't use all the local shellfish available to them. My children and I would comb the beaches and tidal flats of Wellfleet to collect three other wonderful shellfish Cape Codders don't eat, namely, mussels (I have no idea why they don't eat them), razor clams, and whelks. Periwinkles are popular too, but only with natives and they are usually eaten as an appetizer. Since so many of our seafood leftovers ended up in casseroles, we always had a dinner ready.

Corn and Oyster Casserole

T his casserole is well known along the East Coast from Boston to Savannah. The casserole ends up being a kind of pudding, and if you love corn and oysters, well this is the one for you. I don't use many canned products, but this is one recipe that works well with canned creamed corn. You could of course make your own creamed corn. I can't tell you how many oysters you'll need because they are all different sizes, but figure on at least eighteen. • **Makes 4 servings**

One 15-ounce can creamed-style corn, drained well
½ cup half and half
1 large egg, beaten to blend
⅛ teaspoon celery salt
Salt and freshly ground black pepper
1 cup crushed soda crackers or fresh bread crumbs
    fried in 1 tablespoon of butter until crispy
1 cup shucked oysters with their liquid,
    cut in thirds or more if larger
2 tablespoons unsalted butter, cut into small cubes
¼ teaspoon hot paprika

1 Preheat the oven to 350°F. Butter a 9-inch round baking casserole.

2 In a bowl, fold together the creamed corn, half and half, egg, and celery salt. Season with salt and pepper. Stir in the soda crackers or bread crumbs, then fold in the oysters and a tablespoon of their liquid, and mix thoroughly.

3 Pour the mixture into the baking casserole. Top with the cubes of butter and sprinkle with the paprika. Bake until the casserole has set and is no longer runny, 45 to 50 minutes. Serve hot.

Pasta and Noodle Casseroles

Baked Ziti with Broccoli

When I was a kid, one of my favorite dishes was my mom's baked ziti. She never cooked it like this, but her baked ziti and the baked pastas I've had in southern Italy are the inspiration for this recipe. Besides, this is a pretty dish and especially delicious with a good quality caciocavallo cheese. The pasta you use here is not the short-cut tubes of ziti but the long tubular strands of macaroni called *ziti lunghe*—it's actually kind of fun to eat and is perfect for a baked pasta dish. It's the same pasta the Greeks use to make Pastitsio (page 87). You're more likely to find it in an Italian market than a supermarket, but you can use any ziti you find. • **Makes 4 servings**

½ pound *ziti lunghe*
1¼ pounds broccoli, florets reserved, stems saved for another purpose
½ cup freshly grated Parmesan cheese
1 large garlic clove, finely chopped
1 tablespoon extra-virgin olive oil plus more for drizzling
Salt and freshly ground black pepper
2 tablespoons unsalted butter
2 tablespoons all-purpose flour
¾ cup whole milk, warmed
¾ cup heavy cream, warmed
¼ pound caciocavallo cheese or provolone cheese, sliced
2 tablespoons dry bread crumbs

1 Preheat the oven to 350°F. Lightly butter a 9 × 5-inch-deep round baking casserole or oven-proof terrine.

2 Bring a large pot of abundantly salted water to a vigorous boil and add the pasta. After about 5 minutes, add the broccoli and cook until the pasta is three-quarters cooked (follow the package instructions) and then drain well. Toss the pasta and broccoli with the Parmesan, garlic,

and 1 tablespoon of olive oil. Season lightly with salt and pepper. Place in the baking casserole.

3 In a small saucepan, melt the butter over medium-high heat. Add the flour and stir to form a roux. Continue to cook, stirring, for 2 to 3 minutes. Remove from the heat and slowly whisk in the warm milk and cream. Return the saucepan to medium heat and cook the white sauce, stirring occasionally, until dense, 10 to 15 minutes.

4 Layer the caciocavallo cheese over the pasta and cover with the white sauce. Sprinkle the top with the bread crumbs and drizzle some olive oil over the top. Bake until the top is golden brown, 30 to 35 minutes. Serve hot.

Caciocavallo Cheese

Caciocavallo is a hard, spun-curd cheese made from cow's milk. A spun-curd cheese, or *pasta filata* in Italian, is so-called because the drained curd is soaked in hot whey and then in water and finally stretched, molded, and spun by the cheese maker. Among these string-like Italian cheeses that are all spun-curd are mozzarella, provolone, and scamorze. When finished, caciocavallo cheese is hung in the form of two gourds tied together. The outside is a smooth pale yellow while the inside is nearly white. The cheese itself is very dense. Provolone cheese is made in an identical way but contains more fat. Caciocavallo cheese, of which there are many varieties, is mostly made in southern Italy and Sicily. Caciocavallo cheese is eaten as a table cheese for the first six months, while aging it up to a year produces a sharper cheese for grating. Caciocavallo cheese is found exclusively in Italian markets and gourmet cheese shops or on the Internet at agferrari.com, esperya.com, or pastacheese.com. Provolone cheese is an acceptable substitute.

Baked Ditali and Mortadella with Mozzarella

ere's another great casserole preparation inspired by the baked pasta dishes of Naples and the Campania region of Italy. Mortadella is a cold cut that one normally associates with an antipasto or a sandwich. In this recipe it is marinated in milk to remove some of the salty taste, and then it is baked with the small macaroni called *ditali*, which is usually used in minestrone. If you can't find *ditali,* use elbow macaroni. • **Makes 4 servings**

¼ pound mortadella, diced

1¼ cups whole milk

1 cup ricotta cheese

3 tablespoons freshly grated Parmesan cheese

1 large egg

6 ounces *ditali* pasta (about 1¼ cups)

1 tablespoon extra-virgin olive oil

2 large garlic cloves, finely chopped

3 tablespoons finely chopped fresh parsley

2 teaspoons fresh thyme leaves or ¾ teaspoon dried thyme

Salt

6 ounces fresh mozzarella cheese, sliced

1. Place the mortadella in a nonmetallic bowl and cover with 1 cup of milk. Marinate for 1 hour, then drain well. Meanwhile, beat the ricotta, Parmesan, egg, and the remaining ¼ cup of milk together in a bowl.

2. Preheat the oven to 400°F. Lightly butter a 12 × 9 × 2-inch baking casserole.

3. Bring a large pot of abundantly salted water to a vigorous boil and add the pasta. Boil until half-cooked (follow the package instructions) and drain well. Transfer the pasta to the bowl with the ricotta cheese mixture.

4. In a skillet, heat the olive oil over medium-high heat, then add the mortadella, garlic, parsley, and thyme. Cook, stirring, until sizzling, about 1 minute. Scrape this mixture into the ricotta mixture and stir to blend well. Check the seasoning and add more salt if necessary.

5. Pour the macaroni mixture into the baking casserole and cover with the mozzarella. Bake until the cheese is beginning to brown on top, 25 to 30 minutes. Serve hot.

Stuffed Rigatoni

This preparation is not only a winner but you'll impress everyone with your meticulous work, as rigatoni seems impossible to stuff. And it is impossible to stuff without a pastry bag. So if you don't have a pastry bag, get one at a baking or kitchen supply store, as you will find it useful for a multitude of tasks from cupcake decorating to making deviled eggs. This preparation sounds a lot more labor-intensive than it really is, and yes, it's a little work, but the reward is without question very much worth it, as the dish is simply luscious. The one important thing to remember is not to overcook the rigatoni, otherwise it may rip or collapse when stuffing them. Also, make sure the pastry bag is fitted with a $\frac{1}{4}$-inch-wide conical nozzle. Now, that having been said, if you ignore my advice and try to stuff the rigatoni without a pastry bag you'll want to use the handle end of a teaspoon and stuff and tamp it down with your pinky—after stuffing the rigatoni this way you'll realize that you should have taken my advice and used a pastry bag.

• Makes 6 servings

1 tablespoon unsalted butter
¾ pound rigatoni
8 ounces (about 1 cup) ricotta cheese, pushed through a sieve
One 7-ounce can imported tuna in oil, drained
1 cup heavy cream
2 cups (about 5 ounces) freshly grated Parmesan cheese
Salt and freshly ground black pepper
1 tablespoon finely chopped fresh parsley (optional)

1. Coat a 12 × 9 × 2-inch baking casserole with 1 tablespoon of butter.

2. Bring a large pot of abundantly salted water to a vigorous boil. Add the rigatoni and boil until half-cooked (follow the package instructions). Drain and then transfer the rigatoni to a large bowl of cold water as you continue the preparation.

3. Blend the ricotta and tuna in a food processor until soft and smooth. In a medium bowl, mix the cream and Parmesan, then season with salt and pepper and set aside.

4. Fill a pastry bag with the tuna mixture and squeeze it into the opening of the rigatoni, filling it to the opening. Arrange the stuffed rigatoni in orderly rows in the casserole. Pour the cream mixture over the stuffed rigatoni and refrigerate for 3 hours.

5. Preheat the oven to 400°F.

6. Remove the rigatoni from the refrigerator and let rest at room temperature for 30 minutes. Bake uncovered until brown and bubbling on top, about 25 minutes. Serve hot with the parsley sprinkled on top, if desired.

Baked Rigatoni with Sausages

This is a classic of Italian-American cooking; a type of Sunday dish that my mom made and one that I was crazy about as a kid. She wouldn't have used the Béchamel sauce, but I've incorporated it since it's typically Neapolitan and where one finds the roots of this casserole. The preparation starts with what the Italians call a *soffritto*, a finely chopped mixture of onion and pancetta cooked in lard and olive oil that initiates a sauce or ragout. Mixing lard and oil is typical of the cooking of Campania, the region of which Naples is the capital, but you can leave out the lard if you wish and use butter instead. This dish will be all the better if you are able to make your own sausages, otherwise search out the very best (see page 69 for sausages ideas).

• Makes 6 servings

2 tablespoons pork lard (preferably) or unsalted butter

2 tablespoons extra-virgin olive oil

1 large onion, finely chopped

2 tablespoons chopped pancetta

2 pounds sweet Italian sausages, cut into 1-inch pieces

1 cup dry red wine (such as Chianti)

2 pounds canned whole tomatoes, with their liquid, chopped

5 large garlic cloves, finely chopped

Bouquet garni, consisting of 10 sprigs of fresh parsley
    and 10 sprigs of fresh thyme (or 1 teaspoon dried thyme),
    tied in cheesecloth

Freshly ground black pepper

1 pound rigatoni

1 pound fresh mozzarella, diced or shredded

2 cups Béchamel sauce (page 211)

Béchamel Sauce

3 tablespoons unsalted butter

3 tablespoons all-purpose flour

2 cups hot or warm whole milk

Salt and freshly ground white pepper

Pinch of nutmeg

In a medium saucepan, melt the butter over medium-high heat. Add the flour and stir to form a roux. Continue to cook over medium heat, stirring, for 1 minute. Remove the saucepan from the heat and slowly whisk in the milk until it is all blended. Season with salt, white pepper, and nutmeg. Return the saucepan to the heat, reduce to medium-low, and cook, stirring almost constantly, until thick, about 12 minutes.

• Makes about 2 cups

1. In a large flame- and oven-proof enameled cast-iron casserole, melt the lard with the olive oil over medium heat, then add the onion and pancetta, and cook, stirring occasionally, until golden, about 10 minutes. Add the sausages and cook, tossing, until browned, about 8 minutes.

2. Pour in the wine to deglaze the casserole, scraping up the bits on the bottom of the casserole, then add the tomatoes and their liquid. Add the garlic and bouquet garni, and season with black pepper. Reduce the heat to very low and simmer uncovered, stirring occasionally, until dense and unctuous, about 4 hours.

3. Preheat the oven to 400°F.

4. Bring a large pot of abundantly salted water to a vigorous boil, and add the rigatoni. Cook until al dente and then drain. Transfer the rigatoni to the casserole and toss with the sausage-tomato sauce. Sprinkle the mozzarella over the top, then spread the Béchamel sauce evenly over that. Bake until the top is dappled with brown spots, about 30 minutes. Remove from the oven, let rest 5 to 10 minutes, and serve.

Baked Rigatoni with Meatballs

T his is a rich wintery Italian-American preparation that is, frankly, an improvement on my mom's recipe. She wouldn't have gotten as involved, nor would she have used balsamic vinegar, but this is a great recipe. Although there is admittedly a bit of work in preparing this dish, I think it is worth it for two reasons. First, it really tastes great with crusty Italian bread, and is enjoyable to assemble on a blustery cold winter Sunday. Second, if you have leftovers, they make great meatball heros for lunch. • **Makes 6 servings**

For the ragù

5 tablespoons extra-virgin olive oil

¾ pound lean ground beef

½ pound sweet Italian sausages, casings removed and meat crumbled

¼ pound pork tenderloin, chopped with a knife

1 small onion, finely chopped

2 large garlic cloves, finely chopped

1 cup dry red wine (such as Chianti) plus more as needed

2 pounds canned whole tomatoes, with their liquid, chopped

One 6-ounce can tomato paste

½ cup water

3 tablespoons balsamic vinegar

1 tablespoon dried oregano

1 tablespoon sugar

1 teaspoon dried rosemary

Salt and freshly ground black pepper

For the meatballs

½ pound white part of French baguette or Italian country loaf

1 cup heavy cream

1 pound very lean ground beef

¼ cup finely chopped onion

2 tablespoons finely chopped fresh parsley

1 large egg, beaten to blend

It's not a bad idea to make more meatballs than needed, as long as you're making them anyway. To make use of the leftover raw meatballs (or cooked ones), arrange them in a casserole that's lightly smeared with olive oil. Pour some tomato sauce, if you have any, over the meatballs. If you don't have any tomato sauce, cut three large tomatoes in half, squeeze the seeds out, and grate the tomato flesh against the largest holes of a box grater down to the peel and over the meatballs. Cut half a pound of mozzarella cheese into small cubes and push them down into the sauce (or grated tomatoes). Cover the top with slices of provolone cheese and sprinkle with Parmesan cheese, then bake for 45 minutes at 350°F.

Salt and freshly ground black pepper

2 tablespoons unsalted butter

2 tablespoons extra-virgin olive oil

For the zucchini

1 tablespoon extra-virgin olive oil

1 medium zucchini, peeled and quartered lengthwise,
     each quarter cut into 10 pieces

Assembling and garnishing the rigatoni

1 pound rigatoni

Extra-virgin olive oil for drizzling

1 tablespoon finely chopped fresh parsley

¼ cup (less than 1 ounce) freshly grated Parmesan cheese

¼ cup (less than 1 ounce) freshly grated pecorino cheese

1. To make the ragout, in a skillet, heat 1 tablespoon of olive oil over medium heat, then add the chopped beef, crumbled sausage, and chopped pork. Cook, stirring and breaking up the meat with a wooden spoon, until the pork loses its color, about 10 minutes. Drain well using a slotted spoon and set aside. Discard the fat.

2. In a large flame- and oven-proof enameled cast-iron casserole, heat the remaining 4 tablespoons of olive oil over medium heat, then add the onion

and garlic and cook, stirring, until translucent, about 6 minutes. Add the cooked meat to the onion mixture and cook for 2 minutes. Pour in 1 cup of red wine and cook, stirring occasionally, until it is reduced by a third, about 10 minutes. Add the tomatoes, tomato paste, water, balsamic vinegar, oregano, sugar, and rosemary. Season with salt and pepper. Reduce the heat to low and cook, stirring occasionally, until dense, about 3 hours. Add small amounts of water or wine if the ragout gets too thick.

3 Meanwhile, make the meatballs. In a small bowl, soak the bread in the cream until all the bread is moistened but not dripping wet, about 1 minute. In a larger bowl, knead together with your hands the soaked bread, ground beef, onion, parsley, and egg, and season with salt and pepper. Form into 14 to 16 balls with wet hands (so the meat doesn't stick). In a large skillet, melt the butter and olive oil over low heat. Add the meatballs and cook until browned, shaking the pan occasionally, about 30 minutes. When finished, let the meatballs sit in the skillet until needed.

4 Preheat the oven to 400°F.

5 To prepare the zucchini, in a small skillet, heat 1 tablespoon of olive oil over medium-high heat, then add the zucchini and cook, stirring, until dappled with brown spots, about 5 minutes. Set aside.

6 Bring a large pot of abundantly salted water to a vigorous boil. Add the rigatoni and boil until the rigatoni is al dente and then drain. Transfer the rigatoni to the casserole and stir in the ragout, mixing well and moistening with some additional red wine. Spread the cooked zucchini and meatballs on top.

7 Drizzle some olive oil on top of the meatballs. Bake until lightly browned on top, 15 to 20 minutes. Remove and serve with a sprinkle of parsley, grated Parmesan and pecorino cheese.

Baked Macaroni

One will often hear southern Italians say that the word *macaroni* comes from the Greek word meaning "divine food." In fact, scholars have no idea where the word *macaroni* came from, except we do know that in the tenth century it may have meant "idiot" in the slang of Naples. Whatever its roots, I think that macaroni is indeed a food of the gods, and you'll never feel like an idiot for making it. This casserole is a simple *maccheroni al forno*, "baked macaroni" in Italian, which is the name for hundreds of similar casseroles. It's a rich casserole, so you need to accompany it only with a green salad. The young pecorino cheese called for in the ingredient list is sometimes known as fresh, soft, eating, or table pecorino and is usually less than six months old. It can be found in Italian markets, cheese stores, gourmet shops, and some better supermarkets. The pecorino cheese you are probably familiar with (sometimes called pecorino Romano) is older than a year and is used for grating. • **Makes 8 servings**

¾ pound very lean ground beef
1 cup fresh bread crumbs (see Note 1)
¼ cup finely chopped fresh parsley
2 large garlic cloves, finely chopped
5 large eggs (1 raw; 4 hard-boiled, shelled and sliced)
Salt and freshly ground black pepper
2 tablespoons extra-virgin olive oil plus more as needed
2 tablespoons pork lard or unsalted butter
½ pound mixed *salume* (see Note 2), diced small
1 medium onion, chopped
1 fresh red finger-type chile, finely chopped
3 pounds canned whole tomatoes, with their juice, chopped, or
    fresh ripe tomatoes, cut in half, seeds squeezed out, and flesh grated
    against the largest holes of a box grater down to the peel

1 pound 2-inch-long tubular pasta (such as penne, ziti,
　　mostaccioli, or rigatoni),
6 ounces young pecorino cheese, shredded
¼ pound caciocavallo cheese or sharp aged provolone cheese,
　　diced small or broken into pieces

1 Preheat the oven to 350°F.

2 Place the beef in a food processor and blend for 15 seconds. Add the bread crumbs, 1 tablespoon of parsley, half the chopped garlic, and the raw egg. Season with salt and pepper. Blend until pasty, about 1 minute. Form into hazelnut-size meatballs. Place the meatballs in a 13 × 9 × 2-inch casserole. Bake until browned, about 15 minutes. Transfer to a bowl and set aside until needed. Clean the casserole for the next step unless you have two casseroles.

3 Increase the heat of the oven to 400°F. Lightly oil a 13 × 9 × 2-inch baking casserole.

4 In a large skillet, heat the olive oil with the lard over medium heat until the lard melts, about 3 minutes. Add the *salume*, onion, chile, and the remaining parsley and garlic. Cook, stirring, until the onion is translucent, about 8 minutes. Add the tomatoes and cook, stirring, until the mixture is a little denser, about 10 minutes. Set aside until needed.

5 Meanwhile, bring a large pot of abundantly salted water to a vigorous boil. Add the pasta and boil until half-cooked (follow the package instructions), stirring occasionally to keep them separate. Drain. (If you cook the macaroni earlier in the day, keep it in a pot of cold water until needed, and drain before using.)

6 Arrange half of the macaroni in the lightly oiled casserole. Spoon half of the tomato sauce over the macaroni and then top it with half of the pecorino cheese, all the pieces of caciocavallo cheese, the sliced hard-boiled eggs, and then the meatballs. Cover with the remaining macaroni.

Pour the remaining tomato sauce over the macaroni and sprinkle with the remaining pecorino cheese, mixing them slightly. Cover with aluminum foil. Bake until the cheeses are melted and the mixture is very hot, about 1 hour. Remove from the oven, let rest for 15 minutes, and serve.

Note 1: This amount can be made from crumbling two ½-inch-thick slices of 5¼ × 3-inch French or Italian bread in a food processor.

Note 2: In Italian *salume*, the plural of *salami*, means "cold cuts," but of the Italian variety, of course. So choose three of the following *salume*, preferably from an Italian deli: *pancetta, guanciale,* prosciutto fat, *capocollo, coppa, soppressata*, Genoa salami, Naples salami, Milano salami, or other salami.

What's a Finger-type Chile?

Although there are only five species of cultivated chiles and one of those species makes up about 95 percent of the chiles you'll see in an American market, there are hundreds of different cultivars and they all have different names depending on where you live. This creates a great headache for me when I try to specify a chile to use, so I just specify the shape, namely, a finger-type chile, which is a long narrow red or green chile. Chiles also have different amounts of capsaicin, the active ingredient that resides in their placenta (the white inner rib of the chile) that accounts for how piquant they are. So, for example, bell peppers and cubanelle have no piquancy at all, while poblano, Anaheim, New Mexico, and pasilla chiles are hot; jalapeño and serrano chiles are very hot; Thai, bird's eye, finger-type, cayenne, Tabasco, and de arbol are extremely hot; and, finally, habanero, Scotch bonnet, and African bird chiles are ridiculously hot. Certain chiles have the same name wherever you live, such as jalapeño chiles, and for those chiles I'll specifically call for them throughout the book.

Baked Macaroni with Broccoli

This is a preparation that is well suited to a small dinner party, and when you want good food that can be prepared ahead of time and isn't too much trouble. Virtually, the entire dish can be prepared in advance and then simply put into the oven until you want to serve it. • **Makes 8 servings**

4 tablespoons (¼ stick) unsalted butter plus
    2 tablespoons melted butter
1½ pounds broccoli, stems removed then peeled and
    cut into 1-inch lengths, florets broken up
1 pound 2-inch-long tubular pasta (such as penne,
    ziti, mostaccioli, or rigatoni)
6 tablespoons finely chopped shallots
3 tablespoons all-purpose flour
2 cups whole milk, warmed
½ cup heavy cream, warmed
Salt and freshly ground black pepper
3 cups freshly grated fontina cheese or mild white cheddar cheese
3 tablespoons dry bread crumbs

1. Preheat the oven to 375°F. Coat a 13 × 9 × 2-inch baking casserole with 1 tablespoon of butter.

2. Bring a large pot of abundantly salted water to a vigorous boil, then add the broccoli stems and cook for 4 minutes. Add the macaroni and cook for 3 minutes, then add the broccoli florets and cook until the macaroni is al dente or even a little harder, about another 5 minutes. Drain well, and rinse under cold running water if you think the broccoli and macaroni do not need any more cooking, otherwise set them aside in a colander to drain.

Leftover Idea

Have you ever had plastic storage bags filled with leftover spaghetti? Well, depending on how much you've got, you can make a nice individual casserole or a large one for the family. Toss the spaghetti with some chopped garlic (half a garlic clove per person), leftover cooked broccoli (whatever you have) and drizzle with olive oil (1½ teaspoons per person). Arrange in a casserole and cover with whatever leftover steak or ground meat you have and heavy cream or beef broth (2 tablespoons per person). Cover with 1 cup of grated Swiss cheese and bake in a 350°F oven until the cheese is dappled golden on top, about 35 minutes.

③ In a saucepan, melt the remaining 3 tablespoons of butter over medium-high heat, then add the shallots and cook, stirring, until softened, about 3 minutes. Add the flour and cook, stirring, to form a roux, for about 2 minutes. Remove the saucepan from the heat and whisk in the milk and cream. Season with salt and pepper. Return the saucepan to the heat and bring the sauce to a boil, stirring. Reduce the heat to medium and continue to cook for 3 minutes. Add 2 cups of cheese and once it has melted, continue to cook, stirring, for another 2 minutes.

④ Mix the cheese sauce in a large bowl with the cooked macaroni and broccoli. Transfer to the casserole. Smooth the surface so it is even, sprinkle the remaining cheese on top, then sprinkle the bread crumbs over and drizzle the 2 tablespoons of melted butter on top. Bake until the top is crispy and slightly golden, about 25 minutes. Serve hot.

Baked Macaroni, Eggplant, and Broccoli

This is a satisfying dish with assertive flavors inspired by the baked lasagne dishes of the Campania region of southern Italy. A small amount of steak is used just to give flavor rather than dominate the dish, which is really about the eggplant and broccoli. Although there is some work involved in preparing this casserole it can be made ahead of time and re-heated. • **Makes 4 servings**

¼ cup extra-virgin olive oil

Salt

1 pound broccoli, stems cut off, peeled, and cut
    into ½-inch pieces, florets left whole

1 pound eggplant, sliced into ⅜-inch-thick rounds

6 cups inexpensive olive oil for deep-frying

6 to 8 ounces skirt, flank, sirloin tip, or rib eye steak,
    sliced in 1 × ¼-inch pieces

½ pound 2-inch-long tubular pasta (such as penne,
    ziti, mostaccioli, or rigatoni)

3 large garlic cloves, finely chopped

1½ teaspoons red chile flakes

Freshly ground black pepper

⅓ cup (about 1 ounce) dry or fresh bread crumbs (see Note)

⅓ cup (about 1 ounce) freshly grated Parmesan cheese

⅓ cup (about 1 ounce) freshly grated pecorino cheese

1. Preheat the oven to 425°F. Coat a 12 × 9 × 2-inch baking casserole with 2 teaspoons of extra-virgin olive oil.

2. Bring a large saucepan of water to a vigorous boil, salt lightly, and cook the broccoli stems for 4 minutes. Add the florets and cook until they are bright green and tender, about 6 minutes and not more. Drain and plunge into ice water or pass under cold running water to stop it from cooking. Set aside.

I find that when I teach cooking classes even experienced cooks get nervous about deep-frying. Now that kitchen appliance manufacturers have come out with a variety of great and safe home-use regulated deep-fryers, cooks should take advantage of them and not be intimidated. However, if you are nervous about deep frying, in all recipes that call for deep-fried eggplant, you can alternatively brush the eggplant with olive oil and either griddle it or bake it in a hot oven until it reaches the doneness as indicated by the recipe.

3 Lay the eggplant pieces on some paper towels and sprinkle with salt. Leave them to drain of their bitter juices for 30 minutes, then pat dry with clean paper towels.

4 Preheat the 6 cups of inexpensive olive oil to 375°F in a deep-fryer or an 8-inch saucepan fitted with a wire fry basket insert. Deep-fry the eggplant slices until golden brown, 3 to 4 minutes on each side. Drain on a platter lined with paper towels. Set aside.

5 In a small cast-iron skillet, heat 1 teaspoon of extra-virgin olive oil over high heat for 10 minutes, then brown the steak on both sides, about 2 minutes total cooking time. Remove the steak from the skillet and set aside.

6 Bring a large pot of salted water to a vigorous boil. Add the pasta and boil until it is half-cooked (follow the package instructions), stirring occasionally to keep them separate. Drain. Toss the pasta in the casserole with the steak, broccoli, eggplant, garlic, red chile flakes, black pepper, and 2 tablespoons of extra-virgin olive oil. Using a spatula or your hands, press down on the pasta so the top is even and flat.

7 In a bowl, mix the bread crumbs, Parmesan cheese, and pecorino cheese together and sprinkle the mixture on top of the macaroni. Drizzle with the remaining 1 tablespoon of extra-virgin olive oil. Bake until the top is golden brown, about 20 minutes.

Baked Macaroni with Fried Eggplant and Mozzarella

In Naples, they often call this kind of oven-baked macaroni casserole a "macaroni pie." Well, there is no pie crust with this macaroni pie, just the illusion of one from a scrumptious golden crust waiting for a big serving spoon to be plunged into it and serve forth the rich melting flavors of fried eggplant, pasta, and mozzarella. The ideal macaroni to use here is a long tubular macaroni with a large opening called *zitoni*, but use whatever macaroni is available. It may sound odd, but I love the leftovers for breakfast.

• Makes 8 servings

3 eggplants (about 3 pounds total),
    cut into ¼-inch-thick slices
Salt
6 cups inexpensive olive oil for frying
8 tablespoons (1 stick) unsalted butter
2 tablespoons extra-virgin olive oil
1 small onion, finely chopped
1 large garlic clove, finely chopped
2 cups tomato puree
4 fresh basil leaves
Freshly ground black pepper
1 pound 2-inch-long tubular pasta (preferably *zitoni*)
½ cup (about 1½ ounces) freshly grated Parmesan cheese
¾ pound fresh mozzarella cheese, thinly sliced

1. Preheat the oven to 350°F. Lightly butter a 12 × 9 × 3-inch deep baking casserole or lasagne pan.

2. Lay the eggplant slices on some paper towels and sprinkle with salt. Leave them to drain of their bitter juices for 30 minutes. Pat dry with clean paper towels.

3. Preheat the 6 cups of inexpensive olive oil to 375°F in a deep-fryer or an 8-inch saucepan fitted with a wire fry basket insert. Add some of the eggplant slices to the hot oil and cook until golden on both sides, turning once, about 4 minutes a side. Remove from the oil and transfer to a paper towel-lined platter to drain while you cook the remaining eggplant slices.

4. Prepare the tomato sauce in a large saucepan or stove-top casserole by melting 5 tablespoons of butter with 2 tablespoons of extra-virgin olive oil over medium-high heat, then add the onion and garlic and cook, stirring, until softened, about 4 minutes. Add the tomato purée and basil, and season with salt and pepper. Cook, stirring and reducing the heat if the sauce sputters too much, about 5 minutes.

5. Meanwhile, bring a large pot of abundantly salted water to a vigorous boil. Add the pasta and boil until al dente. Drain the pasta without rinsing. Transfer the pasta to the tomato sauce with 3 tablespoons of the Parmesan cheese.

6. Arrange half of the macaroni mixture on the bottom of the casserole, then arrange half of the eggplant on top of the macaroni. Now layer half of the mozzarella cheese over. Layer the remaining macaroni, eggplant, and mozzarella, in that order, then sprinkle the remaining 5 tablespoons of Parmesan cheese over the mozzarella. Dot the top with the remaining 3 tablespoons of butter. Spoon any remaining tomato sauce over the mozzarella. Bake uncovered until golden brown, 50 to 55 minutes.

Baked Macaroni with Ground Lamb

When my children were little, a family dinner would often include friends and their kids, meaning all of a sudden I might be feeding eight or more people. This is a very attractive casserole that is ideal for serving two families—I often make it when I have to feed that many and when it's not a formal dinner. The golden crust that develops at the end of the baking time is appetizing, the flavors are aromatic, and kids like it too.

• Makes 6 to 8 servings

1½ pounds ground lamb
Salt and freshly ground black pepper
3 tablespoons extra-virgin olive oil
1 small onion, finely chopped
4 large garlic cloves, finely chopped
One 28-ounce can crushed tomatoes
1 cup dry red wine
1 tablespoon dried rosemary
1 pound 2-inch-long tubular pasta (such as
       penne, ziti, mostaccioli, or rigatoni)
4 ounces (½ cup) ricotta cheese
¾ pound fresh mozzarella cheese, sliced

1. Preheat the oven to 400°F. Lightly oil a 12 × 9 × 2-inch baking casserole.

2. Put the ground lamb in a skillet and turn the heat to medium-high, then cook the lamb until it browns, breaking it up with a wooden spoon as you cook, about 8 minutes. Remove the lamb with a slotted spoon, pressing out all the fat and liquid. Discard any fat and liquid remaining in the skillet. Season the lamb with salt and pepper and set aside.

3. In a flame-proof casserole, heat the olive oil over high heat, then add the onion and garlic and cook, stirring constantly so the garlic doesn't burn, until the onion turns translucent, about 4 minutes. Add the tomatoes, wine, and cooked lamb, then reduce the heat to medium and cook, stirring occasionally, until denser, about 30 minutes. Stir in the rosemary. Season the tomato sauce to taste with salt and pepper.

4. Bring a large pot of salted water to a vigorous boil. Add the pasta and boil until it is very al dente. Drain. Transfer the pasta to the flame-proof casserole and toss with the tomato sauce. Stir in the ricotta cheese.

5. Pour the pasta mixture into the lightly oiled casserole. Cover the top of the casserole with the mozzarella cheese. Bake until the top is completely golden, about 25 minutes. Remove and serve hot.

Baked Bucatini with Porcini Mushrooms

The pasta used in this casserole is bucatini, the thick spaghetti-like pasta with a hole in the middle that also goes by the name *perciatelli*. Dried porcini mushrooms carry a lot of flavor once they are rehydrated, and therefore, you don't need to use a lot. The entire dish can be prepared ahead of time and plopped in the oven fifteen minutes before serving.

• Makes 6 servings

7 tablespoons extra-virgin olive oil

1½ ounces (about 2 loosely packed cups)
    dried porcini mushrooms

6 tablespoons finely chopped fresh parsley

Salt and freshly ground black pepper

6 salted anchovy fillets, rinsed and pounded in a
    mortar or finely chopped

2 large garlic cloves, thinly sliced

¼ cup dry bread crumbs

1 pound bucatini (*perciatelli*)

1 Preheat the oven to 350°F. Coat a 12 × 9 × 2-inch baking casserole with 1 tablespoon of olive oil.

2 Soak the mushrooms in a bowl with enough tepid water to cover until soft, about 15 minutes. Remove the mushrooms and slice them, saving the soaking water.

3 In a large skillet, heat 3 tablespoons of olive oil over medium-heat, then add the mushrooms and cook for about 1 minute. Add 3 tablespoons of the reserved mushroom soaking water and 5 tablespoons of the parsley. Season with salt and pepper, and stir. Reduce the heat to low, add the anchovies, and stir. Add the remaining 3 tablespoons of olive oil, the garlic, and another 3 tablespoons of the mushroom soaking water to the mushroom mixture. Cook the mushroom sauce, stirring, for 2 minutes.

4 Sprinkle half of the bread crumbs over the casserole, shaking the casserole so the crumbs coat the bottom completely.

5 Meanwhile, bring a large pot of abundantly salted water to a vigorous boil. Add the bucatini and boil until al dente. Drain the bucatini, transfer it to the skillet with the mushroom sauce, and toss well. Transfer the seasoned bucatini to the casserole. Sprinkle the top with the remaining bread crumbs, a grinding of pepper, and the remaining parsley. Bake until crispy and golden, 15 to 20 minutes. Serve hot.

The Glutton's Cannelloni

There is a difference between a gourmet (*buongustaio* in Italian) and a gourmand (*ghiottone*). A gourmet is a connoisseur of food and the gourmand is someone excessively fond of eating—in other words, a glutton. So what are we to make of the name of this sumptuous dish called *cannelloni del ghiottone* in Italian? I suspect that it means that it's worthy of a gourmet but you'll end up a glutton because you'll probably eat more than your fair share. The cannelloni you will want to buy have one-inch-diameter openings. Some cannelloni shells are "no-boil," so read the package to make sure you are buying the right cannelloni. • **Makes 6 to 8 servings**

½ cup extra-virgin olive oil

1 medium onion, chopped

½ pound sweet Italian sausages, casings removed,
    meat crumbled

½ pound pork loin or leg, cut into small pieces

½ pound veal loin or leg, cut into small pieces

1 sprig fresh rosemary

Salt

½ cup dry white wine

½ pound veal sweetbreads, poached in very gently
    bubbling water for 20 minutes until firm and white,
    drained, cut into small pieces

½ cup chicken or veal broth

2 large eggs

1½ cups (about 5 ounces) freshly grated Parmesan cheese

Pinch of nutmeg

¾ pound cannelloni or manicotti shells

4 cups Béchamel sauce (page 211)

1. Preheat the oven to 350°F.

2. In a skillet, heat the olive oil over medium-high heat, then cook the onion, stirring, until translucent, about 5 minutes. Remove the onion with a slotted spoon and set aside. Add the sausage, pork, veal, and rosemary to the skillet and cook, stirring, until the meat browns, about 5 minutes. Season with salt and stir in the wine. Cook until the wine is almost evaporated, about 15 minutes. Add the sweetbreads and cook for a couple of minutes, then add the broth and continue to cook until it evaporates too, about 12 minutes. Remove and discard the rosemary sprig.

3. Remove the meats from the skillet and pass through a meat grinder or pulse in a food processor along with the reserved onion until it looks very finely chopped or almost smooth. Transfer to a bowl and add the eggs, 1 cup of the Parmesan cheese, and the nutmeg, stirring well to mix.

4. Meanwhile, bring a large pot of abundantly salted water to a vigorous boil, then drop the cannelloni into the boiling water and cook for about 1 minute less than half-cooked (follow the package instructions). If you are using no-boil cannelloni, cook them for 2 minutes in boiling water, stirring occasionally to keep them separate, and then remove

Cannelloni and Manicotti

Although cannelloni and manicotti are the same thing, some manicotti manufacturers make theirs with slightly larger openings than cannelloni. Both are sold in supermarkets. Cannelloni derives from the Italian word for cinnamon stick, which they resemble, while manicotti is purely an Italian-American word derived from the Italian word for muff (hand-warmer).

them immediately from the boiling water. Transfer the cannelloni to a bowl of cold water while you continue with the preparation.

5 Stuff the cannelloni with the meat filling, using your fingers or a small spoon, until they are three-quarters full.

6 Spread the bottom of a 13 × 9 × 2-inch baking casserole with a ½-inch-thick layer of Béchamel sauce. Arrange the stuffed cannelloni on the layer of sauce and cover with half of the remaining Béchamel sauce. Add another layer of stuffed cannelloni, spread the remaining Béchamel sauce over, and sprinkle with the remaining Parmesan cheese. Bake, covered, until the cannelloni shells are cooked through, about 30 minutes. Uncover and bake until dappled light golden on top, about 15 minutes. Serve hot.

Some Béchamel Sauce History

Béchamel sauce is nothing but white sauce. White sauce begins with the forming of a roux—the mixing of melted butter and flour over heat—and then it is thinned with scalded milk and simmered until a dense sauce is formed. It is the foundation for many compound sauces in classical French cooking. In fact, those cans of Campbell's cream of mushroom or cream of celery soups that are ubiquitous in 1950s American casseroles were used as a substitute for French compound sauces. A white sauce is so easy to make that in this book I've banished the preservative-laced can of condensed creamed soups.

The traditional and modern history of Béchamel sauce attributes its invention to François Pierre de La Varenne (1615–1678), chef to Louis XIV, who named it after the king's honorary steward, the Marquis Louis de Béchameil.

Another theory, promoted by the late Waverly Root, reports that the town of Cesena in Emilia-Romagna claims the sauce as its own, as there are documents from the fourteenth century that mention *balsamella* sauce at a celebration for Cardinal Albornoz.

I believe the real history of this sauce is much older. The earliest source mentioning what came to be known as Béchamel sauce, or white sauce, can be traced to the ancient Greeks. For we have the Alexandrian writer of scurrilous verse, Sopater of Paphos (circa 300 B.C.), describing a "white sauce"—a sauce we don't know much about except that it "covers a stew of sow's miscarried matrix." (Man, they ate differently then!)

Whatever the true history of the sauce, the first written French recipe was in La Varenne's cookbook and the first written Italian recipe with this name appears in Francesco Leonardi's *L'apicio moderno* published in 1790, where it seems to be a sauce used in different forms for stuffing purposes. The use of Béchamel in Neapolitan cooking was introduced in the late eighteenth century by the French-influenced chefs of aristocratic and bourgeois families, and is more prominent in Neapolitan cooking than one might think.

Cannelloni with Spinach and Ricotta

Cannelloni are fun to make partly because you can really stuff them with whatever you like. I recommend getting inventive and experimenting. In fact, this dish came about as a way of using up some leftovers and little chunks of cheese. • **Makes 6 to 8 servings**

1¼ pounds spinach leaves without stems, rinsed well

12 ounces ricotta cheese

2 large egg yolks

⅛ teaspoon ground nutmeg

Salt and freshly ground black pepper

6 tablespoons unsalted butter plus more as needed

¼ cup all-purpose flour

4 cups hot whole milk

½ cup (about 1½ ounces) freshly grated Parmesan cheese

½ cup (about 1½ ounces) freshly shredded Swiss cheese

½ pound cannelloni or manicotti shells (about 14)

1. Preheat the oven to 350°F. Lightly butter a 13 × 9 × 2-inch baking casserole.

2. Place the spinach in a large pot with only the water adhering to it from its last rinsing. Cover and cook over high heat, stirring occasionally, until the spinach wilts, 4 to 5 minutes. Transfer the spinach to a strainer to drain, squeezing out the excess water with the back of a wooden spoon. Chop the spinach finely.

3. Pass the ricotta cheese through a sieve, strainer, or food mill and into a large bowl. Stir in the chopped spinach, 1 egg yolk, and half of the nutmeg. Season with salt and pepper.

4. Prepare a Béchamel (white) sauce by melting 4 tablespoons of butter in a medium saucepan over medium-high heat, then sprinkle in the flour, stirring to form a roux. Cook for 1 minute, then remove the saucepan from the heat. Slowly whisk in the hot milk. Stir in the remaining nutmeg and season with salt and pepper. Return the saucepan to low heat and continue to cook, stirring, until denser, about 12 minutes. Add half of the Parmesan cheese, all of the Swiss cheese, and 1 tablespoon of butter. Simmer, stirring frequently, until the sauce is thicker, about 8 minutes. Remove from the heat and quickly beat in the remaining egg yolk.

5. Meanwhile, bring a large pot of abundantly salted water to a vigorous boil. Add the cannelloni shells and boil until half-cooked, 6 to 7 minutes. (If using no-boil shells, cook them about 2 minutes.) Transfer the cannelloni to a bowl of cold water so they don't stick to each other. Drain well.

6. Using a small spoon, stuff the cannelloni with the ricotta mixture. Arrange the cannelloni in the casserole. Cover the cannelloni with the Béchamel sauce. Sprinkle the top with the remaining Parmesan cheese, and dot with the remaining butter. Bake until bubbly and slightly golden, about 45 minutes. Remove from the oven and let rest 10 minutes before serving.

Stuffed Shells # 1

This stuffed pasta casserole from the Italian province of the Marche is traditionally made with the large stuffable macaroni known as *tuffoli*, also known as *pipe* in other areas of Italy, and looks like the top part of a tuba. They can sometimes be found in Italian markets, but if you are relying on your supermarket, then you'll need to get jumbo shells. You could boil the entire one-pound box of jumbo shells and freeze half of it to use later.

• Makes 6 servings

8 tablespoons (1 stick) unsalted butter,
  7 tablespoons melted
½ small onion, chopped
2 ounces twice-ground veal
1 cup dry white wine
Salt and freshly ground black pepper
6 ounces boneless turkey breast, diced
½ pound cooked ham, diced
6 ounces chicken livers, sinews removed,
  livers cut up into smaller pieces
2 tablespoons heavy cream
½ pound *tuffoli* or jumbo pasta shells
¼ pound Gruyère cheese, shredded

1. Preheat the oven to 350°F. Butter a 12 × 9 × 2-inch baking casserole.

2. In a large skillet, melt 1 tablespoon of butter over medium-high heat, then add the onion and cook, stirring, until softened, about 3 minutes. Add the veal and cook, stirring and breaking up the meat with a wooden spoon, until it has turned color, 1 to 2 minutes. Add the wine and cook until it has reduced by half. Season the veal sauce with salt and pepper, stir, and cook a minute more. Set the veal sauce aside.

3. Make the stuffing. In a food processor, blend the turkey, ham, and chicken livers until a paste forms. Pass this mixture through a food mill so it is very smooth. Alternatively, push it through a colander. Transfer the turkey mixture to a bowl and stir in the cream. Season with salt and pepper.

4. Meanwhile, bring a large pot of abundantly salted water to a vigorous boil. Add the *tuffoli* and boil until half-cooked (follow the package instructions). Drain the *tuffoli* and transfer to a bowl of cold water so they don't stick together. Drain well. Stuff the *tuffoli* with the turkey mixture and arrange them in the casserole.

5. Cover the stuffed *tuffoli* with the veal sauce and the Gruyère cheese. Pour the 7 tablespoons of melted butter over everything. Cover and bake until the cheese has melted into the shells and the butter is bubbling vigorously, about 50 minutes. Let rest for 5 minutes, then serve.

Stuffed Shells # 2

This Italian-American dish is an easy way to use up the remaining shells that you haven't used from the preceding recipe. In this preparation you don't completely stuff the shells; rather, you accidentally let them stuff themselves. What I mean is, as you toss all the ingredients the meat will find its way into the shells without your having to purposely stuff them. I know that sounds confusing, but you'll see what I mean when you do it. This is quite a scrumptious casserole and there is a danger that you may eat far more than your portion. Skip Step 2, obviously, if you already have leftover parboiled shells from the previous recipe. • **Makes 4 servings**

½ pound jumbo pasta shells

1¼ pounds ground beef

1 small onion, chopped

1 zucchini, diced small

Salt and freshly ground black pepper

One 6-ounce can tomato paste

¾ cup water

10 ounces sweet Italian sausages (about 3 links),
    casings removed, meat crumbled coarsely

¼ cup extra-virgin olive oil

½ cup (about 1½ ounces) freshly grated Parmesan cheese

1½ cups (about 5 ounces) shredded Swiss cheese

1. Preheat the oven to 350°F. Lightly oil a 10-inch round baking casserole (preferably earthenware).

2. Meanwhile, bring a large pot of abundantly salted water to a vigorous boil. Add the pasta and boil until half-cooked. Drain the pasta and transfer to a bowl of cold water so they don't stick together. Drain well.

3. In a large bowl, mix the ground beef, onion, and zucchini together. Season with salt and pepper. In a small bowl, dissolve the tomato paste in the water, then add to the beef mixture along with the sausage and pasta shells. Toss gently, using your hands if desired, allowing some of the meat mixture to go into the cavities of the shells. It doesn't matter if some of the shells are broken or if some are not stuffed. Transfer the shells to the casserole.

4. Drizzle the oil over the top of the shells, then sprinkle with ¼ cup of the Parmesan cheese and all of the Swiss cheese. Cover the casserole and bake until the cheese is completely melted and the casserole is bubbling vigorously, about 50 minutes. Remove from the oven, let rest 10 minutes, and serve with the remaining Parmesan at the table.

Lasagna # 1

Does lasagna need any explanation? There are many different lasagne (ending in "a" when singular, "e" when plural) and, in fact, I wrote a book several years ago devoted exclusively to lasagne from all the regions of Italy, called *Lasagne* (Little, Brown & Co., 1995). This recipe is your basic lasagna, nothing fancy, just the rich, deep tastes of a luscious lasagna that you could eat all week. In this recipe, I assume you'll use the packaged no-boil lasagne that come with three aluminum pans. If you decide to use the optional pork skin for added flavor, you can find it in two places at the supermarket. If the market sells pork shoulder they often leave the skin on, so you can use that, but you'll have to buy the whole shoulder and freeze it afterwards. Supermarkets also sell salt pork that usually has an edge with the skin on and you can use that too. • **Makes 6 servings**

1 pound ground beef
½ pound (2 links) sweet Italian sausages,
    casings removed, meat crumbled
Extra-virgin olive oil for drizzling
1 medium onion, chopped
½ green bell pepper, seeded and chopped
3 large garlic cloves, finely chopped
Two 4-inch squares pork skin (optional, see headnote)
One 28-ounce can crushed tomatoes
1 cup water
½ cup dry red wine
1 tablespoon dried oregano
1 bay leaf
½ pound no-boil lasagne
1 pound fresh mozzarella cheese, sliced
8 ounces ricotta cheese
Freshly grated Parmesan cheese for sprinkling

1. Preheat the oven to 400°F. Lightly oil the bottom of three 9 × 9-inch aluminum baking pans.

2. In a skillet, cook the ground beef and sausage over medium-high heat, breaking up the meat with a wooden spoon, until browned, about 8 minutes. Remove the meat with a slotted spoon and squeeze out the excess meat fat with the back of a wooden spoon. Set the meat aside. Discard all but 1 tablespoon of accumulated fat from the skillet.

3. In the skillet with the tablespoon of reserved fat, add the olive oil and heat over medium heat. Add the onion, bell pepper, garlic, and pork skin, if using, and cook, stirring, until the onion and bell pepper are softened, about 10 minutes. Add the cooked meats, tomatoes, water, wine, oregano, and bay leaf, and cook, stirring occasionally, until denser, about 30 minutes. Discard the pork skin. Set the sauce aside.

4. Divide all your ingredients by three, so you don't run out as you assemble the lasagna. In each pan, layer the lasagne, then some sauce, mozzarella, ricotta, more sauce, and finally, the Parmesan cheese. Continue layering in that order until the ingredients are used up. You should have about 4 layers of lasagna sheets in each pan.

5. Cover the baking pans with a piece of tented aluminum foil and bake until the cheese is melted and the sauce on the sides of the pan is bubbling vigorously, about 45 minutes. Serve hot or let cool and freeze for future re-heating.

Lasagna # 2

There are as many lasagne as there are families, and this could easily be called Lasagna # 305. The careful assembly of lasagne, attention to the quality of each ingredient, and their relative proportions is what makes a great lasagna. This Neapolitan-inspired recipe is another one that I make for my family on a regular basis. Not all cooks use wine in their sauces, but if you do, use a full-bodied Chianti. If you are using the so-called instant no-boil lasagne you need not go through Step 2, and can just begin layering the uncooked lasagne in a casserole. You can use one large lasagna pan or the three 9 x 9-inch aluminum pans that come in the "no-boil" lasagne package.

- Makes 6 servings

1 pound lasagne
1 tablespoon extra-virgin olive oil
1 pound sweet Italian sausages, casings removed, meat crumbled
1 cup dry red wine
2 cups Tomato Sauce (page 243)
2 tablespoons dried oregano
1 tablespoon sugar or to taste
2 teaspoons dried rosemary
1 teaspoon dried thyme
½ teaspoon fennel seeds
Salt and freshly ground black pepper
2 large eggs
¾ cup (about 4 ounces) freshly grated Parmesan cheese
16 ounces ricotta cheese
1 pound mozzarella cheese, thinly sliced

1. Preheat the oven to 400°F.

2. Bring a large pot of abundantly salted water to a vigorous boil. Add the lasagne and boil until half-cooked (follow the package instructions).

Peeling Tomatoes Quickly

Many recipes in this book, and probably many of the cookbooks you own, call for peeled tomatoes. Although canned tomatoes are already peeled, and they are perfect for winter cooking, fresh summer tomatoes need to be peeled in many cases because their hard-to-digest peels roll up unappealingly and unattractively in the casserole. Typically, a recipe will instruct you to plunge the tomato into boiling water for a minute to loosen the skin, which then is pinched off. If the recipe calls for coarsely chopped tomatoes, that's what you will have to do. But if it doesn't, there is a quicker and easier way to peel a tomato. Take out your four-sided standing grater, cut the tomato in half, gently squeeze out the seeds with a quick jerk over the sink, and then grate the flesh of the tomato against the largest holes of the grater, keeping your palm flat and using the peel to protect your hand.

Drain and keep them in some cold water until needed to prevent them from sticking together.

3. Meanwhile, in a deep flame-proof casserole or a large saucepan, heat the olive oil over medium-high heat, then cook the sausage until browned, breaking it up further with a wooden spoon, 5 to 6 minutes. Pour in the red wine and let it evaporate for 5 minutes, then pour in the tomato sauce. Add the oregano, sugar, rosemary, thyme, and fennel seeds. Season the sauce with salt and pepper and stir to blend. Reduce the heat to medium-low and cook until the sauce is slightly dense, 20 to 40 minutes. (The range in time depends on how liquidy your tomato sauce is.)

4. Meanwhile, as the sauce cooks, beat the eggs in a large bowl. Add the Parmesan to the eggs and then beat in the ricotta cheese. Season with salt and pepper and set aside.

5. Lightly oil a lasagna pan. Layer the lasagne, ricotta cheese mixture, lasagne, sauce, and mozzarella, in that order, finishing the top layer with a little mozzarella and sauce. Cover the top with a tented piece of aluminum foil and bake until the cheese is melted and the sauce on the sides of the pan is bubbling, about 35 minutes. Serve hot.

Lasagna with Breaded Fried Eggplant and Spinach

This Sicilian lasagna is usually a big hit, because it's so delicious and unfamiliar. Most people think of lasagne as mozzarella and meat sauce layered up, yet this lasagna shows how versatile they can be. If using the so-called instant no-boil lasagne there is no need to boil them first. Some no-boil packages come with three 9 × 9-inch aluminum pans which you can use. • **Makes 8 servings**

1 pound lasagne

16 ounces ricotta cheese

¼ cup water

3 tablespoons freshly grated pecorino cheese

½ teaspoon salt plus more as needed

1 small eggplant (about ¾ pound), stem removed and
    eggplant cut crosswise into ⅜-inch-thick slices

¼ cup extra-virgin olive oil

1 medium onion, finely chopped

2 large garlic cloves, finely chopped

2 pounds ripe tomatoes, cut in half, seeds squeezed out,
    and flesh grated against the largest holes of a box grater
    down to the peel

Bouquet garni, consisting of 6 sprigs each of fresh thyme
    and fresh basil, tied in cheesecloth

1 tablespoon dried oregano

Freshly ground black pepper

10 ounces spinach leaves without stems, rinsed well

6 cups inexpensive olive oil for deep-frying

1 large egg, beaten to blend

Dry bread crumbs for dredging

1 pound fresh mozzarella cheese, thinly sliced

Tomato Sauce

This is a basic tomato sauce that can be used in all recipes calling for sauce rather than tomatoes. In the summer, use fresh tomatoes, but in the winter, use canned tomatoes.

¼ cup extra-virgin olive oil
3 large garlic cloves, finely chopped
2 pounds tomatoes, cut in half, seeds squeezed out, and flesh
   grated against the largest holes of a box grater down to the peel,
   or canned crushed tomatoes
1 sprig fresh basil
Salt and freshly ground black pepper

In a saucepan, heat the olive oil over medium heat with the garlic. Once it starts sizzling, stir in the tomatoes and basil sprig. Once it starts to spurt, reduce the heat to low, then cook until a bit denser, about 20 minutes. Season with salt and pepper, remove and discard the basil sprig, if desired. Use the sauce as required, or cool and refrigerate for up to 1 week, or freeze until needed. • Makes 3 cups

1. Preheat the oven to 350°F.

2. Bring a large pot of abundantly salted water to a vigorous boil. Add the lasagne and boil until half-cooked (follow the package instructions). Drain and keep them in some cold water until needed to prevent them from sticking together.

3. In a bowl, stir the ricotta, water, pecorino cheese, and ½ teaspoon of salt together.

4. Lay the eggplant pieces on some paper towels and sprinkle with salt. Leave them to drain of their bitter juices for 30 minutes, then pat dry with clean paper towels.

5. In a medium skillet or flame-proof casserole, heat 3 tablespoons of extra-virgin olive oil over medium-high heat, then add the onion and garlic and cook, stirring frequently so the garlic doesn't burn, until translucent, about 6 minutes. Add the tomatoes, bouquet garni, and oregano. Season

with salt and pepper. Cover and cook, stirring occasionally, until the sauce is a bit denser, about 12 minutes. Reduce the heat to low and continue to simmer until the sauce is denser still, about 10 minutes more. Set aside.

5. Meanwhile, heat the remaining 1 tablespoon of extra-virgin olive oil in a saucepan and add the spinach with a pinch of salt. Sauté the spinach over medium heat, tossing frequently, until it wilts, about 5 minutes. Set aside.

6. Preheat the inexpensive olive oil to 375°F in a deep-fryer or an 8-inch saucepan fitted with a wire fry basket insert. Dip the eggplant slices in the egg, then dredge in the bread crumbs to coat, shaking off any excess. Deep fry the breaded eggplant slices until golden brown, about 2 minutes per side. Drain on paper towels and set aside.

7. Ladle a few tablespoons of tomato sauce on the bottom of two 9 × 9 × 2½-inch casseroles, then layer the lasagne, ricotta mixture, fried eggplant, tomato sauce, lasagne, spinach, and mozzarella, in that order until all the ingredients have filled both pans, with the top and final layer being spinach and mozzarella. Cover the pans with a piece of tented aluminum foil and bake until the cheese is melted and the sauce is bubbling on the sides of the pan, about 45 minutes. Serve hot.

Lasagna with Eggplant, Spinach, and Lamb Sauce

This preparation, inspired by the cooking of the Abruzzo region of Italy, looks wonderful cooked in a large earthenware dish with the contrasting colors of the white ricotta and mascarpone cheeses and the green spinach. This is a preparation that is very flavorful, a favorite with kids, and one of which you are unlikely to have leftovers. You can use canned crushed tomatoes instead of fresh in this preparation too, if it happens to be winter. If using no-boil lasagna sheets you can skip Step 6. If you don't want to deep-fry the eggplant slices, brush them on both sides with some olive oil and bake at 425°F until golden brown, about 35 minutes. • **Makes 6 servings**

1 large eggplant (about 1¼ pounds), peeled and cut
   crosswise into ⅜-inch-thick slices
Salt
6 cups inexpensive olive oil for deep-frying
2 pounds spinach leaves without stems, rinsed well
3 tablespoons extra-virgin olive oil plus more for drizzling
1 small onion, finely chopped
2 large garlic cloves, finely chopped
1 pound ground lamb
1½ pounds ripe fresh tomatoes, cut in half, seeds squeezed out,
   and flesh grated against the largest holes of a box grater
   down to the peel
1 cup (about 2 dozen) pitted imported black olives
½ cup dry red wine
Freshly ground black pepper
3 tablespoons finely chopped fresh basil
1¼ pounds lasagne
8 ounces mascarpone cheese
16 ounces ricotta cheese
Freshly grated pecorino cheese for serving

1. Lay the eggplant on some paper towels and sprinkle with salt. Leave them to release their bitter juices for 30 minutes, then pat dry with clean paper towels.

2. Preheat the inexpensive olive oil to 375°F in a deep-fryer or an 8-inch saucepan fitted with a wire fry basket insert. Fry the eggplant slices in batches until golden brown, about 4 minutes a side. Drain and transfer to a paper towel-lined platter to drain further.

3. In a large saucepan or stockpot, place the spinach with only the water adhering to it from its last rinsing. Cover and cook over high heat, turning once or twice, until it wilts, about 4 minutes. Transfer to a strainer and drain well by pressing out the excess water gently with the back of a wooden spoon.

4. In a large casserole, heat 3 tablespoons of extra-virgin olive oil over medium heat, then add the onion and garlic and cook, stirring so the garlic doesn't burn, until translucent, 5 to 6 minutes. Add the lamb and cook, stirring to break up the meat, until browned, 3 to 4 minutes. Add the tomatoes, fried eggplant, olives, and red wine. Season with salt and pepper. Cook, gently stirring occasionally, until the sauce is thick and unctuous, about 1 hour. Add the basil and cook another 5 minutes. Set the sauce aside.

5. Meanwhile, preheat the oven to 350°F.

6. Bring a large pot of abundantly salted water to a vigorous boil. Add the lasagne and boil until almost al dente. Drain most of the cooking water, keeping the lasagne in some warm water so they don't become sticky. Drain well.

7. Layer the bottom of a large earthenware casserole or a 12 x 9 x 2-inch baking casserole with a few tablespoons of sauce. Cover with a layer of

lasagne, then the spinach, a few randomly placed dollops of both mascarpone and ricotta, the sauce, and then another layer of lasagne. Continue in this order, finishing with a top layer of spinach, dollops of cheese, and sauce. Drizzle the top very lightly with olive oil. Cover the casserole with aluminum foil and bake for 20 minutes, then serve with pecorino cheese.

"Johnny Marzetti"

One can hardly believe that a casserole recipe exists that is unique to the U.S. Panama Canal Zone. But if you were to ask all those servicemen and military brats who were raised in the Canal Zone before it was turned over to Panama under President Jimmy Carter about casseroles they would say without hesitation Johnny Marzetti (sometimes Johnny Mazetti). So who is Johnny Marzetti? No, the question should be what is Johnny Marzetti? Johnny Marzetti is the name of a beef noodle casserole that was either born in or became identified with the Canal Zone. Jean Anderson in her *American Century Cookbook* says that Johnny Marzetti is a casserole created in the 1920s by the owner of the Marzetti Restaurant in Columbus, Ohio, and named after his brother Johnny. How it got to the Canal Zone and how it became a memorable favorite of Americans who raised families in the Canal Zone are mysteries. The casserole is made with wide flat noodles, hamburger meat, diced onions, chopped green bell peppers, celery, tomatoes, black olives, green olives, mushrooms, Worchestershire sauce, cheddar or colby cheese (or Velveeta in the 1950s), and Arturo sauce which was bought at the base commissary. Arturo sauce was a canned sauce that makes many nostalgic for the old Canal Zone. You can still find it by visiting www.saucearturo.net. It was made with finely chopped mushrooms, water, tomato sauce, soy sauce, apple cider vinegar, brown sugar, salt, garlic, pepper, ginger, and nutmeg. The only reason I don't have a recipe for Johnny Marzetti is because it sounds, if I may be honest and my apologies to those with memories of lost foods, awful.

Mushroom Lasagna

This delicate summer preparation is called *Dantesche* in Italian. We don't know where the dish comes from or what the name means other than it is probably some Tuscan chef's fantasy dish inspired by Dante Alighieri. It would be best to use your own homemade lasagna noodles, but store-bought lasagne will be fine if you buy the thin no-boil variety, although you will boil them briefly in this recipe. If you do make your own lasagne, cut them into 4 x 2½-inch rectangles. Because the lasagna is so simple, you must use the finest ingredients, especially ripe, sweet tomatoes off the vine, or from a farmers market, but do not use supermarket tomatoes. The shiitake mushrooms should be fresh but should not be wrapped in plastic; brush them clean, but don't rinse them. Remember too that fontina Val d'Aosta cheese, the best of the fontina cheeses, is not sold sliced, so you will have to buy the wedge of cheese and use a cheese slicer, not a knife, to get the thin slices. • **Makes 4 to 6 servings**

> ½ pound thin no-boil lasagne or thin homemade lasagne
> 3 tablespoons unsalted butter, at room temperature
> 10 ounces shiitake mushrooms, stemmed, thinly sliced
> ½ cup freshly grated Parmesan cheese
> Salt and freshly ground black pepper
> 1¾ pounds ripe tomatoes, peeled and thinly sliced
> ½ pound fontina Val d'Aosta cheese, thinly sliced

1. Preheat the oven to 350°F. Lightly butter a 13 × 9 × 2-inch baking casserole.

2. Bring a large pot of abundantly salted water to a vigorous boil. Add the lasagne and boil until they are soft and pliable, 4 to 5 minutes. Drain the lasagne. Set them aside in a pan filled with water so they don't stick together. When you are ready to assemble the lasagna, dry each lasagna sheet on a kitchen towel.

3. Arrange a layer of lasagne in the casserole. Spread about 1 tablespoon of butter over the lasagna sheets and then cover with a third of the mushrooms. Sprinkle with a third of the Parmesan cheese and season with salt and pepper. Lay a third of the tomato slices, and finally lay a third of the fontina cheese on top. Follow this order for the next two layers. Cover the casserole with a tented piece of aluminum foil and bake until bubbly, about 45 minutes. Serve hot.

Baked Lasagnette with Shrimp, Swiss Chard, and Ricotta

In southern Italian cooking, one popular pasta is called *lasagnette*, a kind of flat pasta about three-quarters of an inch wide with one crinkly edge. *Lasagnette* is a great pasta for an earthy dish like this. Some pasta makers call it *malfadine*, which is what you might find on the label. In any case, use the widest flat pasta available, and if that happens to be fettuccine, then use that. I often made this *lasagnette* when my kids were younger, and they always gobbled it up. Once, my oldest son Ali, who was about 10 at the time, asked me what the green stuff was. I said, "Swiss chard." He asked, "What's Swiss chard?" and I said, "Oh, it's like the poor man's spinach." He responded, "Well, why don't we just use spinach?" • **Makes 4 servings**

¾ pound *lasagnette* pasta
1¾ pounds Swiss chard, heavy stems removed,
    washed and cut into strips
5 tablespoons extra-virgin olive oil
4 large garlic cloves, finely chopped
6 tablespoons finely chopped fresh parsley
Salt and freshly ground black pepper
1½ pounds large shrimp, peeled
12 ounces ricotta cheese

1. Preheat the oven to 350°F. Generously oil a 12 × 9 × 2-inch baking casserole.

2. Bring a large pot of abundantly salted water to a vigorous boil. Add the lasagnette and boil until half-cooked (follow the package instructions), then add the Swiss chard and cook until the lasagnette are al dente. Drain well.

3. In a large skillet, heat 3 tablespoons of olive oil over medium heat with half of the garlic and half of the parsley until sizzling. Add the lasagnette and Swiss chard, season with salt and pepper, and mix well. Transfer to the casserole.

4. Place the shrimp in a medium skillet with the remaining 2 tablespoons of olive oil and the remaining garlic and parsley. Turn the heat to high and cook, stirring, until the shrimp have turned red or orange, 4 to 5 minutes.

5. Transfer the shrimp to the casserole and mix slightly with the pasta. Push pieces of ricotta down into the pasta. Bake until the top is very slightly browned, about 20 minutes. Serve hot.

Baked Angel Hair Pasta with Sausages and Smooth Tomato and Artichoke Sauce

Angel hair pasta, called *capellini* in Italian, is a very thin, delicate pasta used for very specific purposes, and usually tossed with smooth sauces. Baking angel hair pasta in the manner of baked macaroni is not very common—in fact, I never ran across a baked *capellini* in Italy. But I like to prepare this dish that's inspired by the baked pastas of Campania because both the texture and taste are alluring. If you can make your own sausages this dish will be even better. Also, fresh artichoke hearts (or bottoms) would be great to use, but lacking that, the marinated ones give a tangier taste.

• Makes 4 to 6 servings

2 pounds (about 8 links) sweet Italian sausages

4 bay leaves

½ cup extra-virgin olive oil

1 small onion, very finely chopped

1 celery stalk, very finely chopped

¼ cup finely chopped fresh parsley

3 large garlic cloves, very finely chopped

3 large ripe tomatoes (about 1½ pounds total),
      peeled (see page 241), seeded, and finely chopped

½ red bell pepper, seeded and finely chopped

5 marinated or fresh artichoke hearts (bottoms), chopped

Salt and freshly ground pepper

1 pound angel hair pasta (*capellini*)

Freshly grated Parmesan cheese for garnish

1. Preheat the oven to 350°F. Lightly oil a 12 × 9 × 2-inch baking casserole.

2. Place the sausages in the casserole. Stick the bay leaves between some sausages and place the casserole in the oven until the sausages are fully cooked, about 30 minutes. Remove the sausages from the casserole and set aside.

3. In a skillet, heat the olive oil over medium heat, then add the onion, celery, parsley, and garlic, and cook, stirring frequently, until softened, about 6 minutes. Add the tomatoes, bell pepper, and artichoke hearts. Season with salt and pepper. Reduce the heat to low, cover, and cook, stirring occasionally, until denser, about 50 minutes. Pass the sauce through a food mill or strainer and set aside.

4. Bring a large pot of abundantly salted water to a vigorous boil. Add the pasta and boil until half-cooked (follow the package instructions), about 1½ minutes. Drain well and toss the pasta with the sauce. Arrange the pasta in the empty casserole that the sausages were cooked in and place the sausages attractively in rows on top of the pasta. Bake until the top of the pasta begins to get a little crunchy, 20 to 25 minutes. Sprinkle the Parmesan cheese liberally over the casserole and serve.

Angel Hair Pasta au Gratin

A ngel hair pasta, *capellini* in Italian, is so called because it is so light and fine. Because of its thinness, it is used only with certain kinds of preparations and sauces. In this simple recipe, inspired by the kind of pasta dishes one might fine in Nice or elsewhere in Provence, the cooked *capellini* is baked for a meal that is quite rich and satisfying. • **Makes 4 servings**

> 6 tablespoons (¾ stick) unsalted butter
> 1 pound angel hair pasta (*capellini*)
> 1 cup heavy cream
> 1 cup half and half
> Salt and freshly ground black pepper
> ¾ cup fresh bread crumbs (see Note)

1 Preheat the oven to 350°F. Coat a 12 × 9 × 2-inch baking casserole with 2 tablespoons of butter.

2 Bring a large pot of abundantly salted water to a vigorous boil. Add the pasta and boil until it is about half-cooked, 2 to 3 minutes, then drain and transfer to a bowl. Add 2 tablespoons of butter and toss well to coat.

3 Arrange the pasta evenly in the casserole . Pour in the heavy cream and half and half, and season with salt and pepper. Sprinkle the top with bread crumbs and dot with the remaining 2 tablespoons of butter. Bake the pasta until the top is golden, about 30 minutes.

Note: this amount can be made from crumbling two ½-inch-thick slices of 5¼ × 3-inch French or Italian bread in a food processor.

Chicken Tetrazzini

James Beard, the famous American chef and cookbook author, claimed that this dish was named after the fabulous coloratura Louisa Tetrazzini (1871–1940) who was born in Italy and reigned supreme in the San Francisco opera in the early part of the twentieth century. He thought the dish was invented in San Francisco where she loved to sing and to eat. But how was it invented? The research of Andrea Niosi, of the Alice Statler Library of the Culinary Arts and Hospitality Studies Department of the City College of San Francisco, points to the dish being invented either by Chef Pavani at the Knickerbocker in New York City around 1912 or by Chef Ernest Arbogast at the Palace Hotel in San Francisco around 1908. Christiane Romani, on the other hand, believes her great-grandfather, Nicolas Sabatini, invented it while he worked at the Mayflower Hotel in New York. I'm in favor of its San Francisco origins. Given the name of the dish, I would guess that it was created in honor of Louisa Tetrazzini at a San Francisco hotel after she sang a free concert to 250,000 people at the Lotta Fountain at Kearney and Market streets in San Francisco on December 24, 1910. One candidate for this honor of invention was the Palace Hotel which was famous at the time for its rich French cuisine typical of the nineteenth century, and the velouté sauce used in tetrazzini is definitely not Italian. The problem with this theory is that the Palace Hotel burned down in 1906, although it was rebuilt. In any case, Louisa Tetrazzini was unaware she had a dish named after her because she never mentions this in her autobiography. Chicken tetrazzini is a recipe that has gone out of favor, which is a shame because even though it's old-fashioned it is delicious. It is often made with turkey too. • **Makes 6 to 8 servings**

One 3-pound chicken

1 small onion, cut in half

1 celery stalk, cut up

1 carrot, cut up

2 whole cloves

1 bay leaf

2 tablespoons salt plus more as needed

Water as needed

7 tablespoons unsalted butter

1 large garlic clove, crushed

½ pound white button mushrooms, sliced

¾ pound fettuccine

¼ cup all-purpose flour

1 cup heavy cream

2 tablespoons dry sherry

Freshly ground pepper

1 cup (about 3 ounces) freshly grated Parmesan cheese

1 Place the whole chicken in a stockpot with the onion, celery, carrot, cloves, bay leaf, and 1 tablespoon of salt. Add enough water to cover. Bring to a near boil over high heat. Just as the water begins to gently bubble, reduce the heat to low and simmer until the chicken is tender and almost falling off the bone, about 2 hours, making sure the broth never boils, which would only make the chicken tough. The water should only shimmer on the surface. Remove the chicken from the pot and once it is cool enough to handle, discard the bones and skin and shred the meat. Strain the broth. You should have more than 4 cups of broth. Return 2 cups of broth to the stockpot. Add 2 quarts of water to the broth in the stockpot and return to the heat and keep at a low simmer. Set aside the remaining 2 cups of broth for making the sauce in Step 5.

2 Preheat the oven to 375°F. Coat a 13 × 9 × 2-inch baking casserole with 1 tablespoon of butter.

3 Meanwhile, in a medium skillet, melt 1 tablespoon of butter over medium-high heat with the garlic. Add the mushrooms and cook, stirring, until softened, about 5 minutes. Reduce the heat to medium-low, season with salt, and cook, stirring occasionally, until dark and wilted, about 5 minutes longer. Set aside.

4 Bring the simmering broth in the stockpot to a vigorous boil over high heat and add about 1 tablespoon of salt. Add the fettuccine and boil until al dente. Drain, transfer to a bowl, and toss with 1 tablespoon of butter.

5 In a saucepan, melt the remaining 4 tablespoons of butter over medium heat, then stir in the flour to form a roux, cooking for 2 minutes while stirring. Add the reserved 2 cups of chicken broth in a slow stream, stirring or whisking while you do. Continue to cook, stirring occasionally, until dense, about 12 minutes. Remove from the heat and pour in the cream and sherry, stirring as you do. Return to medium-low heat and simmer, stirring, until thick, about 12 minutes. Season with salt and pepper. Add half of this sauce to the reserved shredded chicken and mix the other half of the sauce into the mushrooms.

6 Pour the fettuccine into the casserole. Arrange the shredded chicken mixture over the pasta. Scatter the top with the mushroom mixture. Sprinkle with the Parmesan cheese. Bake until the top is golden, about 25 minutes. Serve hot.

Bacon Noodle Bake

This recipe makes a wonderful impression on guests as it is rich and luscious. The real key to the dish is the bacon. It is best to forget about the watery, shriveled supermarket bacon that does not have the depth of flavor needed. To me, supermarket bacon tastes of salt, sugar, and artificial flavoring, and has too much fat and water. There is a lot of properly cured bacon being produced in this country today by, for lack of a better term, artisanal producers. The first time you cook artisan bacon you will notice that it doesn't shrivel, but instead, it maintains its shape and is very flavorful. The best known of the artisan producers is Niman Ranch. You can buy their center-cut applewood-smoked bacon at stores like Whole Foods or Trader Joe's, or at their Web site, nimanranch.com. But there are many others and a visit to nichepork.org will be very rewarding. If you must use supermarket bacon, look for slab bacon or at least the thickest cut of unflavored bacon they have. • **Makes 4 servings**

2 tablespoons unsalted butter, melted

2 cups (about 6 ounces) shredded Gruyère, Cantal, or Comté cheese

1 cup heavy cream

¼ cup mascarpone cheese

¼ cup mayonnaise

½ pound wide egg noodles, such as pappardelle or lasagne

¾ pound thick-cut bacon

¼ cup (less than 1 ounce) freshly grated Parmesan cheese

½ teaspoon sweet paprika

Salt and freshly ground black pepper

1 cup fresh bread crumbs (see Note)

1. Preheat the oven to 350°F. Coat a 12 × 9 × 2-inch baking casserole with 1 tablespoon of butter.

2. In a bowl, stir together the Gruyère cheese, heavy cream, mascarpone cheese, and mayonnaise. Set aside.

3. Bring a large pot of abundantly salted water to vigorous boil. Add the noodles and cook, stirring occasionally, until al dente. Drain and transfer the noodles to a bowl. (If using lasagne, cut or break them into 1½-inch-long strips.) Add the cheese mixture and toss with the noodles.

4. In a large skillet, cook the bacon over medium heat until almost crispy, about 10 minutes. Remove the bacon from the skillet and cut into 1-inch pieces. Toss half of the bacon with the noodle mixture. Arrange the noodle mixture in the casserole. Sprinkle the Parmesan cheese over the noodle mixture, then cover with the remaining bacon. Season with the paprika, salt, and pepper. Toss the remaining 1 tablespoon of melted butter with the bread crumbs and then sprinkle the buttered bread crumbs over the casserole. Bake until bubbly, golden, and crispy on top, about 30 minutes. Serve hot.

Note: This amount can be made from crumbling two ½-inch-thick slices of 5¼ × 3-inch French or Italian bread in a food processor.

Tuna Noodle Casserole

The old tuna noodle casserole popular in the 1950s was a quick dinner that many mothers prepared with cooked noodles, a can of tuna, and a can of condensed cream of mushroom soup. It was baked in a hot oven, and perhaps topped with crushed corn flakes or potato chips. We might remember it as comfort food, but in fact, it was awful. As Russ Parsons, food columnist for the *Los Angeles Times*, said, "it's gotten so that the mere phrase 'tuna fish casserole' has become a kind of punch line." But he also traces the history of the preparation, reminding us that it had noble beginnings in the nineteenth century as a way of using up leftover salt cod or fresh cod. It was called cod à la Béchamel in *Mrs. Beeton's Every Day Cookery and Housekeeping Book* published in 1865, and was bound with Béchamel sauce and topped with bread crumbs before baking. Tuna was first canned commercially in 1903 and soon replaced the disappearing salt cod. In 1934, Campbell's Soup Company introduced canned cream of mushroom soup, and by 1939 the tuna noodle casserole, made with canned tuna, canned soup, and noodles, appeared in Irma Rombauer's *Streamlined Cooking*. This recipe takes that classic "comfort" food of the fifties and gives it all the freshness it deserves, yet it takes no longer to prepare than the original version. Some cooks use elbow macaroni, but I like the delicate taste of flat egg noodles.

• Makes 4 to 6 servings

½ pound wide flat egg noodles

12 ounces canned tuna in water, drained and flaked apart

2 cups (about 6 ounces) shredded Swiss cheese

1 cup heavy cream

¼ cup crème fraîche or sour cream

¼ cup mayonnaise

1 cup fresh or frozen peas

6 tablespoons chopped onion

¼ cup chopped fresh chives

¼ cup diced green bell pepper

Salt and freshly ground black pepper

2 tablespoons unsalted butter, melted

1 cup fresh bread crumbs (see Note)

1. Preheat the oven to 425°F. Butter a 12 × 9 × 2-inch baking casserole.

2. Bring a large pot of abundantly salted water to a vigorous boil. Add the noodles and boil until al dente. Drain the noodles, then transfer them to a large bowl with the tuna, and toss.

3. Meanwhile, in a saucepan over medium heat, combine the cheese, heavy cream, crème fraîche or sour cream, and mayonnaise with the peas, onion, chives, and bell pepper, and cook, stirring, until smooth, about 7 minutes. Toss the sauce with the noodle mixture. Season with salt and pepper and toss again.

4. Spread the noodle mixture evenly in the casserole. Toss the butter with the bread crumbs and sprinkle on top of the noodles. Bake until bubbling and golden and crispy on top, about 20 minutes. Serve hot.

Note: This amount can be made from crumbling two ½-inch-thick slices of 5¼ × 3-inch French or Italian bread in a food processor.

Oyster and Noodle Casserole

This utterly rich casserole from the mid-twentieth century was first offered by Mrs. Peter O'Donnell for a Junior League of Dallas cookbook published probably in the 1930s. In some ways, we wish this had become more popular than tuna noodle casserole, as it is just magnificent and so simple—but you've got to like oysters to make it. My recipe has modernized the original by reducing the heaviness but keeping the richness. To make it less rich, reduce the butter by half and use milk instead of cream.

• **Makes 4 to 6 servings**

8 tablespoons (1 stick) unsalted butter

½ pound wide flat noodles, such as pappardelle

2 cups shucked whole oysters with their liquid
    (about 48 oysters or 1 pound frozen whole oysters)

2 large eggs, beaten to blend

2 cups finely ground plain cracker crumbs
    (such as water crackers, oyster crackers, or Saltines)

Salt and freshly ground black pepper

1 cup crème fraîche or sour cream

1½ cups heavy cream

1 Preheat the oven to 325°F. Coat a 9 × 2½-inch-deep round baking casserole with 1 tablespoon of butter.

2 Bring a large pot of abundantly salted water to a vigorous boil. Add the noodles and boil until al dente. Drain the noodles and toss them in a bowl with 2 tablespoons of butter.

3 Cover the casserole with half of the noodles. Drain the oysters; reserving their liquid. Working with one at a time, dip the oysters in the egg, and then dredge them in the cracker crumbs. Cover the noodles with half of the coated oysters. Season with salt and pepper. Cover the oysters with the remaining noodles and then place the remaining coated oysters on top of the noodles. Season with salt and pepper. Dot the top with the remaining 5 tablespoons butter.

4 In a bowl, mix any egg remaining from dipping the oysters, with the crème fraîche, cream, and reserved oyster liquid. Pour over the noodles and bake until bubbly, about 45 minutes. Serve hot.

Macaroni and Cheese

American kids have grown up with macaroni and cheese ever since 1937 when the Kraft Company put it in a box. There can be no doubt that its ultimate origins are Italian, as one finds macaroni and cheese recipes from the late thirteenth century in southern Italy. But the American macaroni and cheese has two claimed lines of ancestry. In the first, it is thought that macaroni and cheese was a casserole that had its beginnings at a New England church supper. In southeastern Connecticut, it was known long ago as macaroni pudding. In the second, and more famous story, and more likely the original story, it is said that the classic American macaroni and cheese was brought to Virginia by Thomas Jefferson after his sojourn in Italy. His daughter, Mary Randolph, became the hostess of his house after Jefferson's wife died, and she is credited with inventing the dish using macaroni and Parmesan cheese. Later, the Parmesan was replaced with cheddar cheese. Anyway, that's one story. It is more likely that Jefferson encountered the dish in Italy and brought back the recipe along with the pasta machine. Although there are many different recipes for macaroni and cheese, there really is no need for so many since it is, in principal, just macaroni and melted cheese in white sauce. A macaroni and cheese should be simple, true, and un-gussied. The key to this dish is the cheese, so it is wise to choose a high-quality, aged, cheddar cheese such as a Vermont Shelburne Farm cheddar. Why isn't my mac and cheese orange? Well, I don't believe in using food coloring and prefer white cheddar cheese, which does not include food coloring. Some cooks add bread crumbs to the top of the casserole, and I like that au gratin finish. With or without the crumb topping, this recipe is a far cry from the one that comes out of a box and a lot better, too. • **Makes 4 to 6 servings**

3 tablespoons unsalted butter

3 tablespoons finely chopped onion

½ garlic clove, finely chopped

3 tablespoons all-purpose flour

3½ cups whole milk

1 pound mild or sharp aged white cheddar cheese, shredded

2 tablespoons Dijon mustard

¾ teaspoon salt plus more to taste

1 pound elbow macaroni or any short tubular pasta

2 tablespoons dry bread crumbs

1. Preheat the oven to 400°F. Butter a 10-inch round baking casserole that is at least 3 inches deep.

2. In a saucepan, melt the butter over medium heat, then add the onion and garlic and cook, stirring, until translucent, about 3 minutes. Add the flour to form a roux, stirring for about 1 minute. Remove the saucepan from the heat and whisk in the milk. Return to low heat and simmer, stirring, until smooth but still liquidy, about 15 minutes. Add the cheese, 1 cup or a handful at a time, stirring frequently, until it melts. Add the mustard and ¾ teaspoon of salt, and stir to blend well.

3. Meanwhile, bring a large pot of abundantly salted water to a vigorous boil. Add the macaroni and boil until half-cooked (follow the package instructions). Drain the macaroni and transfer it to a large bowl. Pour the cheese sauce over the macaroni and stir and toss a bit. Transfer the macaroni mixture to the casserole. Sprinkle the bread crumbs on top and bake until the top begins to turn golden and the sauce is bubbly, about 25 minutes. Let rest for 10 minutes, then serve.

Ukrainian Noodle and Spinach Casserole

This beautiful casserole, called *lokshyna, zapechena z shpynatom* in Ukrainian, is a favorite home-cooked meal in many Ukrainian homes. It is filling, nourishing, and satisfying. Traditionally, the egg noodles are home-made too, but you can use any flat egg noodle. You can prepare the casserole ahead of time, with everything in place except the hard-boiled egg garnish, and store it in the refrigerator until needed. When baking it after it has been refrigerated, remember to keep it in the oven a little longer than called for in the recipe so that it will be hot in the center. Leftovers can be saved for making a secondary casserole (see box). • **Makes 6 servings**

8 tablespoons (1 stick) unsalted butter
½ pound flat egg noodles
¾ cup (about 2½ ounces) shredded Swiss cheese
1 teaspoon salt
2½ to 3 pounds spinach leaves without stems, rinsed well
1 medium onion, finely chopped
Freshly ground black pepper
½ cup fine dry bread crumbs
4 hard-boiled eggs, peeled and quartered

1. Preheat the oven to 350°F. Lightly butter the bottom and sides of a 9 × 3-inch round baking casserole with 1 tablespoon of butter.

2. Bring a large pot of abundantly salted water to a vigorous boil. Add the noodles and cook until al dente. Remove the noodles by pulling them out of the water with tongs or a pasta fork and transfer them to a large bowl; allow the water to continue boiling. Toss the noodles with 2 tablespoons of melted butter, half of the cheese, and ½ teaspoon of salt.

Well, I guess you could call it fusion cuisine, but when I took leftover Veal Roman Style (page 103) and pushed it into a smaller casserole with some leftover Ukranian Noodle and Spinach Casserole (previous page), I got a great casserole dinner out of it. You might want to sprinkle more Swiss cheese over the top before putting it into a 350° oven to bake for 30 minutes.

3 Add the spinach to the boiling salted pasta water, and cook until the spinach wilts, about 1 minute, then drain the spinach in a strainer, squeezing out the excess water with the back of a wooden spoon. Finely chop the spinach and set aside.

4 In a large skillet, melt 3 tablespoons of butter over high heat, then add the onion. Reduce the heat to medium and cook, stirring, until softened, about 4 minutes. Stir in the chopped spinach, increase the heat to high, and cook uncovered, stirring almost constantly, until the moisture in the pan has completely evaporated and the spinach has begun to stick slightly to the pan, about 4 minutes. Stir in the remaining ½ teaspoon of salt and some black pepper.

5 Arrange one-third of the noodle mixture in a layer on the bottom of the casserole. Place half of the spinach on top. Cover the spinach with the next third of the noodle mixture, then cover with the remaining spinach. Add the remaining noodle mixture as the top layer.

6 In a medium-size skillet, melt the remaining 2 tablespoons of butter over high heat, then remove from the burner and stir in the bread crumbs and remaining cheese. Quickly sprinkle the bread crumb mixture on top of the noodles. Bake until golden brown, about 30 minutes. Garnished with the hard-boiled eggs, and serve immediately.

Noodles and Ham Casserole

This is a classic Austrian ham and cheese casserole called *schinkenfleck-erln* that is something akin to a noodle quiche. Some cooks like to add a cup of diced Swiss cheese to this recipe. The square noodles may by hard to find, so use any wide and flat noodles. I also like to use cooked Black Forest ham in this recipe, since this dish demands the best of ingredients.

• **Makes 6 servings**

½ pound square egg noodles

4 tablespoons (½ stick) unsalted butter, at room temperature

1 medium onion, chopped

2 large eggs

¾ cup heavy cream

2 cups (about ½ pound) diced cooked or smoked ham

½ teaspoon caraway seeds

¼ teaspoon freshly ground black pepper

1 tablespoon dry bread crumbs

1 teaspoon hot or sweet paprika

1 medium tomato, sliced

2 tablespoons finely chopped fresh parsley

1. Preheat the oven to 350°F. Lightly butter a 12 x 9 x 2-inch baking casserole.

2. Bring a large pot of abundantly salted water to a vigorous boil. Add the noodles and boil until al dente. Drain the noodles and transfer to a bowl.

3. Stir the butter and onion into the noodles while the noodles are still hot. In a bowl, beat the eggs into the cream, then add to the noodles with the ham and caraway seeds. Season with black pepper and mix well.

4. Sprinkle the bread crumbs evenly on the bottom of the casserole, then pour in the noodle mixture. Sprinkle with the paprika. Bake until the mixture has set, like a pudding, about 40 minutes. Serve hot, garnished with sliced tomato and chopped parsley.

Rice and Grain
Casseroles

White Rice and Black Beans with Roast Orange Duck

In the Spanish region of Valencia, as well as in Latin America, there is a dish called *moros y christianos*, Moors and Christians, alluding to the contrast between the swarthy Moors (black beans) and the white Christians (rice). This recipe adds duck to the rice and beans to make an elegant and extravagant casserole. When you see duck and oranges you probably think of the famous French duck à l'orange, but you may not know that the French learned this preparation from the Spanish, and it's possible the Spanish learned it from the Arabs since the Arabs were responsible for bringing both rice and oranges to Spain. This is a casserole to make for a special occasion; it's not an everyday casserole. • **Makes 4 servings**

For the duck

One 5-pound duck, cut into half lengthwise
1 teaspoon freshly ground cumin
Salt and freshly ground black pepper
2 tablespoons extra-virgin olive oil
1 cup freshly squeezed orange juice

For the beans

½ pound (about 1 cup) dried black beans
1 quart cold water
1 small onion, cut in half
3 large garlic cloves, crushed
1 bay leaf

For the bean seasoning

2 tablespoons extra-virgin olive oil
½ cup diced slab bacon or pancetta

1 medium onion, finely chopped

2 large garlic cloves, finely chopped

1 teaspoon all-purpose flour

1 teaspoon sweet paprika

1 teaspoon salt

1 cup dry white wine

For the rice

1 tablespoon unsalted butter

¾ cup medium-grain rice

1½ cups chicken broth

1 teaspoon finely chopped fresh tarragon,
    or ½ teaspoon dried

1 teaspoon salt

¼ teaspoon dried oregano

Finely chopped fresh parsley for garnish

1 Preheat the oven to 350°F.

2 To prepare the duck, prick the skin of the duck all over with the tip of a knife or a corn cob holder so the fat can run out while the duck is roasting. Sprinkle the duck halves with cumin and arrange them in a roasting pan, skin side up. Season with salt and pepper, and drizzle some of the olive oil and about ½ cup orange juice over the duck. Bake until the skin is golden brown and crispy, about 1½ hours, basting with the remaining ½ cup orange juice and olive oil. Set aside once cooked.

3 Meanwhile, to prepare the beans, place the beans in a large pot with the water, onion halves, garlic, and bay leaf. Bring to a boil over high heat, then reduce the heat to very low, partially cover, and simmer until tender, about 45 minutes. Drain, if necessary, and set aside.

4 To prepare the bean seasoning, heat the olive oil in a medium skillet over medium-high heat, then add the bacon, onion, and garlic, and cook,

stirring frequently, until the onion is translucent, about 5 minutes. Add the flour, paprika, and salt, mix well, and stir in the reserved beans and the wine. Simmer until the beans are a little more tender, about 20 minutes. Once the beans are cooked, drain any remaining liquid and set aside. Remove and discard the onion halves and bay leaf.

5. To prepare the rice, in a small, heavy flame-proof casserole or saucepan, melt the butter over medium-high heat, then cook the rice, stirring, for 1 minute. Add the chicken broth, tarragon, salt, and oregano, and stir to combine. Reduce the heat to low, cover, and cook until the broth is absorbed and the rice is tender, about 15 minutes, but check for doneness after 12 minutes. Turn the heat off and let sit, covered, for 10 minutes. All the components of the casserole can be refrigerated at this point and assembled later, if desired.

6. In a large baking casserole, preferably round, arrange the beans in the center and surround them with the rice. Cut the duck halves in half and arrange on top of the rice. Place in the oven until crispy, about 20 minutes. Sprinkle with parsley and serve hot.

Rice

There are many varieties of rice and they are used for different purposes, usually depending on the culinary culture. In Spanish cooking, the favored rice is medium-grain rice, sometimes called Calrosa or Calrose. Most Japanese and Thai rice dishes use medium-grain rice too. Short-grain rice, such as Arborio or Vialone, is used for risotto, stuffing vegetables, and desserts. Long-grain rice is used for making pilaf. All three sizes of rice grains are now easily found in supermarkets. Other specialty rice does exist, but they are not used in this book

Baked Rice Pilaf with Carrots

This Lebanese-style rice pilaf is called *ruzz wa'l-jazar* in Arabic which simply means "rice with carrots." But this preparation is a little more than that because the grains of rice are separate and fluffy, and not sticky like Asian rice or wet like risotto. It's important that the rice be washed or rinsed, otherwise it will not cook separately. When my children were young they loved this baked rice, especially when I made it along with fried turkey nuggets dusted with ground cumin. It is best to use long-grain rice, such as basmati rice, for this recipe, as converted rice will not work here. The heavy enameled cast-iron Le Creuset casseroles are excellent to use for this recipe too.

• Makes 4 servings

3 tablespoons unsalted or clarified butter
½ cup diced peeled carrot
1 cup long-grain rice, soaked in tepid water for 30 minutes
    or rinsed in a strainer under running water, drained
1½ cups water
1 teaspoon salt
Freshly ground black pepper

1 Preheat the oven to 350°F.

2 In a heavy 2-quart flame- and oven-proof casserole with a heavy lid, melt the butter over medium-high heat, then cook the carrot and rice together, stirring frequently, for 2 minutes. Add the water and salt, and sprinkle with pepper. Bring to a boil. Cover and bake in the oven until the water has been absorbed, about 20 minutes. Remove from the oven, uncover, and place a paper towel over the casserole to replace the lid. Let rest for 20 minutes, then serve.

Rice Pilaf with Spiced Turkey and Baby Lima Beans

This rice pilaf is a convenient and delicious way to use up leftover turkey. It's a grand rice casserole that imitates the way chefs of the Ottoman court in Istanbul would try to impress the sultan with magnificent dishes. The palace kitchens of the Ottomans in the seventeenth century were feeding about 10,000 people a day, so it was a significant job. If you have any leftover lentils, stir them into the leftovers of this dish, then cover the whole casserole with Turkish yufka pastry instead of the casserole lid, and bake it until the top of the pastry is golden. You can purchase yufka pastry through the Internet, such as at www.tulumba.com. You can use phyllo pastry too. • Makes 4 to 5 servings

1 teaspoon turmeric powder

½ teaspoon ground allspice

2½ teaspoons salt

½ teaspoon freshly ground black pepper

¼ teaspoon ground cloves

½ pound boneless turkey breast, diced, or leftover cooked turkey breast, diced

4 tablespoons (½ stick) unsalted butter

1½ cups long-grain rice, soaked in tepid water for 30 minutes or rinsed in a strainer under running water, drained

1 carrot, peeled and chopped

2¼ cups boiling water

½ cup fresh or frozen baby lima beans

1. Preheat the oven to 350°F.

2. In a bowl, mix together the turmeric powder, allspice, ½ teaspoon of salt, the pepper, and cloves. Add the turkey and toss to coat with the spice mixture.

3. In a skillet, melt 2 tablespoons of butter over medium-high heat, then add the turkey and cook, stirring or shaking the pan frequently, until the turkey is white and firm, about 5 minutes. Remove the skillet from the heat and set aside, keeping the turkey warm.

4. In heavy 2-quart flame- and oven-proof casserole with a heavy lid, melt the remaining 2 tablespoons butter over medium-high heat. Add the rice and carrot, and cook, stirring and turning the rice to coat it with butter, about 4 minutes. Add the boiling water, lima beans, and the remaining 2 teaspoons of salt. Return to a boil. Cover and bake in the oven until all the water is absorbed and the rice is tender, about 20 minutes. Remove from the oven, uncover, and place a paper towel over the casserole to replace the lid. Let rest for 20 minutes, then serve.

Why So Many Spanish Recipes?

While writing this book, I tested many more recipes than are actually in the book. Many recipes didn't make the final cut because they were beaten out by the better tasting ones. In this chapter, I noticed only after I had finished writing it that nearly all the recipes were Spanish. I didn't do this intentionally; it just turned out that the best recipes were Spanish. So be it. It's just like when the Russians sweep the figure skating championships.

Baked Rice with Ham, Pork, and Sausage

This rustic casserole comes from the Spanish region of Andalusia where they call it *arroz con jamón, cerdo y longaniza*. It is an evocative recipe of a deep-rooted love for the land and its produce exemplified in culinary preparations that are fanciful, rich in meats and vegetables, and spiced in an exotic, almost North African, way. This preparation is pure home cooking and you are unlikely to come across it in a restaurant. The sausage suggestions in the ingredient list are listed in the order of ease of finding them in a supermarket, but you can also buy them from Internet vendors, such as arnolds-sausage.com, and they all can be shipped to your door. The best pork meat for this stew is pork butt, so use it here. Traditionally, this dish is cooked in an earthenware casserole called an *olla* or *cazuela* in Spanish.

• Makes 6 servings

¼ cup extra-virgin olive oil

1 small onion, finely chopped

6 large garlic cloves, finely chopped

3 tablespoons finely chopped fresh parsley

½ pound cooked ham, cut into ½-inch cubes

½ pound pork stew meat, cut into ½-inch cubes

½ pound sweet Italian sausage, Polish kielbasa, chicken sausage, turkey sausage, Portuguese chouriço sausage, Spanish chorizo sausage, or Spanish longaniza sausage, cut in half

1 tablespoon tomato paste

4 cups water

2 pinches saffron threads (about ½ teaspoon), crumbled

2 turnips (about ¾ pound total), peeled and diced

1 teaspoon sweet paprika or mild Spanish paprika (*pimentón*)

½ teaspoon dried thyme

1 bay leaf

Freshly ground black pepper

2 cups medium-grain rice

2 teaspoons salt

6 ounces snow pea pods

1 Preheat the oven to 425°F.

2 In a heavy, 10-inch-round baking casserole (preferably earthenware), heat the olive oil over medium heat, then add the onion, garlic, parsley, ham, pork, and sausage, and cook, stirring, until the onion is softened and the pork turns color, about 8 minutes. (If you are using an earthenware baking casserole, set it over a heat diffuser, and cook over high heat.)

3 Meanwhile, dissolve the tomato paste in the water. Add the saffron and let it steep for 5 minutes. Add the tomato paste mixture, turnips, paprika, thyme, and bay leaf to the baking casserole. Season with the black pepper and stir well. Cook until the turnips are al dente, about 12 minutes. Add the rice and salt, submerging the rice in the liquid, but without stirring. Scatter the snow pea pods over and submerge them slightly in the liquid.

4 Cover the casserole and bake until the liquid is absorbed, about 20 minutes. Remove from the oven, let rest for 20 minutes, covered, and then serve.

Baked Rice with Sausages and Potatoes

This impressive casserole is from the Spanish region of Albacete, the southwest hinterland of Valencia, and is known simply as *arroz al horno* or baked rice. As you can imagine, there are many variations of this dish as every family will add something different. Along the coast, cooks use seafood, while inland in the plains and hills, cooks use sausages and other meats, as we see in this recipe. There is an enormous amount of flavor in this dish, so you will want to stick to the recipe and use two different kinds of sausage. Ideally, you will use morcilla, the blood sausage that's popular in Spain, and a Spanish chorizo sausage. Both can be bought through Internet sources such as donajuana.com. Many local supermarkets carry blood sausage too, usually already cooked and typically sold near the bacon. If these sausages are not available, you can use some of the substitutes I recommend in the recipe. Normally, I suggest substitutes for pork lard in cooking, but in this recipe it's such an important part of the flavor I recommend highly that you use it in the specified amount. • **Makes 8 servings**

For the tomato sauce

1 tablespoon extra-virgin olive oil
1 small onion, finely chopped
1 small carrot, peeled and finely chopped
½ celery stalk, finely chopped
3 large leaves fresh basil, finely chopped
1 tablespoon finely chopped fresh parsley
2 cups chopped and peeled (see page 241) fresh or canned tomatoes
Salt and freshly ground black pepper

For the rice

1 cup pork lard

1¾ pounds potatoes, peeled and sliced ¼ inch thick

¾ pound Canadian bacon, diced

1 head garlic, cloves separated and peeled

1½ pounds cooked blood sausages, sliced ½ inch thick

¾ pound Spanish chorizo sausage, Portuguese *chouriço* sausage,
    Polish kielbasa, Italian turkey sausage, or sweet Italian sausage,
    sliced ½ inch thick

2½ cups medium-grain rice

5 cups boiling chicken broth

3 ripe tomatoes (about 1¼ pounds), peeled (see page 241) and
    seeded (2 chopped and 1 sliced)

2 tablespoons finely chopped fresh parsley

½ teaspoon slightly crumbled saffron threads

1 teaspoon salt

1 teaspoon freshly ground black pepper

1 To prepare the tomato sauce, in a saucepan, heat the olive oil over medium-high heat, then add the onion, carrot, celery, basil, and parsley. Cook, stirring, until softened, about 5 minutes. Add the chopped tomatoes, reduce the heat to medium-low, and simmer until denser, 25 to 30 minutes. Season with salt and pepper and set aside.

2 To prepare the rice, in a large baking casserole (preferably earthenware) set over a heat diffuser or in a flame- and oven-proof casserole with sides that are at least 2 inches high, melt the lard over high heat. Add the potatoes and cook, turning carefully so you don't break the slices or at least don't break them too much, until they are golden, about 10 minutes. (If you are not cooking with earthenware and a diffuser, cook over medium-high heat and check for doneness sooner.) Add the Canadian bacon, garlic cloves, blood sausage, chorizo sausage, and the reserved tomato sauce. Reduce the heat to low and cook until the chorizo sausage looks tender, about 30 minutes.

③ Meanwhile, preheat the oven to 425°F.

④ Gently but thoroughly fold the rice into the sausage mixture. Add the boiling broth, chopped tomatoes, parsley, and saffron, and stir gently again. Season with salt and pepper. Arrange the sliced tomatoes on top of the casserole and bake uncovered until the rice is cooked and the liquid is nearly all absorbed, about 20 minutes. Let the casserole sit covered at room temperature for 15 minutes, then serve.

Allioli

Allioli is a special garlic mayonnaise used predominantly as a condiment for anything from rice dishes to fish soups in the cookery found along the Mediterranean Riviera from Valencia in Spain to Nice in France. In Catalonia, probably the home of allioli, it appears to have an ancestry that goes back to the first century A.D. In Provence and Languedoc, aïoli and aillade, respectively, are made as a garlic mayonnaise. The true Catalan allioli (*all*, "garlic," *i*, "and," *oli*, "oil") is prepared without eggs, using only garlic, olive oil, and salt. But today, most cooks make it with eggs.

5 large garlic cloves (about 1½ ounces), peeled
½ teaspoon salt
1 large egg
1 cup extra-virgin olive oil

1. In a mortar, mash the garlic and salt together with a pestle until mushy. Transfer the garlic paste to a food processor. Add the egg and process for 30 seconds.

2. With the machine running, slowly drizzle in the oil in a very thin stream through the feed tube until it is absorbed and the mixture is well blended. Cover with plastic wrap and refrigerate for 1 hour before using to let the emulsion solidify a bit. Keep refrigerated for up to 2 weeks. • Makes 1½ cups

Baked Rice with Vegetables

This simple baked rice dish is typical in the Valencia province of Spain. It all gets mixed together and baked, and usually served with a fish or shellfish preparation, although it is certainly satisfying enough on its own. It is best to use fresh artichokes in this recipe, in which case you boil them first until they are tender, about 45 minutes, then remove the leaves, properly called bracts. The flesh on the inside of the leaves can be scraped off with a spoon and combined with the rice if desired. Trim the bottoms and remove the fuzzy choke and any tough woody sections with a small paring knife. • **Makes 6 servings**

1½ cups medium-grain rice
½ pound fresh or frozen peas
½ pound green beans, trimmed and cut into 1-inch lengths
4 freshly cooked medium artichokes or canned artichoke hearts
    (also called bottoms or foundations), quartered
2 medium tomatoes, peeled, seeded, and chopped
1 medium onion, chopped
2 large garlic cloves, finely chopped
6 tablespoons extra-virgin olive oil
1½ teaspoons salt
Pinch of saffron, crumbled in a mortar
Freshly ground black pepper
2 cups water
Allioli (page 280)

1 Preheat the oven to 350°F.

2 In a 10- to 12-inch round baking casserole (preferably earthenware), combine the rice, peas, green beans, artichokes, tomatoes, onion, garlic, olive oil, salt, and saffron. Season with black pepper. Pour in the water and stir to mix. Bake, uncovered without stirring, until the water is absorbed and the rice is tender, 45 to 60 minutes. Keep checking the rice; it and the green beans should be tender. Serve hot with the Allioli.

Baked Rice with Shrimp, Ham, and Chicken

The southern Spanish region of Andalusia has two distinct cuisines, one from the mountains and one from the coast. Every coastal community has some kind of rice and seafood dish to offer. This particular casserole is absolutely magnificent if you have access to freshly caught shrimp—that is, shrimp with their heads and that have never been frozen. These fresh shrimp are admittedly rare even in areas of the U.S. where they catch shrimp, such as Florida's west coast, Maine, California, and Louisiana. If you can get fresh shrimp leave their heads on, otherwise use frozen shrimp that have been defrosted in the refrigerator, which is the best way to defrost shrimp. See the note below for making shrimp broth which you should do first.

• Makes 6 servings

2 tablespoons extra-virgin olive oil

1 small onion, finely chopped

3 scallions, white and light green parts only,
    trimmed and thinly sliced

4 large garlic cloves, finely chopped

½ pound cooked Polish kielbasa or Portuguese
    linguiça sausage, sliced

¼ pound cooked ham, diced

¼ pound Canadian bacon, diced

¼ pound boneless skinless chicken breast, diced

1 cup medium-grain rice

2 pounds fresh large shrimp with their heads, shells removed, or
    1 pound headless uncooked large shrimp, defrosted, shells
    removed, shells saved for making broth

2 cups shrimp broth (see Note below)

½ cup frozen or fresh peas

2 teaspoons salt

1 teaspoon freshly ground black pepper

1 teaspoon sweet paprika or mild Spanish paprika (*pimentón*)

½ teaspoon saffron threads

1. Preheat the oven to 475°F.

2. In a large baking casserole (preferably earthenware) set over a heat diffuser, heat the olive oil over high heat. Add the onion, scallions, and garlic. Cook, stirring, until softened, about 10 minutes. (If you are not cooking with earthenware you will not need a heat diffuser; the flame-proof casserole you use should cook over medium heat and you should check for doneness sooner.) Add the sausage, ham, Canadian bacon, and chicken. Cook, stirring, until they turn color, about 5 minutes. Remove the meats with a slotted spoon and set them aside. Add the rice to the casserole and cook, stirring, until the grains are glazed, about 2 minutes.

3. Return all the meats to the casserole. Add the shrimp, shrimp broth, peas, salt, pepper, paprika, and saffron. Continue to cook over high heat until the broth begins to bubble around the edges, submerging all the shrimp in the broth, about 5 minutes. (This will happen sooner if you are not using earthenware.) Reduce the heat to low and cook, uncovered without stirring, until the broth is absorbed, about 30 minutes. Bake in the oven for 5 minutes. Remove and let rest, covered, for 10 minutes before serving.

Note: To make the shrimp broth, place the shrimp shells in a saucepan. Add 3 cups of water and bring to a boil, then simmer until needed, strain, and use.

Rice with Crab

This easily prepared rice casserole is a recipe from the Spanish province of Valencia, where they might also make it with lobster. Everything goes into the casserole and then gets baked, and that's it. Remember that once the rice goes into the oven you do not do anything—don't stir, don't poke. If you decide to serve this casserole with something, it would go great with a piece of sautéed firm-fleshed white fish, such as monkfish, cooked in olive oil with some chopped tomatoes. • **Makes 4 servings**

1½ pounds live blue crabs or 2 cooked king crab legs
1½ cups medium-grain rice
½ green bell pepper, sliced into thin rings, rings cut in half
1 medium tomato, sliced
2 tablespoons extra-virgin olive oil
1 large garlic clove, thinly sliced
1 teaspoon salt
1 teaspoon sweet paprika or mild Spanish paprika (*pimentón*)

1. Preheat the oven to 350°F.

2. If using live crabs, bring 4 cups of water to a boil in a large saucepan over high heat, then boil the crabs until they are cooked through, about 15 minutes. Cool and remove the meat. Return the shells to the saucepan and simmer for an hour. Strain the broth, reserving 2 cups of it. If using cooked king crab legs, crack the shells and try to keep the pieces of meat in ½-inch chunks as you remove it from the shells, and set it aside. Place the shells in a saucepan filled with 4 cups of water and bring to a boil over high heat, then reduce the heat to low and simmer for an hour. Strain the broth, reserving 2 cups of it.

3. Place all the ingredients including the broth and crab meat in a 10-inch round baking casserole that is at least 2 inches deep, and stir to blend. Bake uncovered without stirring until all the broth has been absorbed and the rice is tender, about 35 minutes. Serve hot.

Rice with Cockles

C ockles are small clams that can, in this recipe, be replaced with the smallest littleneck clams you can find. This baked rice is easy to make because everything goes into the casserole, and that's it. Much of the flavor comes from the garlic and the juice from the clams. The fish broth can come from a number of sources. You could make a quick broth with the salmon bones from the Salmon and Potato Casserole (page 185) if you are making it at the same time, or you could use any fish broth, either homemade or from a can, or a bouillon cube. And plain water is fine too. • **Makes 4 servings**

16 to 24 cockles (1 to 1½ pounds total)
2 cups fish broth or water
1 cup medium-grain rice
1 ripe medium tomato, peeled (page 241) and diced
3 tablespoons extra-virgin olive oil
4 large garlic cloves, finely chopped
1 tablespoon finely chopped fresh parsley
1 teaspoon salt
½ teaspoon chopped fresh thyme or ¼ teaspoon dried
⅛ teaspoon dried oregano
Freshly ground black pepper

1 Preheat the oven to 350°F.

2 In a 10- to 12-inch round baking casserole (preferably earthenware) or any round or oval baking baking casserole, combine the cockles, broth, rice, tomato, olive oil, garlic, parsley, salt, thyme, and oregano. Season with black pepper. Stir to mix well and place in the oven uncovered until all the broth is absorbed, the rice tender, and the cockles have opened, about 45 minutes. Remove and serve hot.

Rice with Clams

Most people think a Spanish rice dish is called paella. But paella is just one kind of Spanish rice dish, and in fact, a paella is cooked in a paella, the name of the large metal pan used to cook the dish over a burner, and not in a casserole. In Spain, baked rice dishes, of which there are hundreds of varieties, are oven-baked casseroles generically called *arroz al horno* (oven-baked rice). Rice casseroles come from all regions of Spain, but those containing fish or shellfish, such as this one from the Basque country, are found along the coasts. This casserole is called *arroz con almejas*, and although it is not as boldly flavored as those from Andalusia in the south of Spain, it is very satisfying. • **Makes 6 servings**

¾ cup extra-virgin olive oil

1 green bell pepper, seeded and chopped

4 large garlic cloves, finely chopped

2 cups medium-grain rice

2 tablespoons finely chopped fresh parsley

2 teaspoons salt

2 pounds Manila (preferably) clams or small littleneck clams (about 48), washed

½ pound mixed firm-fleshed fish, cut into small cubes

3 cups clam broth or fish broth

① Preheat the oven to 350°F.

② In a 10-inch round baking casserole (preferably earthenware) set over a heat diffuser, heat the olive oil over high heat. Add the green bell pepper and cook, stirring, until it is softened, about 5 minutes. (If you are not cooking with earthenware and a diffuser, cook over medium-high heat and check for doneness sooner.) Add the garlic and stir, then add the rice and cook, stirring, for 2 minutes. Stir in the parsley and salt, add the clams and fish, then pour in the broth.

③ Place the casserole in the oven and bake uncovered until the liquid has been absorbed and the clams are open, about 45 minutes. Remove from the oven, cover, and let rest for 10 minutes before serving.

An Old South Carolina Rice Casserole

John Martin Taylor, in his book *Hoppin' John's Lowcountry Cooking: Recipes & Ruminations from Charleston and the Carolina Coastal Plain*, was able to study the still extant receipt (recipe) book of Harriet Pinckney Horry from her Hampton Plantation in 1770. Her recipe for Rice Pye must certainly be one of the first casseroles from South Carolina. In her recipe "To Make a Casserole or Rather a Rice Pye" she says that "in the first place you must have a copper Pan well tined. A Tin pan will not do.— Boil 3 pints of rice rather softer than you do rice in Common grease the pan well with Butter and press it (the rice) well into the pan round the sides and bottom and top and put to Bake at the fire turning it round constantly as it will burn. When it is done of a good light brown turn it out on a Dish and cut out in the middle in the middle [*sic*] sufficient to make room for a rich Fill as a Beef or veal or anything you please."

Baked Rice with Garlic

his is a well-known cazuela (casserole) from the Valencia region of Spain known simply as *arroz con ajo*, rice with garlic; although, as you can see, it is a lot more than that. A cazuela is simply a "casserole," and when rice is baked or cooked in an earthenware casserole, the dish can be called a cazuela too. When it is cooked over an open flame or fire in a large shallow steel pan it is known as paella, as is the pan it is cooked in. Do not rinse the rice, as the starch that remains is what gives Spanish rice its famous sticky and flavorful quality. If you are using store-bought chicken broth, taste it first to make sure it is not too salty. If it is, you will not need all the salt called for in the ingredient list. Just remember that the better the quality of your ingredients, especially the broth, the better tasting the final dish. The casserole can stay in a turned-off oven for up to 2 hours if you are not eating right away, and makes a great party or potluck dish. • **Makes 10 servings**

1 cup extra-virgin olive oil

1 medium onion, chopped

1 head garlic, cloves separated, peeled, and finely chopped

6 cups boiling chicken broth

4 cups medium-grain rice

4 cooked medium artichoke hearts (also called "bottoms"), quartered

2 red bell peppers, seeded and coarsely chopped

2 ounces (about ½ cup) double-peeled fava beans (see Note), cooked

1 tablespoon salt

½ teaspoon saffron threads, crumbled

① Preheat the oven to 375°F.

② In a 12- to 14-inch round baking casserole (preferably earthenware), heat the oil over high heat using a heat diffuser until nearly smoking. Add the onion and garlic, and cook, stirring frequently, until softened and fragrant, about 5 minutes. (If you are not using an earthenware casserole you will not need a heat diffuser; cook over medium-high heat until the onion and garlic softens, about 4 minutes.) Stir in the chicken broth, rice, artichokes, bell peppers, fava beans, salt, and crumbled saffron, mixing thoroughly.

③ Place the casserole in the oven and bake, uncovered and without stirring, until the liquid is absorbed and the rice tender, about 50 minutes. Serve hot.

Note: Double-peeled means the fava beans are taken out of their pods (first peel) and skinned of the tough light green skin (second peel) that surrounds the bean.

Hominy and Chile Pepper Casserole

At a large potluck supper in Los Angeles, someone brought this simple casserole made of hominy, chiles, and cheese, and I thought it was just great and looked easy to prepare. The best kind of hominy to use in this casserole is the one with "Mexican-style" or "nixtamal" on the label. If you can't find that, use whatever your supermarket carries. Hominy is large kernels of dried white corn made by treating the corn kernels with lye or soaking them in unslaked lime to remove their outer skins, and then boiled. Dry hominy, that is, uncooked hominy, is hard to find and may be available only through mail order. If you do find it, it needs to be boiled for 3 hours first (see page 76 for some tips on cooking it for flavor). But canned cooked hominy is found in every supermarket. • **Makes 6 to 8 servings**

Two 29-ounce cans hominy, drained
8 canned or jarred jalapeño or other green chiles,
    cut into strips
½ pound Monterey Jack cheese, diced
1½ cups sour cream
1 tablespoon unsalted butter
¼ cup dry bread crumbs

Leftover Idea

It's wacky I realize, but it worked for me when I had leftover Sausage, Celeriac, and Apple Casserole (page 74) and Hominy and Chile Pepper Casserole (this page). I mixed the two together and baked it in a 350°F oven until slightly crispy on top, about 25 minutes, and it was great.

1 Preheat the oven to 350°F.

2 In a 12 × 9 × 2-inch baking casserole, spread the contents of 1 can of hominy over the bottom of the baking casserole. Arrange half of the chiles over the hominy and then half of the cheese. Spread half of the sour cream over the cheese and then repeat this layering using the other can of hominy and the remaining ingredients in the same order.

3 In a small skillet, melt the butter over medium-high heat, then toast the bread crumbs, stirring, for about 1 minute. Sprinkle the top of the casserole with the bread crumbs and bake until bubbly and golden on top, about 1 hour. Remove from the oven and let rest for 10 minutes before serving.

Corn Casserole

Although the American corn casserole had its beginnings in the Midwest, probably as a dish Native Americans were making, they are popular everywhere now. Each region gives its own little twist, perhaps oysters in New England, hot chiles in California, red and green bell peppers in the South, ham in Virginia, hot dogs in Nebraska, and cheddar cheese in Wisconsin. There is no doubt that it is a rich dish and should be served with that in mind—that is, keep your accompanying foods simple and lean, such as pan-seared chicken breasts and steamed green beans. Corn casserole, this one being pudding-like, is a versatile preparation because it can be made the day before and re-heated, and it freezes well without much loss in taste or texture. Some cooks like to spice this dish up by using hot red chiles instead of the red bell pepper, and you can do the same. • **Makes 4 servings**

2 cups fresh corn kernels (from 2 corn cobs)
3 large eggs
8 tablespoons (1 stick) unsalted butter, melted
1 cup sour cream
1 cup (about 3 ounces) diced Monterey Jack cheese
½ cup cornmeal
¼ cup diced red bell pepper
¼ cup diced green bell pepper
1½ teaspoons salt

1 Preheat the oven to 350°F. Lightly oil a 9 x 9 x 2-inch baking casserole.

2 Place the corn, eggs, and butter in a blender and blend until smooth. Place the sour cream, Monterey Jack cheese, cornmeal, bell peppers, and salt in a large bowl. Add the puréed corn from the blender and mix well.

3 Pour the corn mixture into the baking casserole and bake until firm and golden, about 50 minutes. Serve hot.

Barley Mushroom Casserole

This delicious casserole begs to be served with roast duck. Anyway, that's how I do it. The flavors are quite intense and every one loves this casserole, wondering why they don't eat barley more often. This is a Czech-American recipe that Czech families call *cerni kuba*, but it is also a popular Eastern European Jewish casserole. Some cooks use chicken broth to cook the barley, but here I use the mushroom soaking liquid. This recipe is adapted from *The Time-Life American Regional Cookbook* (Little, Brown, 1978).

• Makes 4 servings

½ cup dried mushrooms, such as shiitake or porcini
½ cup pearl barley
1½ teaspoons salt
1 small garlic clove, finely chopped
2 tablespoons finely chopped red onion
2 tablespoons melted lard or butter
¼ teaspoon dried marjoram
Freshly ground black pepper

1. Soak the dried mushrooms in 2 cups of tepid water for 30 minutes. Remove the mushrooms from the soaking liquid (reserving the liquid) and chop them finely. Add enough water to the soaking liquid to equal 3 cups total.

2. Combine the soaking liquid, chopped mushrooms, and barley in a heavy, medium flame- and oven-proof casserole. Stir in the salt, and bring to a boil over high heat. Reduce the heat to low and simmer until the barley is soft and the water nearly all absorbed, about 1 hour.

3. Meanwhile, preheat the oven to 350°F.

4. Stir the garlic, onion, melted lard, and marjoram into the barley mixture. Season with black pepper. Cover tightly and bake until the liquid is absorbed and the barley is moist, about 30 minutes.

Wild Rice Hot Dish

A "hot dish" is what they call a casserole in Minnesota and other northern states. This Minnesota casserole is a favorite cold weather dish, and Judith M. Fertig tells us in her *Prairie Home Cooking* that wild rice hot dish is more than a casserole, it is a Minnesotan potluck rite of passage. The state's native wild rice, which is, incidentally, not a rice but a grass, goes into this hot dish that almost always contains mushrooms, either dried or fresh, almonds, and some kind of meat, either beef, sausage, or chicken, or other fowl such as duck, pheasant, or grouse. Both the initial soaking period for the wild rice and the overnight resting specified in the instructions are necessary for a tender wild rice hot dish, so don't skip the steps and begin making the casserole a day ahead. • **Makes 6 servings**

4 tablespoons (½ stick) unsalted butter
6 tablespoons finely chopped onion
¼ cup all-purpose flour
1½ cups chicken broth
1½ cups half and half
1½ pounds very lean ground beef
¼ cup dried porcini mushrooms
1 tablespoon finely chopped fresh parsley
1 bay leaf
½ teaspoon dried thyme
¾ teaspoon seasoning salt (such as Knorr Aromat, Accent, or Dash)
½ teaspoon salt
¼ teaspoon freshly ground black pepper
¼ teaspoon sweet paprika
1 cup wild rice
1 cup slivered almonds, toasted (see page 295)

1. In a large saucepan or stew pot, melt the butter over medium-high heat, then add the onion and cook, stirring, until softened, about 4 minutes. Add the flour to form a roux and continue to cook, stirring, for 1 minute. Remove the saucepan from the heat and slowly whisk in the chicken broth and half and half. Return the saucepan to the heat, reduce the heat to low, and simmer, stirring, for 5 minutes. Add the beef, dried mushrooms, parsley, bay leaf, and thyme. Season the sauce with the seasoning salt, regular salt, black pepper, and paprika, and mix well, mashing the meat. Turn the heat off and set aside.

2. Place the wild rice in a bowl, cover with cold water, and let soak 15 minutes. Drain the rice and mix it into the sauce in the saucepan. Stir in the almonds. Cover with a lid and refrigerate overnight.

3. Preheat the oven to 350°F.

4. Transfer the mixture to a 13 x 10 x 2½-inch baking casserole. Cover and bake until golden brown and the liquid is nearly all absorbed, 1¾ hours. Uncover the casserole and bake another 45 minutes. Serve hot.

Toasting Nuts

Lightly roasting or toasting nuts intensifies their flavor by bringing out their essential oils. There are two ways to do it. The easiest way is to dry-roast in a greaseless small cast-iron skillet over medium-high heat, shaking the pan until the nuts are golden, about 2 minutes for pine nuts and 4 minutes for blanched almonds. Keep a close watch on them as they cook and remove them quickly so they do not burn. You can also put them on a tray in a toaster oven and roast at 400°F until they are golden.

Lentil and Bulgur Casserole

Although this is an American casserole, this type of food is quite typical of Turkish cuisine. It can be assembled quickly and is a delicious counterpoint to some baked lamb. You can stir leftovers into the Rice Pilaf with Spiced Turkey and Baby Lima Beans casserole (page 274) for an impressive repast on another evening. If you like, you can serve it with yogurt on the side. Bulgur, a cracked and sun-parched durum wheat product, is sold in different grades of grinding from # 1, the finest, to # 4, the coarsest, and they are used for different purposes. In this casserole you want to use the coarsest.

• Makes 4 servings

½ cup brown lentils, rinsed and picked over for stones
2 teaspoons salt plus more as needed
2 cups chicken broth
½ cup coarse bulgur (#4), rinsed
1 medium tomato, chopped
½ small onion, finely chopped
1 Anaheim chile (long green pepper), seeded and chopped
4 tablespoons (1/2 stick) unsalted butter, cut into thin slices

1 Preheat the oven to 350°F.

2 Place the lentils in a saucepan and cover with water by several inches. Bring to a boil, season with a little salt, and cook until tender, about 40 minutes. Drain and set aside in a 12 × 9 × 2-inch baking casserole.

3 Stir the chicken broth, bulgur, tomato, onion, Anaheim chile, butter, and 2 teaspoons of salt into the lentils in the baking casserole. Bake, uncovered without stirring, until the broth is absorbed and the bulgur tender, 55 to 60 minutes. Serve hot.

Vegetable Casseroles

with Meat

Sausage and Potato Pie

This is an American casserole, but its inspiration is the potato torta of Italy. You can vary the pie in any number of ways and all will be great. You could use chorizo or andouille sausage, or you could add chopped tomatoes. There's a Catalan dish similar to this one that is made with chopped Swiss chard and bacon. There are other potato and sausage pies around the country, but not all are Italian derived. In Maine, a popular potato and sausage pie is made with kielbasa, wine, and apple cider, but no cheese. This preparation is a delicious and rib-sticking one, so I would accompany it only with some steamed fresh green beans dressed with a little butter and Parmesan cheese, sautéed spinach in olive oil, or a garden salad.

• **Makes 4 to 5 servings**

2½ pounds boiling potatoes (such as Red Bliss or White Rose),
    peeled, cut into large pieces
1 large egg yolk
1 pound hot Italian sausages, casings removed
1 medium onion, chopped
¼ pound fresh mozzarella cheese, cut into ¼-inch cubes
½ cup plus 1 tablespoon freshly grated Parmesan cheese
2 tablespoons finely chopped fresh parsley

1. Preheat the oven to 350°F. Lightly oil a 9-inch deep-dish glass or ceramic pie pan.

2. Place the potatoes in a large saucepan and cover with cold water. Bring to a boil over medium-high heat, then cook at a gentle boil until tender and easily pierced by a skewer, about 40 minutes in all. Drain and set aside. Pass the potatoes through a food mill or colander and beat in the egg yolk. Alternately, you may combine the cooked potato pieces and egg yolk in a large bowl and beat with an electric mixer using the whisk attachment on low speed until smooth.

3. Meanwhile, in a medium skillet, cook the sausage over medium heat, stirring frequently to break up the meat, until browned, 15 to 20 minutes. Transfer the sausage to a bowl with a slotted spoon and set aside. Add the onion to the skillet and cook over medium heat in the sausage fat, stirring, until translucent, about 5 minutes. Transfer the onion to the bowl of sausage with a slotted spoon and set aside.

4. Add the sausage and onion, mozzarella cheese, ½ cup of Parmesan cheese, and parsley to the potato mixture and mix with an electric mixer on low speed. If doing this by hand, use a wooden spoon and mix vigorously.

5. Spoon the potato mixture into the pie pan and spread the mixture evenly around the pan, forming a smooth flat surface. Sprinkle the remaining 1 tablespoon of Parmesan cheese on top and bake until golden yellow, about 40 minutes. Remove from the oven, cool 5 minutes. Cut into pie wedges or squares, and serve.

Hungarian Potato Casserole

In Hungarian, this casserole is called *rakott krumpli*. It is usually made with fresh Hungarian sausage that one can find at some German, Polish, or Hungarian delis. Lacking fresh sausage, this is excellent with smoked Polish kielbasa, which is what I usually use. It is quite a filling dinner, so serve it with a green vegetable, such as green beans steamed with just a little butter and paprika. • **Makes 6 servings**

1½ pounds boiling potatoes
    (such as Red Bliss or White Rose)
6 large eggs
Salt and freshly ground black pepper
½ pound smoked Polish kielbasa,
    cut into ¼-inch-thick slices
1 cup sour cream

1. Preheat the oven to 450°F. Lightly coat a 12 x 9 x 2-inch baking casserole with vegetable oil.

2. Place the potatoes in a large saucepan and cover with cold water. Bring to a boil over medium-high heat, then cook at a gentle boil until tender

Leftover Idea

Take your leftover Hungarian Potato Casserole and spread it on the bottom of a buttered baking casserole. On top of that arrange as much cooked broccoli as you need to cover the potatoes. Sprinkle shredded sharp cheddar cheese on top and bake at 350°F until the casserole is heated through and the cheese has melted.

and easily pierced by a skewer, about 40 minutes in all. You can hard-boil the eggs at the same time in the same pot if you like. Place the eggs in the boiling water for 10 minutes exactly, remove the eggs with a slotted spoon, and set them aside in cold water. Shell the eggs and cut them into slices. Drain the potatoes, then peel and cut them into ¼-inch-thick slices.

③ Layer the potatoes on the bottom of the prepared casserole, season with salt and pepper, then lay the sliced eggs on top. Arrange the sliced sausages on top of the eggs, and sprinkle small dollops of sour cream over the top, using only half of the sour cream. Bake until slightly golden and the dollops of sour cream look like cheese, about 25 minutes. Serve with the remaining sour cream.

Casserole of Red Potatoes, Onions, and Garlic

This potato casserole is the easiest thing in the world to make and I usually serve it as an accompaniment to just about anything, and in particular roast turkey breast, roast Cornish hens, or pork shoulder roast. You can replace the lard with butter, but the lard does give it a delicious earthy taste.

• Makes 4 servings

¼ cup pork lard or butter
10 red-skinned potatoes (about 2 pounds), cut in half
1 large onion, cut into 8 pieces and separated
1 large garlic clove, finely chopped
Salt and freshly ground black pepper

1 Preheat the oven to 350°F.

2 In a 12 x 9 x 2-inch baking casserole, melt the lard in the oven, then remove, add the potatoes, onion, and garlic to the baking casserole, and toss to coat with the lard. Season with salt and pepper. Bake until crispy, about 1½ hours. Serve hot.

Herring and Potato Casserole

My grandmother was Finnish and her husband, my grandfather, was Italian, so my mother grew up with some interesting food. My grandfather worked nights, so their big meal was in the afternoon, which was always an Italian meal. But supper, while he was away at work, was often typical Finnish comfort food that grandma missed and my mother loved. This casserole is in the repertoire of many Finnish home cooks and is called *sillilaatikko*. In Sweden, they love this casserole too and call it *sillgratin*. The herring is usually sold in jars. The one you want to use in this dish is plain or preserved with onions and dill. • **Makes 4 to 6 servings**

3 tablespoons unsalted butter
1¼ pounds potatoes (such as russet), thinly sliced
5 ounces herring pieces (about 12 pieces)
Salt
1 medium onion, chopped
1 large egg
1 tablespoon all-purpose flour
2 cups whole milk
¼ teaspoon freshly ground white pepper

1. Preheat the oven to 375°F. Butter a 12 × 9 × 2-inch baking casserole with half of the butter.

2. Layer half of the potatoes on the bottom of the baking casserole, then place the herring pieces over the potatoes. Season with salt. Sprinkle the onion on top and finish by layering the remaining potatoes. Season the top lightly with salt.

3. In a bowl, beat together the egg and flour, then beat in the milk and white pepper. Pour over the potatoes and dot the top with the remaining butter. Bake until golden brown, 1 hour and 30 minutes to 1 hour and 40 minutes.

Lithuanian Potato Casserole

In the late nineteenth century, waves of Eastern European immigrants made their homes in what became the Rust Belt cities of America, such as Buffalo, Cleveland, Milwaukee, and Chicago. They had appalling hardscrabble lives filled with heartbreak, as so poignantly illustrated in Upton Sinclair's novel *The Jungle*, which first exposed the ghastly working conditions of the Chicago stockyards and meatpacking industry at the turn of the century. The immigrants brought with them their memories of foods from their homelands, and so one finds hearty potato casseroles in the northern Midwest. This potato casserole is a Lithuanian dish called *bublba kosha*. It makes a nice accompaniment to a pork or sausage stew. • **Makes 6 servings**

1 tablespoon vegetable oil
¼ pound salt pork, diced
2½ pounds Yukon Gold, Yellow Finn, or any baking potatoes,
    peeled and shredded
1 medium onion, peeled and grated
2 large eggs, beaten to blend
4 tablespoons (½ stick) unsalted butter, melted
¼ cup whole milk, heated just until starting to bubble around the sides of the pan
1 teaspoon salt
½ teaspoon freshly ground black pepper

1. Preheat the oven to 450°F. Lightly oil a 13 x 9 x 2-inch baking casserole.

2. In a small skillet, heat 1 tablespoon of oil over medium-high heat, then add the salt pork and cook, stirring, until brown and crispy, about 5 minutes.

3. In a large bowl, mix together the salt pork and its fat, the potatoes, onion, eggs, butter, milk, salt, and pepper. Spread the potato mixture in the prepared baking casserole and level the top. Bake for 20 minutes, then reduce the heat to 375°F and continue baking until golden brown, about 40 minutes. Remove from the oven, let cool 5 minutes, then serve.

Potato, Bacon, and Gruyère Casserole

This luscious dish is inspired by the casseroles one finds in Alsace or Savoy in France, where cheese and bacon love each other. This is a popular casserole and would make a nice accompaniment to a simpler meat dish, perhaps some pan-seared chicken breasts. For information about really good bacon, see page 258. • **Makes 4 servings**

3 tablespoons unsalted butter
2 large baking potatoes (such as russet) (about 1¾ pounds),
      peeled and cut into ¼-inch-thick slices
¼ cup finely chopped onion
Salt and freshly ground black pepper
¼ pound (about 1¼ cups) Gruyère cheese, shredded
¼ pound slab bacon, cut into 6 slices
1 cup half and half
½ cup crème fraîche or sour cream

1. Preheat the oven to 325°F. Coat a 10-inch round baking casserole with 1 tablespoon of butter.

2. Arrange half of the potato slices in the buttered baking casserole, slightly overlapping each other. Sprinkle with half of the onion, season with salt and pepper, and top with half of the cheese. Dot with the remaining butter.

3. Arrange the remaining potato slices over the first layer, sprinkle the remaining onion over the potatoes, season lightly with salt and pepper, and cover with the remaining cheese. Arrange the bacon over the cheese.

4. In a small bowl, whisk together the half and half and crème fraîche, then pour over the casserole. Bake until the top is dappled golden brown and bubbling, about 1½ hours. Serve hot.

Stuffed Bell Peppers

In the Mediterranean, on the island of Crete, there is a little taverna called Taverna Pantheon in the local market of Iraklion where shoppers can get a quick lunch. Displayed in a window counter in the front of the taverna as you enter is a huge and inviting casserole of baked *piperies yemisti*, stuffed peppers, as they are known in Greek. The peppers are stuffed with a deliciously seasoned mixture of ground lamb and rice and crowned with an inviting layer of baked Béchamel sauce and garnished with a tomato slice.

- **Makes 4 main-course servings or 8 appetizer or side-dish servings**

1 pound ground lamb
1 medium tomato, cut in half, seeds squeezed out,
    and the flesh grated against the largest holes of a
    box grater down to the peel
3 tablespoons finely chopped fresh parsley
2 tablespoons medium-grain rice
1 garlic clove, finely chopped
1 teaspoon ground allspice berries
½ teaspoon ground cinnamon
½ teaspoon ground cloves
Salt and freshly ground black pepper

For the Béchamel (white) sauce

3 tablespoons unsalted butter
3 tablespoons all-purpose flour
2 cups whole milk
Salt and freshly ground black pepper
Pinch of nutmeg

For the bell peppers

4 large bell peppers of any or multiple colors,
    cut in half lengthwise, seeds removed
Salt and freshly ground black pepper
1 large tomato, thinly sliced

1. Preheat the oven to 350°F. Lightly oil a 12 × 9 × 2-inch baking casserole.

2. In a bowl, mix together the lamb, tomato, parsley, rice, garlic, allspice, cinnamon, and cloves with your hands until well blended. Season with salt and pepper.

3. To prepare the Béchamel sauce, melt the butter in a small saucepan over medium-high heat, then add the flour stirring to form a roux. Cook for about 1 minute, then remove the saucepan from the heat and slowly whisk in the milk. Season with salt, pepper, and nutmeg. Return to the heat and simmer over low heat, stirring, until dense, about 15 minutes.

4. To prepare the bell peppers, arrange the pepper halves in the prepared baking casserole. Lightly salt the peppers. Stuff the peppers with the meat mixture. Spoon the white sauce on top. Garnish each with a slice of tomato and season with salt and pepper. Bake until the peppers can easily be skewered, about 1¼ hours. Let rest 10 minutes, then serve.

Cabbage Casserole # 1

B est baked in a casserole that is at least four inches deep, this cabbage casserole is usually served as a main course accompanied by mashed potatoes or buttered noodles on the side. It's very simple to prepare, has very little fat, and needs only to be salted properly. If you like, you can serve apple sauce, sour cream, or lingonberry preserves on the side. See page 381 for Cabbage Casserole #2 and page 382 for Cabbage Casserole #3.

• Makes 4 servings

3 tablespoons unsalted butter
1 medium onion, chopped
1 celery stalk, chopped
¾ pound lean ground beef
Salt
1 head green cabbage (about 2 pounds), cored and thinly shredded
2 Granny Smith apples, cored and thinly sliced

1 Preheat the oven to 350°F.

2 In a large skillet, melt the butter over medium-high heat, then add the onion and celery, and cook, stirring, until softened, about 6 minutes. Add the beef, season with salt, and cook, stirring and breaking up the meat with a wooden spoon, until browned, about 3 minutes.

3 Spread half of the cabbage in a large round or oval baking casserole that is at least 4 inches deep and has a heavy lid. Cover the cabbage with half of the apples and all of the meat mixture. Add the remaining cabbage and apple slices. Cover and bake until the cabbage is tender, about 1 hour. Serve hot.

Red Cabbage, Potato, and Apple Casserole

This recipe from Madrid is called *lombarda de San Isidro. Lombarda,* which means Lombardy (the region in northern Italy), is the word for red cabbage in Castile. Although this casserole makes for a very nice side dish with meat, it is traditionally served as a tapa at tapas bars in Madrid. If you do decide to make this as a tapa, remember that tapa servings are very small, so this recipe will yield twenty tapa servings.

• **Makes 8 side-dish servings and 20 tapas**

¼ cup pork lard or unsalted butter

2 medium onions, chopped

1 red cabbage (about 2 pounds), cored, thinly sliced

3 Granny Smith apples, peeled, cored, and finely chopped

¼ pound Canadian bacon, diced

¼ cup white wine vinegar

1 small bay leaf

1 teaspoon salt or more

Freshly ground black pepper

1 cup water

3 baking potatoes (such as russets) (about 1½ pounds total),
    peeled, each cut into 8 pieces

1 Preheat the oven to 350°F.

2 In a large round or oval flame- and oven-proof casserole (12 x 4½ inches deep), melt the lard over medium-high heat, then add the onions and cook, stirring, until softened, about 5 minutes. Add the cabbage, apples, and bacon, and cook for a few minutes, stirring to mix well. Add the vinegar, bay leaf, and 1 teaspoon of salt. Season with black pepper and stir to blend. Then add the water and bring the mixture to a boil.

3 Cover tightly and bake for 1 hour. Remove from the oven and arrange the potatoes pieces on top, then cover again and bake until the potatoes are tender, about 55 minutes. Season to taste with more salt, if desired. Serve hot.

Cabbage with Mascarpone Cheese and Juniper Berries

This casserole, typical of the northern and German-influenced regions of Italy, such as Friuli or Trentino-Alto Adige, is a delicious dinner on its own. But I like to make it to accompany a succulent slow-roasted pork shoulder. Savoy cabbage is a crinkly-leaf cabbage with a more delicate taste than green cabbage, but if you can't find it sometimes Napa cabbage works well, even though Napa cabbage is not a cabbage, but a mustard.

• **Makes 2 to 4 servings**

3 tablespoons extra-virgin olive oil
1 ounce salt pork, chopped
1 small Savoy cabbage (about ¾ to 1 pound),
    cored and very thinly sliced
Salt and freshly ground black pepper
8 dry juniper berries, crushed and coarsely ground in a mortar
¼ pound mascarpone cheese

Leftover Idea

If, when making Cabbage with Marscapone Cheese and Juniper Berries (this page), you've taken my suggestion to slow-roast a pork shoulder to serve with it, then you've got a great potential leftover casserole. Remove any fat from the leftover pork shoulder, cut the meat into small bite-size pieces and toss with the cabbage. Transfer the pork and cabbage to a baking casserole, sprinkle fresh bread crumbs on top, dot with butter, and bake at 350°F until golden.

1. Preheat the oven to 350°F.

2. In a large flame- and oven-proof casserole, heat the olive oil with the salt pork over medium-high heat, stirring, until the salt pork is turning crispy, 5 to 6 minutes. Add the cabbage and toss so it is coated with fat. Season with salt and pepper and sprinkle on the juniper berries.

3. Cover and bake until the cabbage is tender and completely wilted, about 1½ hours. Stir in the mascarpone cheese and bake for a few minutes until it is heated through and melted. Serve hot.

Stuffed Cabbage Rolls—Finland

This Finnish casserole of delicate cabbage leaves stuffed and rolled up with ground pork and rice is called *kaalikääryleet*, and is quite a favorite in both Finland and many parts of the United States, thanks to Finnish immigrants. Stuffed cabbage rolls are also popular in many northern and eastern European countries. These cabbage rolls can be served with boiled potatoes, and you will definitely want to serve them with lingonberry preserves. Leftover rolls can be frozen in resealable plastic bags for up to 3 months.

• Makes 20 to 26 rolls or 6 servings

1 large head green cabbage (about 2¾ pounds),
   central core removed
1 teaspoon salt plus more as needed
1 teaspoon vegetable oil
1 medium onion, chopped
1 pound lean ground pork
¾ cup cooked medium-grain rice (from about ⅓ cup raw rice)
1 teaspoon fresh or dried marjoram
¼ teaspoon freshly ground white pepper
1 tablespoon light corn syrup
1 tablespoon unsalted butter, melted
2 tablespoons all-purpose flour mixed with 1 tablespoon water
3 tablespoons heavy cream

1. Preheat the oven to 400°F. Lightly butter a 13 × 9 × 2-inch baking casserole.

2. Remove and discard any of the outermost leaves of the cabbage if they are blemished or damaged. Bring a large pot of water to a vigorous boil, add some salt, and plunge the whole cabbage into the water. Cook until the leaves can be peeled away without ripping, about 10 minutes. Drain well, saving about 1 cup of the cooking water. When cool enough to

handle, separate the leaves carefully, setting them aside. Chop the small inner leaves nearest to the core until you have about 1 cup of chopped cabbage.

3 In a skillet, heat the vegetable oil over medium-high heat, then add the onion and cook, stirring, until translucent, about 4 minutes. Transfer the onion to a bowl. Add the pork, rice, chopped cabbage, 1 teaspoon of salt, the marjoram, and white pepper, and mix until well blended. If the mixture feels pasty and thick, add ½ cup reserved cabbage cooking water and mix well.

4 Flatten the cabbage leaves and arrange a cabbage leaf in front of you with the harder white stem end closest to you. Place a heaping table-spoonful or more of the pork filling close to the end nearest to you and roll once away from you. Fold the sides in and continue rolling until a nice neat package is formed. Continue with the remaining cabbage leaves. Arrange the cabbage rolls side by side, seam side down, in the prepared baking casserole.

5 Stir the corn syrup and butter together and drizzle over the cabbage rolls. Season the cabbage rolls with salt. (The cabbage rolls can be refrig-erated at this point to bake later.) Bake the cabbage rolls for 30 minutes, then turn them over and continue baking until dappled golden brown on top, about 25 minutes, basting them with the reserved cabbage cooking water.

6 Transfer the cabbage rolls to a serving platter, keeping them warm. Pour the juices from the casserole (you should have about 1 cup, but if you don't, add enough reserved cabbage cooking water to make 1 cup) into a medium skillet and bring to a simmer over medium heat. Stir in the flour-and-water mixture and the cream and simmer until syrupy, about 5 minutes. Pour the gravy over the cabbage rolls and serve immediately.

Stuffed Cabbage Rolls—Poland

This famous Polish casserole of stuffed cabbage rolls is called *gołąbki* (pronounced ga-WUMP-kee), which means "little pigeons" in Polish. They are usually served as an appetizer, and leftovers are just wonderful, so don't be put off by the initial preparation time involved. Many variations of this recipe exist, as it is popular in Russia too. Some cooks mix up the meats differently, or grate some horseradish or carrots into the mixture. Other cooks use raw rice and others season the dish with dill. Whatever you do, you will have a very nice finished casserole. • **Makes 20 to 26 rolls or 6 servings**

1 large head green cabbage (about 2¾ pounds),
    central core removed
1¼ teaspoons salt plus more as needed
¾ cup medium-grain rice
8 tablespoons (1 stick) unsalted butter
1 cup chopped onion
1 pound lean ground beef
1 pound lean ground pork
1 pound ground veal
½ cup (about 3 ounces) finely chopped salt pork
½ teaspoon freshly ground black pepper
¼ teaspoon celery salt
¼ teaspoon dried marjoram
¼ teaspoon freshly ground nutmeg
1 cup ketchup
1 tablespoon Worcestershire sauce
2 cups water
1 cup tomato puree
1 tablespoon brown sugar

1 Preheat the oven to 325°F. Lightly oil a 13 × 9 × 2-inch baking casserole or 2 smaller baking casseroles.

2 Remove and discard any of the outermost leaves of the cabbage if they are blemished or damaged. Bring a large pot of water to a vigorous boil, add some salt, and plunge the whole cabbage into the water. Cook until the leaves can be peeled away without ripping, about 10 minutes. Drain well. When cool enough to handle, separate the leaves carefully, setting them aside.

3 In a small saucepan, bring 1½ cups of water to a boil over high heat and add the rice, ¾ teaspoon of salt, and 1 teaspoon of butter. Return to a boil, then reduce the heat to low, cover, and cook until the water is absorbed, about 10 minutes. Let cool and then fluff with a fork.

4 In a skillet, melt 1 tablespoon of butter over medium-high heat, then add the onion and cook, stirring, until light golden, about 4 minutes. Transfer the onion to a large bowl and mix in the beef, pork, and veal. Add the salt pork to the same skillet used to cook the onion and cook over medium heat, stirring, until crispy, about 4 minutes. Using a slotted spoon, transfer the salt pork to the meats. Season the meat mixture with ½ teaspoon of salt, the pepper, celery salt, marjoram, and nutmeg, mixing well. Add the ketchup, Worcestershire sauce, and cooked rice, and mix thoroughly.

5 Arrange a cabbage leaf in front of you with the stem end closest to you. Place 2, 3, or 4 tablespoons (depending on the size of the leaf) of the meat stuffing on the end closest to you, then roll away once, fold in the sides, and continue rolling away until a nice neat package is formed. Continue with the remaining cabbage leaves. Arrange the cabbage rolls side by side, seam side down, in the prepared baking casserole.

6 In a bowl, mix together the water, tomato puree, and brown sugar, and pour evenly over the cabbage rolls. Dot the top of the cabbage rolls with the remaining butter; cover with a lid or aluminum foil. (The casserole can be refrigerated at this point and baked later.) Bake until the cabbage rolls are very soft, slightly blackened on top and bubbling vigorously, about 2½ hours, moistening with water if the sauce is drying out. Serve by spooning the sauce over the cabbage rolls.

Stuffed Cabbage Rolls—Croatia

These cabbage rolls are a winter specialty, known as *arambašici* in their home of Sinj, a town near the Dinaric Alps on the Dalmatian coast of Croatia. Traditionally, this casserole of stuffed cabbage leaves is made from a whole head of cabbage that has been prepared as sauerkraut. My recipe uses fresh cabbage which is easier to find and is what a cook from Sinj would use in the summer. Each sauerkraut leaf, or as in this recipe, each cabbage leaf, is stuffed with beef, pork, bacon, and flavored with lemon zest, onion, garlic, cloves, and cinnamon. Each cabbage roll is separated from each other with pieces of pršut (Croatian prosciutto) and smoked tongue. *Arambašici* can also be made with grape leaves. Many cooks also like to make the casserole in the evening and then re-heat it the next day, and you should consider doing this since it becomes even more delicious the day after it is made. The casserole cooks a long time so the meats are very tender and the cabbage leaves become silky. The smoked bacon, smoked pork, smoked tongue, and prosciutto can all be picked up at the deli counter of most supermarkets. Beef suet, which is another name for the hard fat around the kidney that yields tallow, can also be found in supermarkets, but not all of them—and you're likely to have to order it from the butcher. Any beef fat is adequate for the recipe, not just suet. • **Makes 20 to 26 rolls or 6 servings**

1 tablespoon unsalted butter or ox kidney suet
1 large head green cabbage (about 2¾ pounds), central core removed
¾ teaspoon salt plus more as needed
1¼ pounds boneless beef neck meat or beef chuck, finely chopped
5 ounces smoked bacon (preferably) or lean slab bacon, finely chopped
2 ounces ox kidney suet, beef suet, or beef fat, finely chopped
6 ounces boneless pork shoulder or neck meat, finely chopped
2 large onions, chopped

3 large garlic cloves, finely chopped

Grated zest from 1 lemon

½ teaspoon ground cinnamon

½ teaspoon ground cloves

½ teaspoon freshly ground black pepper

¼ teaspoon ground nutmeg

Two 2-inch-long beef marrow bones (optional)

1 ounce smoked pork, finely chopped

2 ounces prosciutto, thinly sliced into strips

2 ounces smoked tongue, thinly sliced into strips

1 cup water plus more as needed

1. Preheat the oven to 300°F. Lightly coat a 13 × 9 × 2-inch baking casserole or 2 smaller baking casseroles with 1 tablespoon of butter.

2. Remove and discard any of the outermost leaves of the cabbage if they are blemished or damaged. Bring a large pot of water to a vigorous boil, add some salt, and plunge the whole cabbage into the water. Cook until the leaves can be peeled away without ripping, about 10 minutes. Drain well. When cool enough to handle, separate the leaves carefully, setting them aside.

3. In a large bowl, mix together the beef, bacon, 2 ounces of suet, and pork shoulder meat. Add the onions, garlic, lemon zest, cinnamon, cloves, ¾ teaspoon of salt, pepper, and nutmeg, and mix well with your hands.

The World of Cabbage

I know you'll enjoy the Stuffed Cabbage Rolls (this page), but you've got to take a look at these other memorable cabbage casseroles in the book, such as those on pages 381, 382, and 384. They're just great and sometimes I forget about them too.

④ Arrange a cabbage leaf in front of you with the stem end closest to you. Place 2, 3, or 4 tablespoons (depending on the size of the leaf) of the meat filling on the end closest to you, then roll away once, fold in the sides, and continue rolling away until a nice neat package is formed. Continue with the remaining cabbage leaves. Arrange the cabbage rolls side by side, seam side down, in the prepared baking casserole, making sure you leave some room to include the beef marrow bones, if using. Sprinkle the chopped smoked pork over the cabbage rolls. Place the prosciutto and smoked tongue slices between the cabbage rolls. Pour the water over the cabbage rolls and cover with aluminum foil. (The casserole can be refrigerated at this point to bake later.) Bake until the cabbage rolls are very soft, slightly blackened on top, and bubbling vigorously, about 4 hours. Remove the marrow from the bones if the marrow has not melted out of them already, and spread it around the casserole. Serve hot. The casserole can be cooled to room temperature and refrigerate overnight, then re-heated and served as an appetizer the next day.

Spinach and Chickpea Casserole

This combination of chickpeas and spinach is very popular in Spain, especially in the southern region of Andalusia where it might show up in soups or stews. This casserole is not only hearty and satisfying but it is awfully easy to whip together. Leftovers make great tapas, too. The marrow bones called for in the recipe will add flavor, but nothing great is lost if you don't have them. • **Makes 4 servings**

> 3 tablespoons extra-virgin olive oil
> One 15-ounce can cooked chickpeas, drained
> 2 beef or veal marrow bones (about ¾ pound) (optional)
> 3 large garlic cloves, finely chopped
> 1 teaspoon tomato paste
> ¼ cup water
> Salt and freshly ground black pepper
> 2 pounds spinach, trimmed of heavy stems, washed well

1. Preheat the oven to 400°F.

2. In a large flame- and oven-proof casserole, heat the olive oil over medium heat, then add the chickpeas, marrow bones, if using, garlic, and tomato paste, then the water. Season with salt and pepper. Cover and cook until the marrow inside the bones has softened a bit, about 15 minutes. (Cook 15 minutes even if not using the bones.) Add the spinach and cook until the spinach has wilted, about 5 minutes.

3. Remove the marrow from the bones and stir it into the vegetables. Discard the bones. Bake uncovered until very hot, about 15 minutes, and serve.

Pounti

The Auvergne region of France is noted for its luscious and rustic cuisine. This vegetable flan is cooked in an earthenware baking casserole and is a sterling example of the local cooking. Many cooks in the Auvergne region will also add prunes to the casserole, which makes a nice addition. Although my recipe doesn't include prunes, you can add a handful of them in Step 3, if you like. Traditionally it is eaten either hot or cold, but it is at its best as a leftover when you can cut it into slices and sauté it in butter. I usually like to serve pounti with either grilled garlic sausages or roast pork.

• **Makes 4 servings**

¾ pound Swiss chard with stems, chopped

1 small onion, chopped

2 ounces prosciutto fat or pork fat, chopped

½ cup coarsely chopped fresh parsley

1 teaspoon salt

½ teaspoon freshly ground black pepper

1 cup whole milk

½ cup all-purpose flour

2 large eggs, beaten to blend

Leftover Idea

Cut the leftover pounti into slices that are about the width of your finger. In a skillet, melt some butter over high heat, and once it stops sizzling, sauté the pounti slices a few minutes or until they are golden on the edges. These make terrific appetizers.

1. Preheat the oven to 350°F. Butter a medium baking casserole, preferably a 9-inch round earthenware one.

2. In a food processor, place the Swiss chard, onion, pork fat, and parsley, and blend until very finely chopped and almost paste-like. Do this in batches if your food processor is not big enough to blend the mixture all at once. Blend in the salt and pepper. Set aside.

3. In a large bowl, mix together the milk, flour, and eggs until smooth. Add the vegetable mixture and stir until blended. Transfer to the prepared baking casserole.

4. Bake until the pounti has set and a skewer pushed into the center comes out clean, about 45 minutes. Serve hot, warm, or at room temperature.

Baby Turnip Casserole in Duck Fat

This is my November casserole. The most beautiful young turnips start to show up at my farmers market about that time and I buy a bunch of turnips that are about an inch in diameter at the most. They are very sweet and accompany pork or roast duck quite nicely. I keep duck fat in a container in my refrigerator, saved from whenever I roast a duck, but some markets, such as Whole Foods, sell rendered duck fat. • **Makes 4 servings**

1½ pounds young turnips, trimmed and peeled
2 tablespoons rendered duck fat, melted
Salt and freshly ground black pepper

1. Preheat the oven to 350°F.

2. Place the turnips and duck fat in a medium baking casserole and season with salt and pepper. Stir the turnips so they are all coated with the fat. Bake until they are golden and tender, about 45 minutes, but keep checking if they are of different sizes. Serve hot.

Lima Bean Casserole

This casserole is always a surprise because it really brings out the flavors of the lima beans. It is usually served as a side course. Although salt pork provides a wonderful flavor, you can use slab bacon or pancetta too.

• Makes 4 servings

¼ pound salt pork, diced

1 medium onion, chopped

1 large carrot, peeled and finely diced

3 cups frozen lima beans

½ cup dry white wine

2 tablespoons unsalted butter

1 teaspoon salt

½ teaspoon freshly ground black pepper

1 Preheat the oven to 350°F.

2 In a medium flame- and oven-proof casserole or a skillet, brown the salt pork over medium heat, stirring, until crispy, about 4 minutes. Add the onion and carrot, and cook, stirring, until softened, 4 to 5 minutes. Add the lima beans, wine, butter, salt, and pepper. Cover and bake until the lima beans are tender, about 30 minutes. (If you have used a skillet, transfer the lima bean mixture to a 9 x 9-inch baking casserole before baking.)

Leftover Idea

Combine some leftover Baby Turnip Casserole in Duck Fat (previous page) with leftover Lima Bean Casserole (this page), and then add cubed pieces of cooked chicken or duck, and reheat in a baking casserole until very hot. Delicious and easy.

Hash of Brussels Sprouts with Bacon and Hazelnuts

I lived in New England for nearly fifteen years when my children were young, and as a result, our Thanksgiving dinners are served forth in traditional New England style. Brussels sprouts are traditional for the holiday, but not everyone likes them and I hate to leave them out. So at one Thanksgiving in the mid-1980s, I made up this dish that, believe it or not, gets gobbled up. This is a terrific preparation, and big servings are taken by everyone. This preparation can be made Thanksgiving morning and left in the casserole, with a quick re-heating just before serving. One thing to pay attention to is that you don't overcook the Brussels sprouts, otherwise no amount of bacon will save them. For people who don't like Brussels sprouts, the appealing trick here is that you can't recognize them because they're all chopped up.

• Makes 8 servings

1½ pounds Brussels sprouts, trimmed
4 tablespoons (½ stick) unsalted butter
6 slices maple-cured bacon, chopped
6 tablespoons crushed or chopped hazelnuts
Salt and freshly ground black pepper

1. Preheat the oven to 350°F. Lightly butter a 12 x 9 x 2-inch baking casserole.

2. Bring a saucepan of water to a boil. Blanch the Brussels sprouts in the boiling water for 3 minutes to preserve their bright green color. Drain and plunge them into ice water or cool under running cold water. Bring a saucepan of water to a boil again and cook until the Brussels sprouts are easily pierced by a skewer with only a slight resistance, 8 to 10 minutes. Drain, trim, and chop them coarsely.

3. In a large skillet, melt the butter with the bacon over medium-high heat, then cook, stirring frequently, until the bacon is browned and crispy, about 10 minutes. Drain all but ¼ cup of fat from the skillet. Add the hazelnuts to the remaining fat in the skillet, and cook, stirring, for 1 to 2 minutes. Add the chopped Brussels sprouts, season with salt and pepper, and cook, stirring, for 3 minutes. Transfer to the prepared baking casserole.

4. Let the casserole come close to room temperature, then bake until sizzling, about 25 minutes. Serve hot.

Irish Rutabaga Pudding

Making this delicious casserole as an accompaniment to a roast pork loin on St. Patrick's Day, all washed down with some Guinness Stout, will certainly please your Irish friends, not to mention yourself. It is also quite nice with some pan-seared thick pork chops, corned beef, or Irish stew. • Makes 4 servings

1¼ pounds rutabagas, peeled and cubed

4 slices bacon

3 tablespoons whole milk

2 large eggs, beaten well

1 teaspoon salt

1 teaspoon sugar

Pinch of ground cinnamon

Pinch of ground ginger

¼ cup fine dry bread crumbs

Leftover Idea

A nice filling winter time leftover is a mixture of Irish Rutabaga Pudding (this page) and Meat and Potatoes Hot Dish (page 54). Just place the leftovers from both in a baking casserole, add a few tablespoons of water, then cover and bake at 350°F until very hot.

1. Preheat the oven to 350°F.

2. Place the rutabagas in a large pot and cover with water by several inches. Bring to a boil over high heat, then boil until tender, 35 to 40 minutes. Drain, transfer to a bowl, and mash with a potato masher.

3. Meanwhile, in a skillet, cook the bacon over medium heat until crisp, about 12 minutes, then remove and crumble. Save 2 tablespoons of bacon fat. Add the bacon to the mashed rutabaga along with the milk, eggs, salt, sugar, cinnamon, and ginger.

4. Coat a 12 x 9 x 2-inch baking casserole with 1 tablespoon of the reserved bacon fat. Spread the rutabaga mixture in the bakinig casserole. Sprinkle the bread crumbs over the rutabaga mixture, and then sprinkle with the remaining reserved bacon fat. Bake until golden brown, about 1 hour. Serve hot.

Green Bean Casserole

You wouldn't know it from the name, but the green bean casserole is a favorite American classic. But a classic only since 1955 when it was invented in the test kitchen of the Campbell Soup Company in Camden, New Jersey. As with many of these American classics, the dish has its roots in the cooking of northern Europe, as it is rich and rib-stickingly satisfying. There are literally hundreds of recipes posted on the Internet and they are quite definite in calling for frozen green beans, cans of condensed cream of mushroom soup, Durkee French Fried Onions, and corn flakes or Ritz crackers for the topping. Although many people still gobble down the back label recipe, I've modernized this recipe so you can buy fresh crisp green beans that snap at the farmers market and make a truly delicious casserole that your family will love and ask for again. Water chestnuts, corn kernels, condensed cream of mushroom soup, and ground beef are all popular additions to green bean casserole, but I think bacon is the only meat you should consider in order to give the beans their due. You can also use cream cheese instead of, or in addition to, the Swiss cheese. Although I've modernized the recipe, I didn't want to take away its original purpose, so just remember that it's rich and the serving yield I recommend is a sensible approach. On the other hand, it's delicious, so four of you might polish it off easily. • **Makes 6 servings**

2 tablespoons unsalted butter (1 tablespoon if using
    Ritz crackers for the topping), melted
Salt
2 pounds fresh green beans, trimmed
6 slices bacon
1 medium onion, chopped
Freshly ground black pepper
2 cups sour cream or crème fraîche

½ pound Swiss cheese, shredded

½ cup fresh bread crumbs (see Note) or

    1 roll Ritz crackers (¼ pound), crumbled

1. Preheat the oven to 350°F. Butter a 12 × 9 × 2-inch baking casserole with 1 tablespoon of butter.

2. Bring a large saucepan of water to a boil, salt lightly, then blanch the green beans by cooking them in the boiling water for 3 minutes. Remove the beans with a skimmer, and let the water continue to boil while you rinse the beans under cold water in a colander. Once the water is boiling vigorously again, return the green beans and cook until tender but with a slight crunch, about 6 minutes. Drain and immediately run the beans under cold water in a colander to stop them from cooking. Place the green beans in a large bowl.

3. In a skillet, cook the bacon over medium heat until crispy, about 15 minutes, then crumble the bacon once it is cool enough to handle. Add the crumbled bacon to the green beans. Discard all but 3 tablespoons of bacon fat, then add the onion to the skillet over medium-high heat and cook, stirring, until softened, about 4 minutes. Transfer the onion to the bowl with the beans. Season with salt and pepper and toss well.

4. In a bowl, stir together the sour cream or crème fraîche and the Swiss cheese. Transfer to the bowl with the beans and fold together.

5. Transfer the green bean mixture to the prepared baking casserole, spreading it evenly. If using bread crumbs, toss them first with the remaining 1 tablespoon of melted butter. Sprinkle the buttered bread crumbs or the Ritz crackers over the top of the casserole. Bake until golden brown on top, about 25 minutes. Serve hot.

Note: This amount can be made from crumbling one ½-inch-thick slice of 5¼ × 3-inch French or Italian bread in a food processor.

Belgian Endives au Jambon

This rich casserole of ham-wrapped boiled endives with Mornay sauce comes from northern France. The soft-cooked endives have a pleasant texture and taste that most people are not familiar with because, typically, Belgian endives are used in salads. It is best as an accompaniment to a simple main dish, such as pan-seared chicken breasts. • **Makes 4 servings**

4 Belgian endives, any damaged outer leaves removed
4 thin center-cut slices Black Forest ham
4 tablespoons (½ stick) unsalted butter
5 tablespoons all-purpose flour
2 cups whole milk
1 cup (about 3 ounces) shredded Gruyère cheese
Salt and freshly ground black pepper

1 Preheat the oven to 400°F. Lightly butter a 9 x 9-inch baking casserole.

2 Bring a saucepan of salted water to a boil over high heat, then reduce the heat slightly and blanch the endives for 15 minutes. Remove the endives and drain well by letting them sit and cool in a colander or strainer. Wrap a slice of ham around each endive. Arrange the endives in the prepared baking casserole.

3 In a small saucepan, melt the butter over medium-high heat, then add the flour, stirring to form a roux. Remove the saucepan from the heat and slowly add the milk, stirring continuously, until blended. Reduce the heat to low and simmer, stirring occasionally, until dense, 12 to 15 minutes. Add a third of the cheese and season with salt and pepper.

4 Pour the sauce over the endives and sprinkle the remaining cheese on top. Bake until the cheese is light golden brown, 15 to 20 minutes. Serve hot.

Vegetable
Casseroles
without
Meat

Le Gratin Dauphinois

This famous dish from the Dauphiné, the region around Grenoble in France, is considered by many gourmets to be the finest potato dish ever invented. Interestingly, it not only has many spin-offs in many cultures, but it is also made in both the home and in Michelin-starred restaurants. It's hard to say where the original recipe came from, but this particular recipe is from Le Restaurant Rostang à Sassenage, famous in the 1960s as a 2-star Michelin restaurant on the outskirts of Grenoble, and the ancestral home-restaurant of the famous contemporary Parisian chef Michel Rostang.

- Makes 4 servings

4 tablespoons (½ stick) unsalted butter
1¼ pounds Yukon Gold or Idaho Russet potatoes,
     peeled, cut into ⅛-inch-thick slices
1½ cups whole milk
Salt and freshly ground black pepper
1½ cups heavy cream

1. Preheat the oven to 300°F. Generously butter a 10-inch round baking casserole (preferably earthenware) or flame- and oven-proof casserole with 2 tablespoons of butter.

2. Pat the potato slices dry with paper towels, then layer them in the prepared casserole in overlapping circular layers. Pour in the milk and season with salt and pepper. Place the earthenware casserole on a heat diffuser if it is not flame-proof and bring the milk to a boil over high heat. Pour in ½ cup of cream and dot the top with the remaining 2 tablespoons of butter.

3. Place the casserole in the oven and bake until the cream is all absorbed, the liquid reduced, and the potatoes golden brown without having formed a crust, adding the remaining 1 cup of cream in ¼-cup increments during the baking time, about 2 hours. Serve hot.

Potato and Mushroom Casserole

This eggy Czech-American potato casserole is not as rich as it sounds, but it is satisfying and would be a nice accompaniment to a lighter tasting meat, such as pork chops, pork tenderloin, or even duck. A side of sautéed red cabbage would complete the meal. • **Makes 4 to 6 servings**

> 2 pounds boiling potatoes
> 8 tablespoons (1 stick) unsalted butter
> 1 medium onion, chopped
> 2 pounds white button mushrooms, sliced
> 1½ teaspoons salt
> ½ teaspoon caraway seeds
> 1 cup whole milk
> 2 large eggs, lightly beaten

1 Preheat the oven to 350°F. Lightly butter a 12 × 9 × 2-inch baking casserole.

2 Place the potatoes in a large saucepan and cover with cold water. Bring to a boil over medium heat, about 20 minutes. Once the water reaches a boil, cook the potatoes until tender, about 20 minutes more. Remove the potatoes, then peel and cut them into ¼-inch slices.

3 In a large skillet, melt the butter over medium-high heat, then add the onion and cook, stirring, until softened, about 5 minutes. Add the mushrooms, salt, and caraway, and cook, stirring, until the mushrooms are slightly softened, about 5 minutes.

4 Arrange a third of the potatoes on the bottom of the buttered casserole. Cover with half of the mushrooms. Arrange another third of the potatoes over the mushrooms, cover with the remaining mushrooms, and then finally cover with the last third of the potatoes. In a bowl, mix the milk and eggs together and pour over the potatoes. Bake until the eggs are set, about 45 minutes. Serve hot.

Potato, Caramelized Onion, and Goat Cheese Gratin

This casserole has its roots in Le Gratin Dauphinois (page 332), the famous potato casserole of the Savoy region of France. Potatoes are one of the favorite ingredients in American casseroles and when you mix them with onions, cheese, milk, and butter it can get to be pretty heavenly. This recipe is adapted from one posted in a chat room on the Internet and whose original unnamed author says "you will be using this flavorful side dish quite often!" I like to serve this with a nice roast beef. • **Makes 6 servings**

The Potato Arrives in France

We know that the potato came from South America directly to Spain, and that it was being grown there by 1573. It has been assumed that the potato continued its journey north to France and the rest of northern Europe. In fact, it seems the potato may have come to France from the other direction, from England. English botanists of the time thought the potato was native to Virginia. But as with the Spanish potato, the French potato also began its journey in South America. It went to Virginia first, then to England. The potato then traveled to the continent, first to Belgium, then northern France and to Switzerland. The celebrated French agriculturalist Olivier de Serres devotes a chapter in his *Théâtre d'Agriculture et Mesnage des Champs*, published in 1600, to the potato, and tells us that the potato came to France from Switzerland, arriving first in the Dauphiné and then traveling south to his native Languedoc.

2 tablespoons extra-virgin olive oil

1 large onion, cut in half, then thinly sliced into half-rounds

1 teaspoon dried thyme

Salt and freshly ground black pepper

2 pounds Yukon Gold or White Rose potatoes,
      peeled and sliced ¼ inch thick

2 tablespoons finely chopped fresh parsley

½ pound soft goat cheese

3 tablespoons unsalted butter, cut into 8 slices

1 cup whole milk

1. Preheat the oven to 425°F. Lightly butter a 13 × 9 × 2-inch baking casserole.

2. In a large skillet, heat the olive oil over medium-high heat, then add the onion, season with the thyme, salt, and pepper, and cook, stirring frequently, until golden brown, about 12 minutes.

3. Meanwhile, place the potatoes in a saucepan with enough water to barely cover them. Bring the water to a boil over high heat, about 20 minutes, then reduce the heat to medium and cook until al dente, about another 20 minutes. Drain the potatoes and arrange half of them on the bottom of the prepared casserole. Season with salt and pepper and sprinkle the parsley over the potatoes. Layer the onion mixture over the potatoes. Crumble the goat cheese over the onion layer and add the remaining potatoes to cover the cheese. Dot the top with the slices of butter and more salt and pepper. Pour in the milk and bake until the liquid has evaporated and the sides are bubbling, about 35 minutes. Serve hot.

Potato, Tomato, and Onion Casserole

This Italian casserole from the southern provinces of Basilicata and Apulia is meltingly delicious. "Meltingly" isn't a word, but it should be and you'll see what I mean when you bake this. I like to cook it in an earthenware casserole, but use whatever you have. The three main ingredients get arranged in two layers, with each layer getting a topping of bread crumbs, pecorino cheese, and oregano. I would serve this casserole with a roast veal shoulder, pan-seared veal chops, or a roast chicken. • **Makes 6 servings**

2 pounds Yukon Gold potatoes, peeled and
    cut into ⅛-inch-thick slices
¾ pound onions, cut into thin slices
1 pound tomatoes, peeled, seeded, and chopped
Salt
2 cups (about 5 ounces) freshly grated pecorino cheese
6 tablespoons dry bread crumbs
2 teaspoons dried oregano
6 tablespoons extra-virgin olive oil plus more as needed

1. Preheat the oven to 400°F. Lightly oil a 10-inch round baking casserole (preferably earthenware).

2. Layer half of the potatoes, onions, and tomatoes, in that order, in the prepared casserole, then sprinkle with salt and half of the pecorino cheese, bread crumbs, and oregano, and then drizzle with some olive oil. Repeat this order for the remaining layer. Bake until crispy golden on top, about 45 minutes. Serve hot.

Cauliflower and Carrot Casserole

This is a simple little casserole that is quite nice in the winter with roast chicken. Buy the fattest carrots you can find, and boil the carrots and cauliflower together to cut down on preparation time. • **Makes 4 servings**

2 fat carrots (about 1 pound total), cut in half
1 small head cauliflower (about 1½ pounds), trimmed
3 tablespoons unsalted butter
3 tablespoons all-purpose flour
1½ cups whole milk
6 ounces Colby and/or Monterey Jack cheese, shredded
¼ teaspoon hot paprika
Salt and freshly ground black pepper
2 scallions, white and green parts, chopped

1 Preheat the oven to 350°F. Lightly butter a 12 × 9 × 2-inch baking casserole.

2 In a large saucepan or stockpot, bring lightly salted water to a boil over high heat. Add the carrots and cauliflower and boil together until they are easily pierced by a skewer, 15 to 18 minutes for the carrots and 12 to 15 minutes for the cauliflower. Remove both and let cool. Break the cauliflower into its florets and quarter the stem portion. Cut the carrots into 1½-inch segments. Set aside.

3 Meanwhile, in a saucepan, melt the butter over medium-high heat, then add the flour and stir to make a roux. Continue to cook, stirring, until light brown, 1 to 2 minutes. Remove the saucepan from the heat and slowly pour in the milk, whisking constantly. Return to low heat and cook, stirring, until dense, about 12 minutes. Add the cheese and continue cooking and stirring until the cheese has melted and blended with the sauce. Season with the paprika, salt, and pepper.

4 Arrange the cauliflower and carrots in the buttered casserole. Lightly salt and pepper the vegetables. Sprinkle the scallions over the vegetables. Spread the cheese sauce over the vegetables and bake until bubbly, about 20 minutes. Serve hot.

Potato and Cauliflower Casserole

American casseroles that are heavy on cheese and cream, usually sour cream, point to a northern European heritage. This rib-sticking casserole is rich, but because it is so delicious, a little taste goes a long way and makes it very satisfying when served with a crispy-skinned golden roasted chicken, some pan-seared pork chops, or some meatloaf (pages 36–38).

• Makes 6 servings

    1 pound boiling potatoes
    1 head cauliflower (about 1½ pounds), trimmed
    3 tablespoons unsalted butter
    3 tablespoons all-purpose flour
    1 cup heavy cream
    1 cup (about 3 ounces) shredded Swiss cheese
    Salt and freshly ground black pepper

Leftover Idea

The idea here is to mix two leftover casseroles, the Frankfurter Casserole with Macaroni (page 67) and the Potato and Cauliflower Casserole (this page). Cut up the leftover frankfurters into ½-inch pieces, and with the macaroni that remains, mix with the cooked Potato and Cauliflower Casserole. Arrange in a buttered baking casserole of appropriate size (depending on much leftovers you've got) and bake at 350°F until slightly crispy on top, about 25 minutes.

1. Preheat the oven to 350°F. Lightly butter a 12 × 9 × 2-inch baking casserole.

2. Place the potatoes in a large saucepan and cover with cold water. Bring to a boil over medium heat, about 20 minutes. Once the water reaches a boil, cook the potatoes until tender, about 20 minutes more. Remove the potatoes and cool slightly, then peel and dice them, and set aside.

3. Place the cauliflower in a steamer basket and steam it over boiling water until tender but firm, about 15 minutes. Remove the cauliflower and cool slightly. Break the cauliflower into florets, slice the thicker stem part, and set aside until needed.

4. In a saucepan, melt the butter over medium heat, then stir in the flour to form a roux. Continue to cook, stirring, for 1 minute. Remove the saucepan from the heat and whisk in the heavy cream until blended. Return to medium-low heat and stir in ½ cup of cheese until it has melted, stirring constantly. Season with salt and pepper.

5. Arrange the potatoes and cauliflower evenly on the bottom of the buttered casserole. Pour the cream sauce over the vegetables and sprinkle the remaining cheese on top. Bake until bubbly and lightly browned, about 20 minutes. Serve hot.

Cauliflower Casserole

The use of packaged cereals as an au gratin topping or filler is a mark of an American home cook. I'm sure there are people who roll their eyes when they see a recipe calling for corn flakes, but in this classic American family casserole made in many homes there is a satisfying taste that is just too delicious to pass up. Serving cauliflower casserole with sautéed hamburger steak or any kind of roast is perfect. • **Makes 4 servings**

> 1 head cauliflower (about 1½ pounds), trimmed
> 1 cup sour cream
> 1 cup (about 3 ounces) shredded mild cheddar cheese
> ½ cup crushed corn flakes cereal
> ¼ cup chopped green bell pepper
> ¼ cup chopped red bell pepper
> 1 teaspoon salt
> ¼ cup (less than 1 ounce) freshly grated Parmesan cheese
> 1 teaspoon hot paprika for sprinkling

Foolin' Around with the Cauliflower Casserole

The Cauliflower Casserole on this page is versatile in that you can add and take away at will. Remove the bell peppers and use cream and Gruyère cheese instead. Or give it an Italian twist by adding cooked rice, parsley, and Parmesan cheese and use chicken broth instead of cream. Make the casserole earthy with the addition of nutmeg and pork rinds or keep it colorful with the addition of broccoli florets. Give it color and a kick with cayenne pepper.

1. Preheat the oven to 325°F. Butter a 12 x 9 x 2-inch baking casserole.

2. Place the cauliflower in a steamer basket and steam over boiling water until tender but slightly firm, about 15 minutes. Remove the cauliflower and cool slightly. Break the cauliflower into florets, slice the thicker stem part, and set aside.

3. In a large bowl, stir together the sour cream, cheddar cheese, corn flakes, green and red bell peppers, and salt. Add the cauliflower and mix well, but gently. Transfer to the buttered casserole. Sprinkle the Parmesan cheese and paprika on top. Bake until crispy golden on top, 30 to 35 minutes. Serve hot.

Cauliflower and Fennel Casserole in Cream

A roasted pork loin or chicken would be a perfect match for this luscious casserole. You can prepare the casserole up to the point when the cream is added. Keep it refrigerated and then bake it a little longer than the 20 minutes called for in order to make sure it's very hot before you top it with the Parmesan cheese and place it under the broiler. If you don't have a flame- and oven-proof casserole, you can use a large skillet in Step 2 and then transfer the cauliflower and fennel to a casserole. • **Makes 6 servings**

1 head cauliflower (about 2 pounds), trimmed

4 fennel bulbs (about 2½ pounds total), top portion
    of stalks trimmed, quartered lengthwise

7 tablespoons unsalted butter

1 medium onion, chopped

1 cup heavy cream

Salt

1 cup (about 3 ounces) freshly grated Parmesan cheese

Leftover Idea

It's a lot of great-tasting vegetables all together, but combining some leftover Ukrainian Noodle and Spinach Casserole (page 266) with leftover Cauliflower and Fennel in Cream Casserole (this page) creates a great enjoyable taste that will leave you thinking that anything can be done. Arrange the two mixed casseroles in an appropriately sized lightly buttered casserole and bake at 350°F until bubbly, about 35 minutes.

Sweat the Onion

This is professional cook's talk for slowly cooking a chopped onion in a pan until it is soft and has released much of its water. As the onion softens it is "sweating." You'll use this technique in the Cauliflower and Fennel Casserole in Cream recipe (previous page).

1. Preheat the oven to 350°F.

2. In a large saucepan, bring lightly salted water to a boil over high heat, then cook the cauliflower until a skewer can be pushed easily through the core, about 12 minutes. Remove the cauliflower with a skimmer or slotted spoon and set it aside in a large bowl and let cool.

3. Return the water to a boil, then cook the fennel until tender, about 20 minutes. Drain and set it aside with the cauliflower. Break up the cauliflower into large florets.

4. In a large flame- and oven-proof casserole (11 or 12 inches in diameter), melt 4 tablespoons of the butter over low heat, then add the onion and slowly sweat it, stirring occasionally, until golden and nearly caramelized, about 45 minutes. Add the cauliflower and fennel to the casserole, increase the heat to medium and cook the vegetables until very hot, turning carefully, about 5 minutes. Pour in the cream and season with salt.

5. Place the casserole in the oven and bake uncovered until the cream is thicker, about 20 minutes. Remove the casserole from the oven. Increase the oven heat to "broil." Sprinkle the top of the casserole with Parmesan cheese and dot the top with the remaining 3 tablespoons of butter. Return the casserole to the oven under the broiler and brown the top, about 5 minutes or less. Serve hot.

Casserole of New England Spring Vegetables

Having lived in New England for fifteen years and being a vegetable gardener, I can assure you that when spring had sprung we kept our eye on one important thing, and that was the last frost-free date, which was, after all, guessing. But we would have some magnificent overwintered spring vegetables to choose from for this casserole. There was the pungent garlic aroma of the spring ramps that grew on the embankment of the bike path near my house that you could smell as you walked by. There were the wild asparagus tips poking out of the ground, and there were spring peas, and fiddleheads, a kind of fern, which I left behind when I moved to California. But this casserole can be made wherever there are vegetables in the spring. All you need to do is pick three of the freshest, prettiest, snappiest, and sweetest vegetables that the farmers market offers every spring. If you're buying the vegetables in a supermarket, examine them a little more carefully since supermarket produce sections don't sell fruits and vegetables that are always grown locally and seasonally. • **Makes 4 servings**

2 tablespoons unsalted butter
2 tablespoons all-purpose flour
1 cup whole milk
½ teaspoon salt
½ teaspoon freshly ground black pepper
1 cup green beans, cut into 1-inch lengths
1 cup shelled fresh sugar snap peas
8 young asparagus tips
½ cup fresh bread crumbs (see Note)
1 cup (about 3 ounces) shredded mild cheddar cheese

① Preheat the oven to 350°F.

② In a small saucepan, melt the butter over medium heat, then add the flour and stir to make a roux. Continue to cook, stirring constantly, for 1 minute. Remove the saucepan from the heat and whisk in the milk, salt, and pepper to form a white sauce. Return to medium-low heat and cook, stirring, until thicker, about 12 minutes.

③ Bring a large saucepan of water to a boil and cook the green beans, peas, and asparagus together until all are tender, about 7 minutes. Drain in a strainer and run cold water over the vegetables to stop them from cooking. Set the asparagus aside from the other vegetables. Toss the green beans, peas, and bread crumbs together and place them in a 9 x 9 x 2-inch baking casserole. Cover the vegetables with the white sauce, and arrange the asparagus tips on top. Sprinkle with the cheese. Bake until the cheese is completely melted and bubbling slightly, about 30 minutes.

Note: This amount can be made from crumbling two ½-inch-thick slices of 5¼ x 3-inch French or Italian bread in a food processor.

Sophia Loren's Asparagus Casserole

The Oscar-winning Sophia Loren is considered the most beautiful, talented, and alluring actress of her time. Unknown to many in her legions of fans, she is also an excellent cook. In the late 1960s while she was pregnant with her son Carlo, she was under doctors' orders to rest and not make any movies, and, to keep herself busy, she took the suggestion of a friend to write a cookbook. The book, *In the Kitchen with Love*, is a real cookbook and a charming insight into the favorite dishes of her poor Neapolitan upbringing. In her recipe for asparagus, she tells us that this dish "has won many an Italian heart." I don't doubt it, as it's delicious and makes a terrific antipasto. She says that you "boil the asparagus according to the golden rule," that is, tied in a bundle and steamed upright in an asparagus steamer. • **Makes 4 servings**

¾ pound asparagus (about 12), stalks peeled
3 ounces Swiss or fontina cheese, cut into long thin slices
1 tablespoon unsalted butter
Salt and freshly ground black pepper
5 tablespoons tomato sauce (page 243)

1. Preheat the oven to 350°F. Butter a medium baking casserole.

2. Tie the asparagus spears into a bundle with kitchen twine if they aren't already bundled with a rubber band. Bring several cups of water to a boil in an asparagus steamer or in a saucepan. Cook the asparagus until tender, making sure the tender tips steam and don't boil by keeping the tips above the water line, 6 to 7 minutes. (If you are using an asparagus steamer the bundle will stand upright; if using a saucepan, the bundle will lean to one side.) Remove and separate the spears into smaller bundles of 3 spears each.

3. Wrap each smaller bundle of asparagus with a slice of cheese and then arrange it in the buttered casserole. Season with salt and pepper. Spread the tomato sauce over the top and bake until the cheese is barely melted, about 6 minutes. Serve immediately.

Zucchini Casserole

I like to use young zucchini for this casserole, those that are about 5 inches long, and arrange them in rows and cover them with the sour cream which, when baked, forms a kind of light crust. You can use fresh oregano or mint instead of the dill, if you like. This dish is nice served with a beef or chicken casserole or as a leftover (see box). • **Makes 4 servings**

> 1¼ pounds young zucchini, split in half lengthwise
> Salt and freshly ground black pepper
> 2 cups sour cream
> ¼ cup chopped fresh dill
> 2 tablespoons extra-virgin olive oil

1. Preheat the oven to 350°F.

2. Arrange the zucchini halves in a 13 × 9 × 2-inch baking casserole, cut side up. Season with salt and pepper. In a bowl, stir together the sour cream, dill, and olive oil, then season with salt and pepper. Spoon the sour cream mixture over the zucchini until they are all covered. Bake until the top is a light golden, about 40 minutes. Serve hot.

Leftover Idea

My supermarket regularly sells smoked boneless pork chops that are nothing but the famous German smoked pork preparation called *Kasseler rippchen*. I doubt it will be labeled as such on the package, but these chops are just great. They're usually sold near the bacon. Top leftover Zucchini Casserole (this page) with the chops and heat it in the oven to your liking. You can smear some horseradish sauce, mustard, or sour cream on top.

Zucchini Parmesan

*P*armigiana di zucchini is the poor cousin of the better known eggplant Parmesan. This is unfortunate, because this famous Neapolitan vegetable casserole is a lighter side dish and sometimes is served as an appetizer at room temperature. It involves much less preparation than its eggplant relative, and is a great casserole for late summer when your zucchini plant, if you've got one, is producing like crazy. • **Makes 6 servings**

4 pounds zucchini, cut lengthwise into ¼ inch thick slices
½ cup plus 2 tablespoons extra-virgin olive oil or more if needed
2 cups tomato puree (preferably freshly made)
¼ cup finely chopped onion
¼ cup water
8 large fresh basil leaves, finely chopped
Salt and freshly ground black pepper
¼ cup (less than 1 ounce) freshly grated Parmesan cheese
½ pound fresh mozzarella cheese, sliced

1. Preheat the oven to 425°F. Coat a 13 x 9 x 2-inch baking casserole with some olive oil.

2. Arrange the zucchini slices on a paper towel-lined baking sheet or a platter and leave exposed to the air for 30 minutes. Pat dry with paper towels.

3. In a large skillet, heat ½ cup of olive oil over high heat. Working in batches, fry the zucchini slices until golden on both sides, turning with a fork, 4 to 5 minutes. Remove from the skillet with a fork and set aside on a paper towel-lined baking sheet or platter to drain.

④ Meanwhile, in a saucepan, combine the tomato puree with the onion, water, and basil. Season with salt and pepper. Bring to a simmer over medium heat. Reduce the heat to medium-low and continue cooking, stirring occasionally, until a little denser, about 5 minutes.

⑤ Arrange the zucchini on the bottom of the prepared casserole, with all the slices facing the same direction and overlapping if necessary. Sprinkle the zucchini slices with the Parmesan cheese, salt, and pepper. Spoon half of the tomato sauce over the zucchini, then lay the mozzarella slices over the tomato sauce, and finally spoon the remaining tomato sauce over the mozzarella. (The casserole can be refrigerated at this point to bake later.) Bake until bubbling furiously, about 30 minutes. Remove from the oven and let rest 10 minutes before serving, or serve at room temperature.

Zucchini and Corn Tostada Casserole

One of the things I like about this casserole is that leftovers taste so great. There is some assembly involved, but once you put it together you can keep it refrigerated until time to bake, making it a convenient casserole too. Roasting the chiles beforehand provides lots of extra flavor, so don't skip that procedure. If you want, you can leave out the green tomatillo sauce. And you can bake rather than fry the tortillas, although I think frying them is better because it gives you an opportunity to eat some while you're cooking. For some more information on the chiles needed for this recipe, see page 217. • **Makes 4 servings**

½ pound tomatillos, husks removed and tomatillos washed
¾ small onion, chopped
2 fresh green serrano chiles, chopped
2 tablespoons finely chopped fresh cilantro leaves
Salt
1 large poblano chile
1 large jalapeño chile
1 cup vegetable oil
Three 8-inch flour tortillas
2 small zucchini (about ½ pound total), diced
1 ear of corn, kernels removed (about 1¼ cups)
1 large garlic clove, finely chopped
½ teaspoon ground cumin
¼ teaspoon cayenne pepper
Freshly ground black pepper
1½ cups (about 5 ounces) shredded Monterey Jack cheese
    or a mixture of meltable Mexican cheeses such as
    queso fresco, queso ranchero, or *queso panela*

1. Bring a medium saucepan of salted water to a boil and cook the tomatillos until they start to become tender, about 8 minutes. Drain, place in a food processor, and puree briefly until a little chunky. Add ⅓ of the onion, serrano chiles, and 1 tablespoon of the cilantro, and blend again. Pour into a bowl, season with salt, and let stand ½ hour before using.

2. Meanwhile, preheat the oven to 450°F.

3. Place the poblano and jalapeño chiles in a baking pan and bake until their skins turn crispy black, 25 to 30 minutes. Cool the chiles slightly, then scrape off their skins and remove the seeds. Cut the poblano into strips and slice the jalapeño into thin rounds. Reduce the oven temperature to 350°F.

4. In a skillet, heat the vegetable oil over medium-high heat for 10 minutes, then cook the tortillas on both sides until they are golden and crispy, 15 to 30 seconds in all. Set aside in a 12 × 9 × 2-inch baking casserole, ripping them to fit.

5. Remove all but 2 tablespoons of the oil in the skillet. To the remaining oil, add the zucchini, corn kernels, remaining onion, and garlic, and cook over medium-high heat, stirring, until the onion is softened, about 5 minutes. Add the reserved chiles, the remaining tablespoon of cilantro, the cumin, cayenne, and some salt and pepper. Continue to cook, stirring, for 2 minutes.

6. Spread the vegetable mixture over the tortillas. Sprinkle the cheese over the top of the vegetables and bake until the cheese is bubbling, about 25 minutes. Serve hot.

A History of Eggplant Parmesan

Although it is commonly accepted that eggplant Parmesan is from Naples, some food writers have claimed that the dish is originally from Parma in the Emilia-Romagna region of northern Italy. They argue that one of eggplant Parmesan's principal ingredients is Parmesan cheese, which is from and named after Parma in northern Italy. I've never been persuaded by that line of thinking for a number of reasons. First, eggplant made its first appearance in Italy in Sicily and the southern regions, not in the north, and it's likely that a dish for eggplant would be invented in the south. Second, the dish is famous in the Campania region in general, Naples in particular, as well as in Sicily and Calabria, and not in Parma. Those who argue against this agree that today eggplant Parmesan is a Campanian or Sicilian dish, but that its name derives from Parmigiano (Parmesan) cheese, the predominant cheese used in the dish. Since Parmigiano is not native to those southern regions and is native to Parma it is likely the dish was originally from that city.

But from at least the fourteenth century Parmesan cheese was a widely traded cheese and found throughout Italy. The first mention of something resembling an eggplant Parmesan is found in "Il Saporetto" by the Medieval Italian poet Simone Prudenzani (1387–1440), whose recipe refers to Parmigiano cheese. The eighteenth-century Neapolitan chef Vincenzo Corrado mentions in his book *Il cuoco galante*, published in 1786, that eggplant can be cooked "alla Parmegiana," meaning the eggplant was seasoned with butter, herbs, cinnamon, and other spices and grated Parmigiano cheese, and covered with a cream sauce made with egg yolks before being oven-baked.

There are some less plausible theories of its origins, such as that of the Sicilian food authority Pino Correnti who suggests that the word actually comes from *damigiana*, a sleeve made of wicker where you put a wine bottle, or in this case, the hot casserole. Another explanation is reported by cookbook authors Mary Taylor Simeti, Vincent Schiavelli, and several others. They suggest that the name has nothing to do with Parmigiano cheese or Parma the city, but derives from the Sicilian word *palmigiana*, meaning "shutters," the louvered panes of shutters or palm-thatched roofs that the layered eggplant slices are meant to resemble, and not from *parmigiana*. Simeti suggests that since the Sicilians have a "probrem" pronouncing the "l" it became *parmigiana*. Another Sicilian food writer, Franca Colonna Romano Apostolo, suggests that the name is *parmiciana*, the equivalent in Sicilian dialect to "Persian," and not *parmigiano*, a cheese that is not important to the original dish. None of these other explanations hold much water though.

Eggplant Parmesan

*P*armigiana di Melanzane, eggplant Parmesan, is one of the classic dishes of Naples and is known in the rest of Campania and Sicily as well. In Sicily, eggplant Parmesan is popular in Palermo, and in other parts of the island, and it is sometimes made with potato slices. The Sicilian version does not emphasize Parmesan cheese, as does the Neapolitan version, and it may be made with raisins and pine nuts too.

The eggplant is cut into slices as thin as paper or as thick as half an inch, although I find the best to be about a quarter inch thick. Different cooks drain the eggplant of its bitter juices in varying amounts of time, ranging from thirty minutes to two hours. Thirty minutes is sufficient. Then the eggplant gets fried—and here recipes diverge. Some cooks dip the eggplant slices in batter or egg before frying, some just fry it, and many flour it before frying, while others more concerned with making the dish light will bake or grill the eggplant slices. If you are frying it, flouring it first is a good method because it will reduce the amount of oil the eggplant absorbs. The tomato sauce is a simple sauce but you must pay attention to get it right. It is a typical tomato sauce made of onions fried in olive oil and then the tomato is cooked with basil, salt, and pepper until quite dense. It is passed through a food mill to make it smooth. At this point the eggplant gets layered. On the bottom of the baking casserole goes a little tomato sauce, then the eggplant, the mozzarella or fiordilatte cheese, some basil, Parmesan cheese, egg slices, and then tomato sauce. One continues in this manner ending with a layer of tomato sauce sprinkled with Parmesan cheese, sliced eggs (sometimes), mozzarella cheese, and more Parmesan, and then it's baked.

Eggplant Parmesan is made a bit differently by Italian Americans, many of whom bread the eggplant before frying it. The traditional eggplant Parmesan is a heavy dish because the eggplant absorbs an enormous amount of oil even after you have blotted and drained it. For this reason, one normally does not serve huge portions, but rather smaller portions which are very filling. Alternatively, some cooks don't bother to fry the eggplant at all, and that will make for a much lighter, but less authentic, preparation. Leftovers can taste even better than the original dish, so go ahead and make this large casserole. • **Makes 8 servings**

4 eggplants (about 4 pounds total), sliced ¼ inch thick
Salt
4 pounds ripe tomatoes or three 28-ounce cans
    whole tomatoes, with juice, peeled, seeded,
    and chopped
3 cups olive oil for frying
All-purpose flour for dredging
¼ cup extra-virgin olive oil
1 medium onion, chopped
1 bunch fresh basil leaves, chopped
Freshly ground black pepper
1 pound fresh mozzarella cheese,
    very thinly sliced or chopped
¼ pound Parmesan cheese, freshly grated
4 large hard-boiled eggs, shelled and sliced, or
    4 large eggs, beaten one at a time as needed

1 Lay the eggplant pieces on some paper towels and sprinkle with salt. Leave them to drain of their bitter juices for 30 minutes, then pat dry with clean paper towels. Place the chopped tomatoes in a colander or strainer and drain for 1 hour.

2 Preheat the oil for frying in a 12-inch skillet over medium-high heat for about 10 minutes or until it reaches 375°F.

③ Working in batches, dredge the eggplant slices in the flour, patting off any excess, and fry them until golden brown, about 4 minutes a side. Drain on paper towels. Change the paper towels at least once; this way you will remove a good deal of residual olive oil.

④ In a large skillet or casserole, heat the extra-virgin olive oil over medium-high heat, then add the onion and cook, stirring frequently, until translucent, about 5 minutes. Add the tomatoes and 2 tablespoons of the chopped basil. Reduce the heat to low and simmer, stirring occasionally, until quite dense, about 30 minutes. Pass the tomato sauce through a food mill and return to a medium saucepan. Season with salt and pepper and cook over medium heat until the remaining water is nearly gone, 8 to 10 minutes.

⑤ Meanwhile, preheat the oven to 400°F.

⑥ Cover the bottom of a 13 × 9 × 2-inch baking casserole with a few tablespoons of tomato sauce, then cover it with some of the eggplant slices. Sprinkle on some mozzarella, Parmesan, basil, a few egg slices or beaten egg, salt, pepper, and tomato sauce. Continue in this order until the eggplant slices are used up, finishing the last layer with a sprinkling of Parmesan cheese. Bake until bubbling and the Parmesan top is beginning to brown slightly, about 20 minutes. Serve hot, warm, or at room temperature.

Eggplant, Tomato, and Ricotta Cheese Casserole

T he ricotta cheese in this casserole doesn't melt. The dollop of ricotta retains its shape and turns an inviting golden brown. I like to make this casserole in September when eggplants and tomatoes are so flavorful. The leftovers make a very nice appetizer served at room temperature the next day, or you can toss the leftovers with just about any other Italian-American casserole to create an entirely new one. • **Makes 6 servings**

2 pounds small Italian or Japanese eggplants,
   peel left on, cubed
Salt
½ cup extra-virgin olive oil
¼ cup finely chopped fresh basil
¼ cup finely chopped fresh parsley
3 large garlic cloves, finely chopped
1 teaspoon dried oregano
3 ripe tomatoes (about 1 pound total) or
   one 28-ounce can whole tomatoes, with
   its juice, peeled and cubed
½ pound ricotta cheese

1. Lay the eggplant pieces on some paper towels and sprinkle with salt. Leave them to drain of their bitter juices for 30 minutes, then pat dry with clean paper towels.

2. Meanwhile, preheat the oven to 375°F. Lightly oil a 13 × 9 × 2-inch baking casserole.

3. In a bowl, stir together the olive oil, basil, parsley, garlic, and oregano. Set the olive oil dressing aside.

4. Arrange the eggplant pieces on the bottom of the prepared casserole. Scatter the tomatoes around evenly. Place spoonfuls of ricotta cheese over the casserole, pushing them in between the eggplant and tomato pieces, then sprinkle the top of the casserole with salt. Pour the olive oil dressing over everything and bake until the eggplant is soft and the ricotta golden, about 1 hour. Serve hot or at room temperature.

Casserole of Eggplant Rolls

T his Sicilian casserole is known as *involtini di melanzane* and there are many variations of the basic recipe. The fact that this particular recipe I collected in Sicily many years ago uses Béchamel sauce indicates that the original recipe was probably a monzù recipe. The monzù were the chefs of the Sicilian and Neapolitan aristocracy in the nineteenth century who were often trained in classical French cuisine and incorporated French culinary techniques into their cooking. Japanese eggplant is one of the names used for the long, narrow, and light purple-skinned eggplant cultivar.

• Makes 4 servings

1½ pounds Japanese eggplant, peeled and cut
 lengthwise into ½-inch-thick slices
Salt
4 to 6 cups olive oil for frying

For the Béchamel (white) sauce

1½ tablespoons unsalted butter
3 tablespoons all-purpose flour
1 cup whole milk
Salt and freshly ground black pepper
½ cup (1 ounce) freshly grated Parmesan cheese
3 ounces fresh mozzarella cheese, cut into small dice
2 ounces provolone cheese, cut into small dice

For the tomato sauce

1 pound ripe tomatoes, cut in half, seeds squeezed out,
 and flesh grated against the largest holes of a box grater
 down to the peel, or one 28-ounce can whole tomatoes,
 drained of juices, chopped
Salt
10 fresh basil leaves

1. Lay the eggplant slices on some paper towels and sprinkle with salt. Leave them to drain of their bitter juices for 30 minutes, then pat dry with clean paper towels.

2. Preheat the oil to 360°F in a deep fryer or an 8-inch saucepan fitted with a wire fry basket. Fry the eggplant until pliable and lightly browned, about 2 minutes. Drain on paper towels and reserve. Let the frying oil cool, strain if necessary, and save for future deep-frying use, if desired.

3. To make the Béchamel sauce, in a small saucepan, melt the butter over medium-high heat, then add the flour and stir to form a roux. Continue to cook, stirring, for about 1 minute. Remove the saucepan from the heat and slowly whisk in the milk. Season the sauce with salt and pepper. Return to low heat and simmer, stirring frequently, until dense, about 15 minutes. Remove from the heat and add the Parmesan cheese. Cover the sauce and cool. Once the sauce is cool, stir in the diced mozzarella and provolone cheese and refrigerate until cold.

4. To make the tomato sauce, put the tomatoes in a large skillet and cook over medium-high heat, stirring frequently, until dense, 15 to 25 minutes, depending how juicy they are. Season with salt. Finely chop half of the basil leaves and stir into the sauce. The sauce should be dense and not liquidy.

5. Meanwhile, preheat the oven to 350°F. Lightly oil a 9 x 9 x 2-inch baking casserole.

6. Lay each slice of cooked eggplant on a work surface in front of you and spread the cold Béchamel mixture over the length of the slice. Roll slices up and arrange snugly in rows in the casserole. Spoon the tomato sauce over the rolls. Snip the remaining basil leaves into thin strips with kitchen scissors, and place half of the remaining basil leaves randomly between the rolls. Sprinkle with black pepper and bake until the cheese is melted and bubbling, about 30 minutes. Serve hot with the remaining basil leaves sprinkled over the top.

Eggplant Cutlet Casserole

Eggplant cutlets are an Italian-American dish. This casserole is handy because it can be assembled beforehand and kept aside until you're ready to bake. It's a real winner, especially if you already love dishes like Eggplant Parmesan (pages 353–355). When I'm not stuffing leftovers of it into a sandwich, I also dice the leftovers and toss them with pasta. • **Makes 4 servings**

1 eggplant (about 1¼ pounds), cut lengthwise
    into ⅓-inch-thick slices
Salt
1 large egg
1½ cups dry bread crumbs plus more as needed
2 to 3 cups olive oil
½ teaspoon dried oregano
Freshly ground black pepper
6 ounces provolone cheese, sliced
1 large tomato (¾ pound), sliced (see Note)
3 tablespoons freshly grated Parmesan cheese

Leftover Idea

Every Italian American knows what you do with a leftover eggplant cutlet (this page). You take an 8-inch-long Italian hero roll and split it down the middle. Tuck the leftover eggplant cutlet in, layer some mozzarella or provolone cheese on top, spoon some tomato sauce (page 243) on top of the cheese, sprinkle the sauce with some Parmesan cheese, then place the hero on a baking tray, and stick into a 450°F oven until the bread is crisp and the cheese dripping. Ohmygod it's good!

1. Lay the eggplant on some paper towels and sprinkle with salt. Leave them to drain of their bitter juices for 30 minutes, then pat dry with clean paper towels.

2. Meanwhile, preheat the oven to 350°F.

3. Beat the egg on a plate and pour the bread crumbs on a piece of wax paper. Dip the eggplant slices in the egg to coat on all sides and then dredge in the bread crumbs.

4. Meanwhile, in a large skillet, heat the olive oil over medium-high heat for 10 minutes, then cook the eggplant cutlets until golden brown on both sides, 6 to 7 minutes in all. Remove from the skillet and arrange in a 13 x 9 x 2-inch baking casserole. The eggplant cutlets can cook in two or three batches, or you could use two skillets. Do not overcrowd the skillet when frying.

5. Sprinkle each eggplant cutlet with oregano, salt, and pepper. Lay a slice of provolone over each eggplant cutlet, and then top each with a slice of tomato. Sprinkle with Parmesan cheese. Bake until the cheese is completely melted and the juice from the tomato is bubbling, about 30 minutes. Serve hot.

Note: Instead of using sliced tomatoes in Step 5, you can use a few tablespoons of tomato sauce (page 243).

Summer Vegetable Casserole from Turkey

Atypical casserole made in the summer by many Turkish families is known as *güveç yaz* (summer casserole), while in the winter they make *güveç kiş* (winter casserole), a winter dish made with winter vegetables such as carrots, potatoes, or rutabagas. *Güveç* means "casserole" or "stew." Because every family makes it differently, there are hundreds of versions. This casserole starts with frying some eggplants, then other typical summer vegetables are layered on top. • **Makes 4 servings**

1 pound eggplant, peeled and cut into cubes
Salt
¾ cup extra-virgin olive oil
1 large red onion, sliced
3 large garlic cloves, finely chopped
2 tablespoons chopped fresh dill
2 tablespoons chopped fresh parsley
Freshly ground black pepper
2 zucchini (about ½ pound total), sliced ¼ inch thick
2 yellow summer squash (about ½ pound total), sliced ¼ inch thick
4 ripe tomatoes (about 1½ pounds total), sliced into rounds
1 large green bell pepper, seeded and sliced into rings
1 teaspoon sweet paprika

1. Lay the eggplant slices on some paper towels and sprinkle with salt. Leave them to drain of their bitter juices for 30 minutes, then pat dry with clean paper towels.

2. Meanwhile, preheat the oven to 350°F.

3. In a large skillet, heat ¼ cup of olive oil over medium-high heat, then cook the eggplant cubes until golden brown on all sides, about 8 minutes in all. Remove with a slotted spoon and set aside.

4. Add another ¼ cup of olive oil to the skillet and heat over medium-high heat, then add the onion and garlic, and cook, stirring frequently so the garlic doesn't burn, until translucent, about 6 minutes. Set aside.

5. Arrange the eggplant on the bottom of a 12-inch baking casserole (preferably earthenware) and sprinkle half of the dill and parsley on top. Season with salt and pepper. Cover with the sliced zucchini and summer squash, then cover with the sliced tomatoes. Sprinkle the remaining dill and parsley over and pour the remaining ¼ cup olive oil over. Arrange the bell pepper over the tomatoes, season with salt and pepper, and sprinkle with the paprika. Bake until soft, about 1½ hours. Let rest about an hour or more, and serve lukewarm.

Leftover Idea

The Summer Vegetable Casserole from Turkey (previous page) is made with lots of olive oil and it makes a very appealing, and authentic, Turkish meze dish the next day served at room temperature with some crusty bread to dunk into the now soft and juicy vegetables.

Pumpkin in Pumpkin Casserole

This fun presentation is a great casserole dish for Thanksgiving, and it's easy on the cook. No washing up! I've adapted this recipe from one by the late Chef Michael Roberts who contributed it to the *Prodigy Guest Chefs Cookbook* many years ago. Michael was one of the founders of what came to be known as California cuisine and was the author of *Parisian Home Cooking* and other cookbooks. As he says, pumpkin dishes don't have to be sweet, and this one is perfect with roast pork. I'd add turkey too. You will need a ten-pound pumpkin for this recipe and you'll peel one half and use that flesh as the stuffing that goes into the other half, which needs to be seeded and acts as an edible casserole dish. • **Makes 6 servings**

> One 10-pound pumpkin
> 1 large white onion, finely chopped
> 2 tablespoons unsalted butter, melted
> 1½ teaspoons salt
> ¼ teaspoon freshly ground white pepper
> ¾ cup whole milk
> ¾ cup ricotta cheese
> 2 large eggs

1. Preheat the oven to 375°F.

2. Cut the pumpkin horizontally into two halves, with one half having the stem. Peel the stem end half with a vegetable peeler or paring knife and remove the stem. Leave the other half with its skin on. Remove the seeds from both halves by scooping them out with a spoon or by scraping with a knife. The peeled stem end half will now look like a bowl with a hole in it. The flesh of the peeled stem-end half will be 1 to 2 inches thick. Cut it into quarters to make further slicing more manageable, then cut the flesh into ¼-inch-thick slices. Place the cut-up pumpkin flesh in a large bowl. Add the onion, butter, 1 teaspoon of salt, and the pepper, and toss well. Salt the inside of the other pumpkin half and place it in a large round baking casserole. Pour the contents of the bowl into the hollow of the pumpkin half. Cover with foil and bake until the pumpkin bottom is easily pierced by a skewer, but has not collapsed, and the pumpkin pieces are tender too, about 3 hours.

3. In a bowl, beat together the milk, ricotta cheese, eggs, and remaining salt until smooth. Remove the baking dish from the oven, remove the foil, and pour the milk-cheese mixture over the top. Bake uncovered until the top turns golden brown, about 45 minutes. Remove from the oven, let cool slightly, and serve.

Pumpkin Casserole

This interesting recipe is called *gratin de potiron d'Arpajon* in French, meaning pumpkin gratin from Arpajon. The town of Arpajon is just outside Paris and is known as a source of the vegetables sold at the city's markets. The casserole was introduced to the American public in 1961 by the publication of Julia Child's *Mastering the Art of French Cooking*, and many cooks added it to their Thanksgiving repertoire. I've adapted the recipe from one published in 1979 in the Junior League of San Francisco's *San Francisco a la Carte*, which gave no background information, but it must be Julia's recipe.

• Makes 4 servings

½ cup dried white beans

1/4 teaspoon salt plus more as needed

5 tablespoons unsalted butter

¼ cup chopped celery

¼ cup chopped onion

2 tablespoons finely chopped peeled carrot

1 pound peeled pumpkin or any winter squash flesh, diced

1 large garlic clove, crushed

1 small bay leaf

⅛ teaspoon dried thyme

1 large egg, lightly beaten

¼ cup heavy cream

1 ounce Swiss cheese, shredded

1. Place the beans in a saucepan and cover by several inches with cold water. Bring to a boil, salt, and cook until tender, about 1¼ hours. Drain and set aside.

2. Preheat the oven to 350°F.

3. In a large flame- and oven-proof casserole, melt 3 tablespoons of butter over medium-high heat, then add the celery, onion, and carrot. Cover and cook, stirring occasionally, until softened, about 6 minutes. Add the pumpkin, garlic, bay leaf, thyme, and ¼ teaspoon of salt. Once it sizzles, cover and bake until tender, about 30 minutes. Remove from the oven and discard the bay leaf.

4. Increase the oven temperature to 425°F. Lightly butter a 9 x 9 x 2-inch baking casserole.

5. Stir the beans into the pumpkin mixture, and then transfer the mixture to a food processor and puree. Spoon the mixture from the food processor into a large bowl and beat in the egg and cream, then season with salt. Spoon the pumpkin mixture into the buttered casserole. Dot the top with thin slices of the remaining 2 tablespoons of butter, and sprinkle the cheese on top. Bake until the top is dappled with golden brown spots, about 30 minutes. Serve hot.

Roasted Vegetables of the Full Moon

This casserole is inspired by a classic Tuscan antipasto called *carabàccia alla luna piena* (meaning "squash of the full moon"), a dish which has its own history. *Carabàccia* is an Italian word that derives from a Spanish and Catalan word for squash or gourd. But in Tuscany, carabàccia is a kind of Florentine-style onion soup, and thought possibly to be the origin of the famous French *soupe à l'oignon* once served at Les Halles market in Paris. Carabàccia is also an antipasto consisting simply of a mirepoix of vegetables, or what the Italians call a *trito* of vegetables that are sautéed and served with a fried egg on top. The name of the dish can be traced back to at least the sixteenth-century *carabazada di cipolle* recipe that appears in the cookbook of Christofaro di Messisbugo, the *Libro novo nel quale s'insegna a far d'ogni sorta di vivande* (New Book Showing How to Make Every Kind of Food). In Messisbugo's recipe the soup is made with onions, almonds, egg yolks, sugar, and cinnamon. That being said, the meaning of the name of this Tuscan preparation is not at all clear. Does a carabàccia of the full moon refer to the sunny-side-up egg looking like a full moon? Or does it have something to do with the Spanish, who sixteenth-century Italians called disparagingly "squash-heads," meaning stupid person because a squash is hollow inside. This recipe is based on the one I had at the Ristorante Carmagnini del '500, located outside Prato. • **Makes 6 servings**

> 1 pound pumpkin or other winter squash, peeled, seeded, and diced
> 6 ounces small fingerling potatoes or other potato, peeled and
>   cut into ¾-inch pieces
> 6 ounces young carrots, peeled and diced or cut into small rounds
> 2 kohlrabi, leaves removed, peeled and diced
> ¾ cup extra-virgin olive oil
> 1 teaspoon salt plus more as needed

1 teaspoon freshly ground black pepper plus more as needed

1 large onion, diced

4 celery stalks, chopped

1 fennel bulb, trimmed of stalks and leaves, diced

3 tablespoons finely chopped fresh parsley

1 tablespoon finely chopped fresh basil

Juice of 1 lemon

1 cup fresh or frozen peas

6 large eggs

1. Preheat the oven to 400°F.

2. Put the pumpkin, potatoes, carrots, and kohlrabi in a 10-inch round baking casserole (preferably earthenware), and toss with ½ cup of olive oil, 1 teaspoon of salt, and 1 teaspoon of pepper. Roast until crispy looking, about 1 hour. Remove 2 tablespoons of flavored oil from the casserole and place it in a large nonstick skillet.

3. Meanwhile, in another skillet, heat the remaining ¼ cup of olive oil over medium-high heat, then add the onion, celery, fennel, parsley, and basil, and cook, stirring, until softened, about 5 minutes. Pour in the lemon juice and season with a little salt and pepper. Reduce the heat to very low, then cover and cook until soft, about 25 minutes. (Use a heat diffuser if your burner doesn't simmer low enough.) Add the peas and continue to cook, stirring occasionally, until soft, about 10 minutes. Turn the heat off and leave covered in the skillet until the roasting vegetables are done.

4. Mix the vegetables in the skillet with the roasted vegetables in their casserole. Keep the mixed vegetables warm in a turned-off oven.

5. In the nonstick skillet with the flavored olive oil, heat the oil over medium heat, then fry the eggs sunny-side up until the whites are set. Remove the casserole from the oven. Carefully lift or slide the eggs, now formed into one round disk with 6 yellow "eyes," out of the skillet and onto the top of the vegetable casserole. (The whole set of eggs will slide out together if you use a nonstick skillet.) Serve hot.

Provençal Greens Casserole

This casserole is a kind of quiche or vegetable pudding that is made in Provence and cooked in an earthenware casserole called a tian. In this recipe, I use three typical Provençal vegetables—spinach, Swiss chard, and zucchini. Other vegetables that appear frequently in the cooking of Provence are tomatoes, eggplants, and artichokes. Some cooks make the dish more substantial by adding rice, typically the red rice that is grown in the Camargue, the marsh land of Provence. • **Makes 4 servings**

2 tablespoons extra-virgin olive oil plus more as needed
1 medium onion, chopped
4 large garlic cloves, finely chopped
2 medium zucchini (about 1 pound total), peeled and grated
2 teaspoons salt
Freshly ground black pepper
1 pound fresh spinach, heavy stems removed, rinsed well
1 pound Swiss chard, heavy stems removed, rinsed well
4 large eggs
1 cup whole milk
Pinch of freshly grated nutmeg
¾ cup (about 2 ounces) shredded Gruyère cheese

1. Preheat the oven to 375°F. Coat a 10-inch round baking casserole (preferably earthenware) with olive oil.

2. In a large skillet, heat 2 tablespoons of olive oil over medium-high heat, then add the onion and garlic and cook, stirring frequently so the garlic doesn't burn, until softened, about 4 minutes. Add the zucchini, season with the salt and pepper, and cook, stirring, until the zucchini has wilted, about 5 minutes.

3. Meanwhile, place the spinach and Swiss chard leaves in a large pot with only the water adhering to them from their last rinsing. Cover, turn the heat to medium-high, and cook until they wilt, turning a few times, 7 to 8 minutes. Drain well in a strainer, pushing out the excess water with the back of a wooden spoon. Chop the greens, then squeeze out as much water as you can with your hands and set aside. It's important that the greens are relatively dry, otherwise the final dish will be slightly watery.

4. In a large bowl, beat the eggs and gradually stir in the milk. Season with salt, pepper, and nutmeg. Add the zucchini mixture and the greens along with the Gruyère cheese. Pour into the casserole and bake until light golden on top, 30 to 35 minutes. Serve hot.

Simple Spinach Casserole

S pinach is one of my favorite vegetables and I like to make this casserole as a side dish because I can put another casserole in the oven at nearly the same time and they both come out golden-crusted and bubbling.

• **Makes 4 servings as a side dish**

2 tablespoons unsalted butter
2 pounds fresh spinach, heavy stems removed, washed well
1½ cups (about 5 ounces) shredded Gruyère cheese
½ cup heavy cream
Salt and freshly ground black pepper
Pinch of nutmeg

1. Preheat the oven to 350°F. Lightly butter a small oval baking casserole.

2. In a large saucepan, melt the butter over medium-high heat. Spin the spinach leaves dry in a salad spinner, then add the spinach to the saucepan. Cook, stirring occasionally, until slightly wilted, 3 to 4 minutes. Remove the spinach and set aside.

3. In a bowl, mix the cheese with the cream. Add the spinach and season with salt, pepper, and nutmeg. Transfer the spinach to the buttered casserole and bake until slightly golden brown on top and bubbling, about 40 minutes. Serve hot or very warm.

Baked Swiss Chard and Spinach with Chickpeas and Feta Cheese

As a fan of leafy green vegetables, I love them every which way. Here's a very pleasant dish that I find satisfying on every level, from taste to texture. The feta cheese never quite melts but becomes very soft and hot. This casserole is one I would serve as an accompaniment to lamb.

• Makes 4 to 6 servings

4 tablespoons extra-virgin olive oil
10 ounces Swiss chard leaves, heavy stems removed, washed well
1 pound spinach, heavy stems removed, washed well
One 15-ounce can chickpeas, drained
4 scallions, white and green parts, chopped
4 large garlic cloves, finely chopped
¼ cup chopped fresh dill
Salt and freshly ground black pepper
3 ounces feta cheese, crumbed

1. Preheat the oven to 350°F. Spread 1 tablespoon of oil over the bottom and sides of a 12 x 9 x 2-inch baking casserole.

2. Add water to a steamer pot and bring to a boil. Place the Swiss chard in the steamer portion and steam until it wilts, about 4 minutes. Add the spinach to the steamed chard and steam until it wilts too, about 4 minutes. Remove both greens and drain, squeezing out the excess water with your hands once it's cool enough to handle. Chop the greens and toss with the remaining 3 tablespoons of olive oil, chickpeas, scallions, garlic, and dill, and season with salt and pepper.

3. Transfer the vegetable mixture to the casserole. Push the feta cheese down into this mixture and bake until it is sizzling, about 35 minutes. Serve hot.

Swiss Chard and Chickpea Casserole

This is a much simpler version of the previous recipe and one I'm likely to make when I want lots of flavor and texture but don't have or don't want to take the time to get involved. Everything goes into a pot to boil and then into the oven. It's as simple as that and makes a very pleasant accompaniment to grilled lamb steaks. • **Makes 4 servings**

1 pound Swiss chard, washed and cut into
    1½-inch pieces including stems
1 cup water
One 15-ounce can chickpeas, drained
3 tablespoons extra-virgin olive oil
Salt and freshly ground black pepper
¼ pound *queso fresco* cheese, farmer cheese,
    or ricotta cheese, crumbled

Leftover Idea

In North Africa, a favorite lunch dish is a thick frittata-like casserole made with eggs, and called either a tagine (a word that also means "ragout" and "casserole") or ma'quda. They are very simple and versatile. To make a version of this specialty, place some leftover Swiss Chard and Chickpea Casserole (this page) in a bowl and season it with a little ground cumin, caraway, cayenne pepper, and salt, if necessary. Mix in some eggs (depending on the amount of leftovers, but probably one or two), then pour the mixture into a well-oiled small casserole that is at least 2 inches deep. Bake in a 350°F oven until the center sets like a pudding, 25 to 30 minutes. Let cool and serve warm or at room temperature as an appetizer or a lunch dish.

1. Preheat the oven to 350°F.

2. Put the Swiss chard in a saucepan with the water, then cover and bring to a boil over high heat. Reduce the heat to low once the leaves have wilted, about 5 minutes. Add the chickpeas and 1 tablespoon of olive oil. Cook, stirring occasionally, until the chickpeas have softened, about 10 minutes. Season with salt and pepper.

3. Transfer the contents of the saucepan with a slotted spoon to a 9 x 9 x 2-inch baking casserole or a medium oval baking casserole. Sprinkle the cheese over the dish. Drizzle the remaining 2 tablespoons of olive over everything. Bake until the cheese is dotted golden, about 30 minutes. Serve hot.

Stuffed Swiss Chard Leaves

In Greece and Turkey, stuffed grape leaves are a very popular meze, but cooks also like to stuff other vegetables, including peppers, zucchini, cabbage leaves, and, in this incredibly delicious dish, Swiss chard leaves, which remain a beautiful dark green color after cooking. As a meze, the leaves are usually cut in half lengthwise before stuffing and rolling, but when making this as a main course the leaves are used whole. This is a vegetarian stuffing, but if you want to add meat cook about ten ounces of ground lamb and add it at the same time as the rice. • **Makes 4 servings**

For the chard and stuffing

2 pounds red or white Swiss chard, heavy stems removed,
    washed well
4 tablespoons extra-virgin olive oil
1 large onion, finely chopped
10 tablespoons water
½ cup medium-grain rice, rinsed well or soaked in
    water for 30 minutes and drained
½ cup coarsely chopped walnuts
Leaves from 1 bunch fresh parsley, finely chopped
½ teaspoon freshly ground allspice berries
Salt and freshly ground black pepper
1 cup fresh tomato juice (squeezed from fresh tomatoes)
¼ cup freshly squeezed lemon juice

For the Béchamel (white) sauce

2 tablespoons unsalted butter
2 tablespoons all-purpose flour
1 cup whole milk
Salt and freshly ground black pepper

① Preheat the oven to 350°F.

② Bring a large pot of water to a boil and plunge the whole Swiss chard leaves in, reduce the heat to medium, and cook until the leaves are wilted, about 5 minutes. Drain through a strainer, rinse with cold water, and set them aside while you continue.

③ In a large skillet, heat 2 tablespoons of olive oil over medium-high heat, then add the onion and cook, stirring, until translucent, 5 minutes. Add 8 tablespoons (½ cup) of water, the drained rice, walnuts, parsley, and allspice. Season with salt and pepper. Reduce the heat to low, stir once to mix, then cook until the rice is al dente, about 12 minutes. Don't stir or touch the rice as it cooks, but after 12 minutes stir and fluff the rice. Remove from the heat and set aside.

④ Carefully arrange the Swiss chard leaves in front of you on a plate, making sure you don't rip them. Take one of the leaves and lay it down with the stem end toward you and the inside of the leaf (the non-shiny side) facing up. Place about 2 tablespoons of stuffing on the end of the leaf and press into a cylindrical shape. Carefully fold the stem over the stuffing and away from you, being careful that you don't rip the leaf. The

The Secret Life of Stems

Many recipes, such as Baked Swiss Chard and Spinach with Chickpeas and Feta Cheese (page 373), call for removing the stems from Swiss chard and spinach. Most of us just throw the stems away, but one can make some nice dishes with these stems. One dish I like to make with them is the stem version of hummus. To make it as I do, boil ½ pound of stems in water, then puree them in a food processor with ¼ cup of tahini (sesame paste) and 3 garlic cloves that have been mashed in a mortar with ½ teaspoon of salt. Then, with the machine running, pour in ¼ cup of freshly squeezed lemon juice through the feed tube. Another preparation is a soup of stems, made with the stems cooked in vegetable or chicken broth.

stem should be a little stiff but soft enough to bend. Fold the sides in and roll up like a cigar.

5 Arrange the rolled Swiss chard leaves tightly in a 10 x 8 x 1½-inch baking casserole. Cover with the remaining 2 tablespoons each of water and olive oil, then the tomato juice and lemon juice. Cover the casserole and bake until bubbling, about 40 minutes.

6 Meanwhile, to prepare the Béchamel sauce, melt the butter in a saucepan over medium-high heat, then stir in the flour to form a roux. Continue to cook, stirring constantly, for about 2 minutes. Remove the saucepan from the heat and stir in the milk until it is well blended. Season with salt and pepper. Return the saucepan to the burner and simmer over low heat, stirring frequently, until dense, 12 to 15 minutes.

7 Remove the casserole from the oven, uncover, spoon the white sauce over the Swiss chard roll-ups, and return to the oven and bake uncovered until light golden on top, about 35 minutes. Serve hot.

Leeks au Gratin

This delicious dish is known as *poireaux à la Savoyarde* in the French Alps, but it also goes by the name *poireaux à la Italienne* too, although it has nothing to do with Italy. I make this gratin dish often in the winter, sometimes using shallots or small onions instead. But you could also make it with cabbage or celeriac. This recipe also fits in nicely with a Thanksgiving meal. Although I had been making this recipe for years, I liked Anne Willan's layered approach from *French Regional Cooking* that I've adapted here.

• Makes 4 servings

3 pounds leeks, white and light green parts only,
    split lengthwise, washed well
1 garlic clove, crushed
3 tablespoons unsalted butter
1 cup (about 3 ounces) shredded Gruyère cheese
¼ cup dry bread crumbs
Salt and freshly ground black pepper
Pinch of nutmeg

1. Preheat the oven to 425°F.

2. Bring a large saucepan of salted water to a boil, and cook the leeks over high heat until tender, about 12 minutes. Drain very well.

3. Rub the inside of a 9-inch oval baking casserole with the crushed garlic clove. Spread the butter over the surface. Spread half of the leeks on the bottom of the casserole and sprinkle with half of the cheese and half of the bread crumbs. Season with salt, pepper, and nutmeg. Cover with the remaining leeks, sprinkle them with the remaining cheese and bread crumbs, and season with salt, pepper, and nutmeg. Bake until golden brown, about 12 minutes. Serve hot.

Fannie Farmer's Vegetables en Casserole

This simple recipe is adapted from Fannie Merritt Farmer's *The Boston Cooking-School Cook Book* (Little, Brown, 1926), a book whose first edition dates to 1896. I was intrigued by the recipe because it looked old-fashioned and a little unusual, but thought what the heck, let's give it a try. I didn't modernize it—I just tweaked measurements and the cooking time a bit. Surprise! It's quite good and very easy to make on top of it. I would serve it with roast chicken or pan-seared chicken breasts or, if you want to stick with the casserole theme, meatloaf (page 36). • **Makes 6 servings**

6 boiling potatoes (about 1¾ pounds), peeled and thinly sliced
1 small turnip, diced
1 medium onion, thinly sliced
¼ cup long-grain rice, rinsed under running water in a strainer
1 cup fresh or frozen peas
1 cup chopped peeled tomatoes
1 teaspoon salt
½ teaspoon freshly ground black pepper
¼ teaspoon freshly ground allspice berries
1 quart beef broth

1 Preheat the oven to 300°F.

2 Layer the potatoes, turnip, onion, rice, peas, and tomatoes, in that order, in a 13 x 9 x 2-inch baking casserole. Season with salt, pepper, and allspice, then pour the beef broth over the vegetables. Cover and bake until bubbling and the potatoes are tender, about 2½ hours. Serve hot.

Cabbage Casserole # 2

This Mediterranean-style casserole uses the crinkly-leafed Savoy cabbage. If you can't find it, you can replace it with Napa cabbage, which is not a cabbage but is a member of the mustard family. In either case, it makes a delightful accompaniment to a variety of main dishes, and leftovers can be put on top of leftover meatloaf and baked for yet another meal.

• Makes 4 servings

¼ cup extra-virgin olive oil

2 large garlic cloves, finely chopped

2 tablespoons finely chopped fresh parsley leaves

1 pound tomatoes, peeled, seeded, and chopped, or
    one 28-ounce can whole tomatoes, drained and chopped

1¼ pounds Savoy cabbage, cored, cut in half, thinly sliced

Salt and freshly ground black pepper

½ pound fresh mozzarella cheese, shredded

1. Preheat the oven to 350°F.

2. In a deep flame- and oven-proof casserole, heat the olive oil over medium heat, then add the garlic and parsley and cook until sizzling, about 1 minute. Add the tomatoes and cook, stirring, until much of their liquid evaporates, 15 to 20 minutes. Add the cabbage and cook until it wilts, about 5 minutes. Season with salt and pepper.

3. Lay the mozzarella cheese on top and bake until dappled with brown spots, 35 to 40 minutes. Serve hot.

Leftover Idea

I mix leftover Cabbage Casserole # 2 (this page) with cooked ground beef and make a new casserole. Or even better, I toss it with cooked macaroni, return it to a casserole, layer some more mozzarella cheese on top, and bake it until the cheese melts.

Cabbage Casserole # 3

There are three kinds of basic cabbage casseroles. The one represented here is a rich and creamy American casserole made with cabbage and white sauce. The second common recipe is sometimes served as a main course and is usually made with meat (page 308) or with rice and tomatoes, and the third is more of a Mediterranean style with tomatoes as the previous recipe. Because this recipe is heavy, it's best to serve it with something light. Notice that the portions you spoon out should be small. • **Makes 10 servings**

10 tablespoons (1⅛ sticks) unsalted butter
1 cup fresh bread crumbs (see Note)
1 head green cabbage (about 1¾ pounds), cored and thinly sliced
⅓ cup all-purpose flour
½ teaspoon salt
Freshly ground black pepper
4 cups whole milk
2 cups (about 6 ounces) shredded mild cheddar cheese

① Preheat the oven to 350°F. Lightly butter a 12 × 9 × 2-inch baking casserole.

② In a medium skillet, melt 2 tablespoons of butter over medium-high heat, then add the bread crumbs and cook, stirring and tossing, until golden, about 4 minutes. Set aside.

③ Bring a large pot of salted water to a boil over high heat, then add the cabbage and cook until bright green and wilted, about 4 minutes. Drain well and transfer to a bowl. Add 2 tablespoons of butter and toss until the butter melts and coats the cabbage. Set aside.

④ In a saucepan, melt the remaining 6 tablespoons of butter over medium heat, then stir in the flour to form a roux. Add ½ teaspoon of salt and season with pepper. Stir until smooth, about 1 minute. Remove the saucepan from the heat and slowly whisk in the milk, stirring constantly. Return to medium-low heat and continue cooking and stirring until thick and bubbly, about 20 minutes.

⑤ Layer half of the cabbage on the bottom of the buttered casserole, then pour half of the white sauce over the cabbage. Add the remaining cabbage and the rest of the white sauce on top of that. Sprinkle the top with the shredded cheese. Sprinkle the bread crumbs over the cheese and bake uncovered until golden and bubbly, 40 to 45 minutes. Serve hot.

Note: This amount can be made from crumbling two ½-inch-thick slices of 5¼ × 3-inch French or Italian bread in a food processor.

Cabbage and Red Potato Casserole

This casserole begs for ultra-fresh cabbage and red potatoes from the farmers market. But you'll enjoy it no matter where the vegetables come from. If your market doesn't sell Savoy cabbage, then use a head of green cabbage. I usually serve this dish with a platter of slow-roasted lamb ribs. Alternately, it goes very nicely with grilled bratwurst.

• Makes 4 servings

3 tablespoons extra-virgin olive oil
1 head Savoy cabbage (about 2 pounds), cored and shredded
1 medium onion, chopped
6 large garlic cloves, finely chopped
2 teaspoons hot paprika
1 teaspoon dried thyme
1 teaspoon ground caraway
Salt and freshly ground black pepper
1 cup vegetable broth
10 small red potatoes (about 1¼ pounds)

1. Preheat the oven to 350°F.

2. In a large flame- and oven-proof casserole, heat the olive oil over medium-high heat, then add the cabbage, onion, garlic, paprika, thyme, and caraway. Season with salt and pepper. Cook, stirring, until the cabbage is well coated with oil and beginning to wilt, about 5 minutes. Add the broth and potatoes.

3. Place in the oven and bake until there is a slight resistance to the piercing of the potato by a skewer, about 1½ hours. Serve immediately.

Sweet Potato Casserole with Praline Topping

The sweet potato casserole is nothing but a version of the sweet potato pie, a dish that was made early on in America and in England, where the first sweet potatoes came from Virginia, probably sometime after 1650. The first recipe I'm familiar with is that found in Hannah Glasse's *The Art of Cookery Made Plain and Easy* published in 1747, and called "Potato-cakes." We don't know if her recipe used sweet potatoes or potatoes, except it was made with sugar, nutmeg, eggs, and cream. This classic of Southern cooking is popular from Georgia to Louisiana, and on Thanksgiving day, it fits the bill for the sweet potato entry far beyond the South. When I began asking around for recipes for this famous casserole I got a million responses. Even my mom had a recipe. So this recipe here is one that tries to capture the true Southern spirit. Like a lot of Southern food, it's sweet. • **Makes 8 servings**

For the streusel

1 cup all-purpose flour
⅔ cup packed brown sugar
¼ cup chopped pecans, toasted (see page 295)
4 tablespoons (½ stick) unsalted butter, melted
½ teaspoon ground cinnamon

For the sweet potatoes

2½ pounds sweet potatoes, peeled and quartered
½ cup sugar
One 5-ounce can fat-free evaporated milk
1 large egg white
1½ teaspoons vanilla extract

1. Preheat the oven to 350°F. Lightly oil a 12 × 9 × 2-inch baking casserole.

2. To prepare the streusel, in a small bowl, combine the flour, brown sugar, pecans, butter, and cinnamon, mixing well.

3. To prepare the sweet potatoes, place them in a large saucepan and add enough water to cover by several inches. Bring to a boil, then reduce the heat a bit and cook until tender, about 30 minutes. Drain well and mash in a large bowl. Stir in 1 cup of the streusel, the sugar, milk, egg white, and vanilla, and mix well.

4. Transfer the sweet potato mixture to the casserole. Spread the remaining streusel over the top of the sweet potatoes then bake until dark brown, about 45 minutes.

Don't Throw Away Broccoli Stems!

Several recipes in this book call for broccoli florets, but that doesn't mean you should throw away the stems. The broccoli stems can be saved for another preparation such as Broccoli and Fennel Gratinate (page 394), or they can be marinated. If marinating the broccoli stems, first peel them, then cut them into ⅛-inch slices. Toss them with salt and let sit to drain in a strainer overnight. Then toss them with a little finely chopped garlic, olive oil, and white wine vinegar, and marinate for 24 hours. Serve the marinated broccoli stems at room temperature as an appetizer or snack.

Broccoli Cheese Dish

As simple as this old-fashioned casserole sounds, it packs a rich and delicious taste. It's so rich and delicious, in fact, that you may be tempted to serve it to two people in a fit of excess. But, be realistic and portion out six servings as I recommend, so you don't overdo it. This casserole is sometimes called broccoli and cheese bake and is typical as a church supper dish. It's best accompanied by something light and simple such as grilled pork chops or chicken breasts cooked in a skillet. • **Makes 6 servings**

1 pound broccoli florets
2 cups heavy cream
1½ cups (about 5 ounces) freshly grated white cheddar cheese
1 small onion, finely chopped
2 large eggs, beaten to blend
⅛ teaspoon ground nutmeg
6 tablespoons (¾ stick) unsalted butter

1 package Ritz crackers (¼ pound), crumbled

1. Preheat the oven to 325°F.

2. Bring a saucepan of salted water to a boil, then cook the broccoli until tender but still bright green, about 6 minutes, but not more. Drain and immediately cool under cold running water to stop it from cooking. Let drain some more in a colander.

3. In a bowl, stir together the cream, cheese, onion, eggs, and nutmeg. Pour this mixture into a 12 × 9 × 2-inch baking casserole. Add the broccoli.

4. Meanwhile, in a large skillet, melt the butter over medium-high heat, then cook the crumbled Ritz crackers, stirring, until crispy and fragrant, about 3 minutes. Sprinkle the crackers over the broccoli, place in the oven, and bake until bubbly, about 30 minutes. Serve hot.

Broccoli-Spinach Casserole

When I told my mom that I was writing a book on casseroles, she immediately began digging into her old file box of handwritten recipes and gave me one for broccoli-spinach casserole. But the instructions were so wacky we couldn't make heads or tails of it. She told me that those handwritten recipes of hers from fifty years ago were really reminder notes more than anything, and so much time had passed that she was clueless as to its meaning, so we discussed how the recipe should look and this is what we came up with. When mom first made it in the 1950s she didn't have access to the extraordinary produce we do today, and this is a recipe begging for the best. Mom would have used store-bought croutons, but I usually make my own because I think they're better. To make your own croutons, cut 2 to 4 slices of Italian or French bread into small cubes that should equal a cup; then fry them in a nonstick skillet in 1 tablespoon of butter until golden. She would have also used Campbell's cream of mushroom soup, but I make my own sauce. If you serve this casserole as a side dish, it is best with a simple main course, such as roast chicken. • **Makes 4 to 6 servings**

¾ pound broccoli florets

1¼ pounds spinach, heavy stems removed, washed well

¼ cup finely chopped onion

¼ pound white button mushrooms

½ cup whole milk

2 tablespoons all-purpose flour

¼ teaspoon salt plus more as needed

¼ teaspoon freshly ground black pepper

¼ cup heavy cream

2 large eggs

¼ cup mayonnaise

1 cup (about 3 ounces) shredded mild white cheddar cheese

1 cup small plain or herbed bread croutons (for stuffing)

1. Preheat the oven to 350°F. Butter a 12 × 9 × 2-inch baking casserole.

2. Bring a large saucepan of lightly salted water to a boil over high heat, then boil the broccoli florets until tender and bright green, 6 minutes and not more. Remove the broccoli with a skimmer or slotted spoon and plunge them into a bowl of cold water to stop them from cooking. Drain the broccoli florets from the cold water after a couple of minutes and transfer them to a large bowl.

3. Meanwhile, keep the water in the saucepan at a boil, then add the spinach and cook until it wilts, about 1 minute. Drain the spinach well, squeezing the excess water out with your hands once it's cool enough to handle. Chop the spinach and set aside in the bowl with the broccoli florets. Add the onion to the bowl and toss the vegetables well.

4. Place the mushrooms, milk, flour, a little salt, and ⅛ teaspoon black pepper in a blender and blend until smooth. Add the heavy cream and blend briefly.

5. In a bowl, beat the eggs, then stir in the mayonnaise, reserved mushroom sauce from the blender, ¼ teaspoon of salt, and ⅛ teaspoon of pepper. Add the cooked vegetables and toss well. Transfer to the buttered casserole.

6. In a bowl, combine the cheddar cheese and croutons, tossing to mix and then sprinkle on top of the vegetables. Bake until the cheese is melted and the edges of the casserole are bubbling, about 20 minutes. Serve hot.

Creamed Broccoli Crêpes Casserole

I'm not sure where I learned to make broccoli crêpes, but I remember they were one of my "specialties" in the late 1960s as a teenage cook. I probably had them on some trip to France and just fell in love with the idea of a savory crêpe. My friends would make fun of me because I made them so often. You can make a good-size batch of crêpes first (page 392) and keep them frozen until you need them. This makes the recipe quite easy too. Broccoli crowns are the topmost floret portion of the broccoli.

- Makes 8 crêpes to serve 4 as a main course or 8 as an appetizer

5 tablespoons unsalted butter
¾ pound broccoli crowns
1 shallot, finely chopped
2 tablespoons all-purpose flour
1 cup whole milk, warmed
Salt and freshly ground black pepper
Pinch of freshly ground nutmeg
½ recipe Crêpes (8 cooked crêpes; page 392)
2 cups (about 6 ounces) shredded Gruyère cheese

Broccoli Alert!

Why do some people hate broccoli so much? I think there is a very simple reason that is rarely mentioned. Bad cooks! Broccoli should never be cooked for long otherwise it will release, as do all cruciferous vegetables, sulfurous compounds such as ammonia and hydrogen sulfide, which interact with the chlorophyll in the broccoli causing it to turn an unappetizing gray and giving off an unpleasant smell. This means, never cook broccoli more than 6 or 7 minutes at a boil, then drain and plunge in cold water immediately to stop it from cooking further.

① Preheat the oven to 375°F. Butter a 13 × 9 × 2-inch baking casserole with 1 tablespoon of butter.

② Bring a large saucepan of lightly salted water to a boil over high heat, then cook the broccoli until tender and bright green, 6 minutes, but not more. Drain and immediately cool under cold running water to stop it from cooking. Set in a colander to drain while you continue the preparation.

③ In a saucepan, melt 3 tablespoons of butter over medium-high heat, then add the shallot and cook, stirring, until soft and translucent, 2 to 3 minutes. Add the flour to form a roux, cooking and stirring for about 1 minute. Remove the saucepan from the heat and slowly whisk in the warm milk until blended. Return to medium heat and cook, stirring, until dense, about 12 minutes. Season with salt, pepper, and nutmeg.

④ Break up the broccoli into smaller florets and dice the remaining stem portion. Fold the broccoli into the white sauce. Season with more salt and pepper, if necessary.

⑤ Place a crêpe in front of you and spoon a few tablespoons and pieces of broccoli in a row toward one edge of the crêpe. Sprinkle about 2 tablespoons of cheese on top of the broccoli and roll up the crêpe up away from you. Place in the buttered casserole. Continue with the remaining 7 crêpes, laying each next to the other in the casserole which will hold all 8 crêpes. Spread the remaining 1 tablespoon of butter over the top of the crêpes and bake until bubbling on the sides, about 25 minutes. Serve hot.

Crêpes

A crêpe is a very thin pancake made by spreading batter over a hot flat cooking surface, either a griddle or a low-sided pan called a crêpe pan. Crêpes are always stuffed and are either savory or sweet. When they are savory the batter does not contain sugar and when they are dessert crêpes it does contain sugar. The word *crêpe* comes from the Latin *crispus* which means a fried thin pancake, the same as today. In Italian, they are known as *crespelle*. Because crêpes freeze so well, this recipe will make about twelve to sixteen 9-inch crêpes. Unlike pancake or waffle batter that gets folded together, crêpe batter gets blended quite vigorously. The actual making of a crêpe is a bit tricky so you will want to pay attention to the direction in the method below. The recipes in the book requiring crêpes will often call for half a recipe (or specify a number), but I advise you to make this whole recipe as the crêpes freeze so well, and having the crêpes already made is handy. The range given in the yield depends on how thick you make the crêpes and whether you rip one or not. • **Makes 12 to 16 nine-inch crêpes**

2 large eggs, slightly beaten
2 cups whole milk
1¾ cups all-purpose flour
2 tablespoons unsalted butter, melted
   (check the recipe you're making to see if it calls for a
   specific kind of butter, otherwise use unsalted butter)
2 tablespoons sugar (only if making dessert crêpes)
½ teaspoon salt
Vegetable oil or butter

① In a blender, blend the eggs for a few seconds, then add the milk, flour, butter, sugar (if making dessert crêpes), and salt, and blend until frothy. You can also blend in a bowl using a hand whisk if you don't have a blender. Pour into a bowl, cover, and let rest for 30 minutes.

② Brush some oil over a 7-inch crêpe pan or nonstick skillet to coat lightly, or use a buttered folded paper towel to lightly coat the pan. Heat the pan over medium-high heat for a few minutes until very hot. Pour in a scant ¼ cup of batter (about three-quarters of a ladleful of batter) and swirl the pan by tilting as you do so the batter spreads quickly to all surfaces of the pan. If necessary, spread further with a spatula, carefully drawing the edge of the spatula over the loose batter until it coats the whole surface and forms a very thin layer. Cook until the top is dry with a few air holes and the bottom is lightly brown. Look by gently and carefully lifting an edge of the crêpe. Cook the second side until brown dots appear everywhere. The first side will be evenly brown and the second side will be spotted brown. Transfer the crêpe to a plate, coat the pan with oil or butter as needed, and continue cooking all the crêpes. Let each crêpe cool down quite a bit before you stack them, otherwise they might stick together. If you're not using the crêpes right away, stack them on a sheet of aluminum foil, then cover with another sheet of aluminum foil and seal the edges well. Freeze until needed and defrost at room temperature before separating them. As you can calculate two stuffed crêpes per serving, you may want to divide the crêpes into serving sizes before freezing them.

Broccoli and Fennel Gratinate

A gratinate is an Italian dish that is cooked au gratin. This simple preparation is interesting in its combination of two distinct tastes that complement each other. You use only the stem portion of the broccoli in this casserole, saving the crowns (florets) for another casserole such as Broccoli Cheese Dish (page 387) or Creamed Broccoli Crêpes Casserole (page 390). I serve this dish with roast chicken or fish. • **Makes 2 to 3 servings**

1 fennel bulb, cut in half
2 broccoli stems, cut up if desired
Salt and freshly ground black pepper
2 tablespoons unsalted butter
3 tablespoons dry bread crumbs
1 tablespoon extra-virgin olive oil

1. Preheat the oven to 400°F. Butter a small baking casserole.

2. Bring a saucepan of water to a boil and cook the fennel until tender, about 10 minutes. Remove with a slotted ladle and set aside. Cook the broccoli until tender in the same water, 6 to 7 minutes, but not more. Drain.

3. Mix the two vegetables together and crush them slightly with a fork. Season with salt and pepper and stir in the butter, which will melt from the heat of the vegetables. Place in the buttered casserole and sprinkle the top with the bread crumbs. Drizzle the olive oil on top and bake until the top is dark brown, about 20 minutes. Serve hot.

Root Vegetables and Fennel Casserole

This is a dish I make often in the fall and winter to accompany roast turkey, duck, or chicken. If I'm roasting duck I usually replace the butter called for with an equal amount of rendered duck fat from the roasting pan—it's a wonderful flavor and greatly improves the overall dish. Of course, it's still excellent with butter too. • **Makes 4 servings**

¼ cup (½ stick) unsalted butter or rendered duck fat, melted
1 russet potato (about 10 ounces), peeled and cut into 1½-inch cubes
1 turnip (about 10 ounces), peeled and cut into 1½-inch cubes
3 large carrots, peeled and cut into large rounds
1 medium onion, cut into eighths
1 fennel bulb, trimmed of leaves and cut into large chunks
3 garlic cloves, finely chopped
Salt and freshly ground black pepper

1 Preheat the oven to 350°F.

2 In a 12 x 9 x 2-inch baking casserole, melt the butter or duck fat in the oven. Add the potato, turnip, carrots, onion, fennel, and garlic to the casserole, and toss to coat. Season with salt and pepper. Bake without stirring or moving the vegetables, until they are tender, about 2 hours. Remove and serve hot.

Baked Fennel and
Tomato Casserole

This simple casserole is just too good to believe that it only has four ingredients. I make this dish a lot and serve it with lamb, but as I often have leftovers, it also makes a very nice vegetarian lunch dish the next day. You can also utilize leftovers for a new casserole of your choosing.

• Makes 4 to 6 servings

3 fennel bulbs, trimmed and quartered
4 tablespoons (½ stick) unsalted butter, at room temperature
8 small ripe plum tomatoes (about 1 pound), peeled (page 241),
    cut in half, seeds squeezed out
Salt and freshly ground black pepper
½ cup (about 2 ounces) freshly grated Parmesan cheese

1. Preheat the oven to 350°F.

2. Bring a large saucepan of salted water to a boil, and boil the fennel until tender, about 10 minutes. Drain well and toss in a bowl with the butter until the butter melts.

3. Arrange the fennel in a medium-size baking casserole and scatter the tomato halves around. Season with salt and pepper. Bake until the tomatoes are soft, about 30 minutes. Remove from the oven, sprinkle the cheese on top, and let rest for 5 minutes before serving.

Dieter's Vegetable Casserole

This is a great casserole to make in late summer when the zucchini and tomatoes are at their best. It's also a great dish to make if you're trying to slim down. Serve the casserole with a slotted spoon so you leave the olive oil behind and just get the vegetables. I usually serve this with a roast turkey breast half, and put the turkey breast and this vegetable casserole in their own baking dishes and bake them for the same amount of time. Spring onions, another name for the young onions of spring that are beginning to develop a bulb, are very rarely available in supermarkets, so you will need to get them at the farmers market. If that's not an option, use small onions cut into quarters rather than scallions. • **Makes 4 to 6 servings**

6 small zucchini (about 1 pound), cut into 1-inch pieces
1 pound tomatoes, peeled (page 241) and cut up, or
    one 28-ounce can whole tomatoes, drained and cut up
½ pound eggplant, cubed
12 spring onions with 1½-inch-wide bulbs (about ¾ pound),
    trimmed of all but 2 inches of their green part
3 tablespoons chopped fresh oregano leaves, or
    1½ teaspoons dried
3 tablespoons finely chopped fresh parsley
Salt and freshly ground black pepper
Olive oil for drizzling

1 Preheat the oven to 300°F.

2 In a 12 x 9 x 2-inch baking casserole, toss together the zucchini, tomatoes, eggplant, spring onions, oregano, and parsley. Season with salt and pepper. Drizzle with olive oil and bake until the vegetables are soft, about 1½ hours.

Carrot Casserole

This is an old recipe from Miss Mary Bobo of Tennessee. She ran a boarding house in Lynchburg, Tennessee, which she took over in 1907. She served midday dinners consisting of two meats, many vegetables and side dishes, homemade breads, desserts, and beverages. She called this dish a garden carrot casserole because the carrots came from her garden. Miss Bobo died in 1983 at the age of 101. The original recipe did not use buttered crushed Ritz crackers, because Ritz crackers were only invented in 1934. But the many versions of this dish made by moms across America do use them. I've made it both ways, with bread crumbs and with Ritz crackers, and the Ritz cracker version is pretty good, but I prefer the bread crumb version, which has a lighter taste. • **Makes 6 to 8 servings**

2 pounds medium carrots, peeled and sliced ¼ inch thick
6 tablespoons unsalted butter (¾ stick), or
    4 tablespoons if using the bread crumb topping
1 cup fresh bread crumbs or crushed Ritz crackers
    (about ¾ packaged roll)
1 large onion, chopped
2 tablespoons all-purpose flour
6 tablespoons whole milk
1 teaspoon dry mustard
½ teaspoon salt or celery salt
1½ cups (about 5 ounces) shredded mild or sharp cheddar cheese

1. Preheat the oven to 350°F. Lightly butter a 12 × 9 × 2-inch baking casserole.

2. Bring a saucepan of water to a boil, then cook the carrots for 7 minutes, drain, and set aside.

3. In a skillet, melt the butter over medium-high heat. Transfer 4 tablespoons of the melted butter if using Ritz crackers and 2 tablespoons if using bread crumbs to a bowl and toss them, respectively, with the butter you removed.

4. To the 2 tablespoons of butter remaining in the skillet over medium-high heat, add the onion and cook, stirring, until translucent, about 4 minutes. Add the flour to the onion, reduce the heat to medium-low, and cook until incorporated and smooth, stirring. Add the milk, mustard, and salt or celery salt, and cook, stirring, until thickened, about 3 minutes. Reduce the heat to very low, add the cheese, and stir until it has melted.

5. Combine the carrots and cheese sauce and place in the buttered casserole. Sprinkle the buttered bread crumbs or Ritz crackers on top and bake until bubbly, about 20 minutes.

Peppers and Tomatoes Casserole

This preparation from Granada, Spain, whose Spanish name means "Arab dish of peppers" (*plato Árabe de pimientos*) is known as a kind of hortaliza, a vegetable preparation made with vegetables grown in the huertas. These huertas, or local truck farms, were originally established in Spain by Arab agronomists during the Islamic period that lasted from 746 to 1492. They revived many of the dormant Roman gardens and established others based on new agricultural technology. There are a great many dishes prepared with vegetables grown in the huertas and they are served as stews, as accompaniments to meat, and as tapas. I like to serve this dish as a room-temperature tapa with toasted slices of French bread rubbed with garlic.

• **Makes 6 servings**

8 green bell peppers (about 2¾ pounds)
4 fresh red finger-type or red jalapeño chiles (about ¼ pound)
8 ripe tomatoes (about 3¼ pounds), peeled (page 241),
    seeded, and quartered
6 tablespoons extra-virgin olive oil
2 bay leaves
Salt and freshly ground black pepper
1 teaspoon freshly ground cumin seeds

1. Preheat the oven to 425°F.

2. Place the bell peppers and chiles on a baking sheet, and roast in the oven, turning the peppers and chiles occasionally so that they cook evenly, until the skins are black, 25 to 30 minutes. Alternatively, if you are grilling, char the peppers and chiles on the grill. Remove the charred skins, stems, and seeds, and quarter all the peppers and chiles.

3. Place the peppers, chiles, tomatoes, olive oil, and bay leaves in a large 12-inch round baking casserole (preferably earthenware). Season with salt and pepper, and toss a bit. Cover and bake for 30 minutes. Remove from the oven, stir in the cumin, and let stand, covered, for 30 minutes. Serve from the casserole or transfer the vegetables with a slotted spoon to a serving platter.

Four-Onion Gratin

This gratin of four onions is a big hit every year at Thanksgiving, although I don't make it when I have small Thanksgivings. You won't believe how much you like onions after tasting this. It all looks so simple that you'll wonder where that great taste comes from. This dish has appeared on our family's Thanksgiving table for at least 25 years. I no longer remember, but I think the original recipe is from an old *Gourmet* magazine from the 1970s. • **Makes 8 servings**

3 tablespoons unsalted butter
½ pound shallots, chopped
1 large yellow onion, peeled, halved lengthwise, and sliced thin
6 leeks, white and light green parts only, split lengthwise, well washed, and chopped
2 garlic cloves, peeled and finely chopped
1 pound small white onions, peeled and left whole
2 cups heavy cream
Salt and freshly ground black pepper
¼ cup finely chopped fresh parsley
1 tablespoon bread crumbs

1. Preheat the oven to 475°F. Butter a 12 x 9 x 2-inch baking casserole.

2. In a large skillet, melt the butter over medium-low heat, then add the shallots, onion, leeks, and garlic, and cook, stirring occasionally, until softened, about 40 minutes. Add the small white onions and cook until just tender, about 15 minutes more. Stir in the cream. Bring to a boil and simmer the mixture until the cream is thickened, 15 to 20 minutes. Season with salt and pepper and stir in the parsley.

3. Spoon the onion mixture into the buttered casserole. Sprinkle the bread crumbs lightly over the top and bake the mixture until the cream is bubbling around the edges and the crumbs are golden, 15 to 20 minutes. Serve hot.

Dessert Casseroles

Cranberry-Apple-Walnut Crisp

Although this dessert casserole is a Thanksgiving favorite in New England, it's actually popular throughout the fall. Americans from other parts of the country often wonder about all the spices one finds in New England desserts. The explanation is easy. In the early nineteenth century, mariners and traders from Salem, Boston, New Bedford, and other New England towns made riches in the spice trade sailing for months to the Indonesian archipelago. That's why Connecticut is known as the Nutmeg State. This crisp is excellent served with vanilla ice cream. • **Makes 6 servings**

2 cups fresh or frozen cranberries, defrosted
4 apples (such as Granny Smith, Cortland, or Empire), cored,
    peeled, and thinly sliced (about 4 cups sliced)
⅓ cup chopped walnuts
⅓ cup fresh orange juice
¼ cup packed light brown sugar
2 tablespoons dark rum
1 teaspoon grated orange zest
1 teaspoon ground cinnamon
⅛ teaspoon grated nutmeg
½ teaspoon salt
1 cup sugar
¾ cup all-purpose flour
5 tablespoons unsalted butter, at room temperature

1. Preheat the oven to 350°F. Lightly butter a 12 × 9 × 2-inch baking casserole.

2. In a bowl, toss the cranberries, apples, walnuts, orange juice, brown sugar, rum, orange zest, cinnamon, and nutmeg together. Pour this mixture into the buttered baking casserole. Sprinkle with salt.

3. In a bowl, blend the sugar, flour, and butter together with a fork or pastry cutter until it looks like coarse dry oatmeal. Spoon this mixture over the fruits, covering them entirely. Bake until the top is brown and the juices around the sides are bubbling, about 40 minutes. Remove from the oven and let cool until it is just warm before serving.

Pear Crisp

Every summer in mid-August I would take my three kids to Cape Cod, and just before leaving we would hope that the fruit from my garden's pear tree in Arlington, Massachusetts, were both nearly ripe and unmolested by the squirrels. I would send the kids into the tree to get the pears and we'd bring them to the Cape with us so we could make this pear crisp. If the pears were too ripe the crisp would be too liquidy. We also always served this for Thanksgiving. It's very nice with ice cream, and can also be made with apples. You can use any kind of pear. • **Makes 6 servings**

4 cups sliced cored and unpeeled near-ripe pears
¼ cup water
1 teaspoon ground cinnamon
½ teaspoon salt
1 cup sugar
¾ cup all-purpose flour
5 tablespoons unsalted butter, at room temperature

1. Preheat the oven to 350°F. Lightly butter a 13 × 9 × 2-inch baking casserole.

2. Place the pears in the bottom of the buttered dish. Sprinkle with the water, cinnamon, and salt.

3. In a bowl, blend the sugar, flour, and butter together with a fork or pastry cutter until it looks like coarse dry oatmeal. Spoon the flour mixture over the pears, covering them entirely. Bake until the top is brown and the juices around the sides are bubbling, about 40 minutes. Serve warm.

Apple Crumble

A crumble is simply a version of a crisp. This recipe is adapted from the apple crumble made by the Stay-Inn-Style Bed & Breakfast in Fayetteville, Arkansas. An apple crumble begs to be served with vanilla ice cream, so consider that part of the dish. You can also use twelve apricots instead of the apples. • **Makes 6 servings**

1 cup all-purpose flour
¾ cup packed light brown sugar
½ cup rolled oats
½ teaspoon salt
4 tablespoons (½ stick) unsalted butter, at room temperature
4 Granny Smith apples, peeled, cored, and cut into wedges
Ground cinnamon for sprinkling
¼ cup water

1 Preheat the oven to 350°F. Butter a 12 x 9 x 2-inch baking casserole.

2 In a large bowl, mix the flour, brown sugar, oats, and salt together. Cut in the butter, using a fork or pastry cutter, until the mixture looks crumbly.

3 Spread half of the dough mixture on the bottom of the buttered baking casserole. Lay the apples wedges in rows on top of the dough mixture. Sprinkle with cinnamon and drizzle the water over. Cover with the remaining dough mixture. Bake until the juices around the sides are bubbling and the top is crispy golden brown, about 40 minutes. Serve warm or at room temperature.

Apple Cobbler

The first known apple orchard in New England was planted prior to 1630 by Reverend William Blackstone, Boston's first settler, who was living there before the establishment of the town in 1630. Blackstone was part of a settling expedition in 1623, three years after the Pilgrims landed at Plymouth. The expedition returned to England, but Blackstone stayed and was responsible for introducing the apple known as the Yellow Sweeting. The orchard was located on the most westerly summits of Trimountain, later known as West Hill, in today's Beacon Hill section of Boston. According to records, it was still bearing fruit in 1765. Nevertheless, some food historians believe that cobbler was first made in the American West in the nineteenth century, utilizing quick biscuit mixes that lined a deep-dish pan in which the apples were placed. This recipe is always a hit, and since not everyone in our family is fond of a heavy pumpkin pie for Thanksgiving, we make apple cobbler. • **Makes 6 servings**

For the dough

1 cup all-purpose flour
2 tablespoons sugar
1½ teaspoons baking powder
¼ teaspoon salt
4 tablespoons (½ stick) cold unsalted butter
¼ cup whole milk
1 large egg, lightly beaten

For the filling

6 Granny Smith apples, peeled, cored, and
    cut into wedges or slices
1 cup sugar

2 tablespoons all-purpose flour

1 teaspoon ground cinnamon

¼ teaspoon grated nutmeg

1 tablespoon unsalted butter

1 Preheat the oven to 400°F.

2 To make the dough, sift the flour, sugar, baking powder, and salt into a bowl, then cut in the butter with a fork or pastry cutter until it looks like a coarse dry oatmeal. In a bowl, mix the milk and egg, then add it to the dry ingredients, stirring just to moisten.

3 To make the filling, in another bowl, combine the apples, sugar, flour, cinnamon, and nutmeg. Place this mixture in a large skillet and cook over medium heat, turning the apples occasionally, until the apples are tender and the whole mixture looks syrupy, about 8 minutes. Pour into a round 9-inch ceramic or glass pie pan or baking casserole and spoon the dough on top.

3 Dot the top with butter and bake until the top is golden brown and speckled black here and there and bubbling, about 20 minutes. Serve warm.

Apple Pandowdy

I've never quite understood what the real difference is between apple cobbler and apple pandowdy, since the name is applied to both methods of drop biscuits as in the Apple Cobbler recipe (page 408) and pre-baked biscuits as in this recipe. One thought is that a pandowdy is simply a dowdy-looking cobbler made in a pan. In Rhode Island, apple pandowdy was made with molasses instead of sugar and it was called cob pie. In any case, apple pandowdy is always served with whipped cream or vanilla ice cream.

• Makes 6 servings

For the biscuits

2 cups sifted all-purpose flour
1 tablespoon baking powder
½ teaspoon salt
5 tablespoons cold unsalted butter
¾ cup whole milk

For the apples

6 Granny Smith apples, peeled, cored, and sliced
½ cup sugar
½ teaspoon ground cinnamon
2 tablespoons unsalted butter

1. Preheat the oven to 450°F. Lightly butter a baking sheet.

2. To prepare the biscuits, sift the flour, baking powder, and salt into a bowl. Add 4 tablespoons of butter, working it into the dough with a fork or pastry cutter, until it looks pebbly. Add the milk and incorporate it to form a soft dough. Turn the dough out onto a floured surface and flip back and forth, kneading gently, until the outer surface looks smooth. Roll out the dough until it is ½ inch thick. Cut out 12 biscuits with a 2-inch round biscuit cutter, reforming the dough when necessary. Place the biscuits on the buttered baking sheet and bake until very slightly golden, 12 minutes. Remove and set aside.

3. Reduce the oven heat to 350°F. Generously butter a 12 x 9 x 2-inch baking casserole.

4. To prepare the apples, arrange them in the buttered baking casserole. Sprinkle with the sugar and cinnamon, and dot with the 2 tablespoons of butter. Cover with the biscuits. Cut several gashes on the tops of the biscuits to allow steam to escape. Dot the tops of the biscuits with the remaining 1 tablespoon of butter. Bake until the tops are golden and the apples are bubbling, about 40 minutes. Serve hot or warm

Peach Delights

This peach casserole is a kind of reverse clafoutis (page 422) in that the fruit goes in first and then a batter is poured over it before baking. Finally, granulated sugar is sprinkled on top after it bakes. I prefer eating this casserole either hot or very warm out of the oven. I usually serve it with vanilla ice cream. You can peel peaches by dropping them into boiling water for about 30 seconds to a minute, then scraping the peel off with a paring knife. • Makes 4 servings

1 tablespoon unsalted butter
½ cup all-purpose flour plus more for dusting
1 large egg
⅔ cup sugar
¼ teaspoon vanilla extract
⅛ teaspoon salt
¼ cup whole milk
1½ pounds ripe peaches, peeled, pitted, and sliced

1 Preheat the oven to 350°F. Coat a 10-inch round baking casserole with 1 tablespoon of butter. Lightly flour the baking casserole, tapping out any excess.

2 In a medium bowl, beat the egg with ⅓ cup of sugar. Slowly add ½ cup of flour, stirring constantly. Once it is blended, stir in the vanilla and salt. Pour in the milk slowly, beating with a fork until it has the consistency of crêpe batter.

3 Layer the peaches in the buttered baking casserole in concentric rings. Cover with the batter. Bake until the top is light golden, about 30 minutes. Sprinkle the top with the remaining sugar and serve hot.

Peach Crumble

In the summer, my local farmers market has the most inviting and juicy peaches that can be eaten only while standing over the kitchen sink to catch the juice running down your chin. But this recipe is perfect for very slightly under-ripe peaches. I would serve the peach crumble with vanilla ice cream. It's also pretty good as a leftover breakfast. • **Makes 6 servings**

2 pounds slightly ripe peaches, pitted and cut into ½-inch-thick slices
¼ cup sugar
1 tablespoon freshly squeezed lemon juice
½ cup all-purpose flour
½ cup packed light brown sugar
¼ teaspoon ground cinnamon
4 tablespoons (½ stick) unsalted butter, cut into smaller pieces
½ cup rolled oats

1 Preheat the oven to 400°F.

2 In a bowl, toss the peaches with the sugar and lemon juice, then spread evenly in a 12 × 9 × 2-inch baking casserole.

3 In a bowl, mix the flour with the brown sugar and cinnamon. Add the butter and blend it with a fork or pastry cutter until the mixture looks crumbly. Add the oats and mix well. Sprinkle this mixture over the peaches. Bake until golden brown and bubbly on the edges, 30 to 35 minutes. Serve hot, warm, or at room temperature.

Stuffed Peaches in Raspberry Sauce

This is a midwinter quick dessert casserole that uses canned peaches and frozen raspberries. As a cook, I am known to make things from scratch and not with canned or frozen foods, so I was teased when I made this casserole. The snickering stopped when they started eating and barely left me any. You can save some of the heavy syrup from the can and use it in the raspberry sauce if you want. • **Makes 8 servings**

1¼ cups sugar

½ cup water

¾ pound frozen raspberries (about 1¼ cups), defrosted

½ pound mascarpone cheese

½ teaspoon vanilla extract

One 29-ounce can cling peach halves in heavy syrup, drained, saving the syrup if desired

½ cup sliced almonds

① Preheat the oven to 375°F.

② In a small saucepan, combine ¾ cup of sugar and the water. Bring to a boil over high heat, and boil, stirring once or twice, until it is very syrupy or reaches 230°F on a candy thermometer. Add the raspberries and stir, then cook until bubbling and frothing vigorously, about 3 minutes. Turn the heat off and let it cool a bit.

③ Pass the raspberry mixture through a food mill or strainer, discarding the remaining pulp and seeds. Return the sauce to a clean small saucepan, bring to a boil over high heat, and boil for 3 minutes. Turn the heat off and let cool. You should have about 1 cup of raspberry sauce.

④ In a bowl, mix together the mascarpone cheese, the remaining ½ cup of sugar, and the vanilla until very well blended. Set aside until needed.

⑤ Spread about ¼ cup of the raspberry sauce over the bottom of an 11 x 7 x 2-inch baking casserole to cover. Arrange the peach halves, cut side up, in the baking casserole. Bake until very hot, about 20 minutes.

⑥ Remove the baking casserole from the oven and stuff the peaches with the mascarpone mixture while they are still hot, dividing the mascarpone mixture evenly among the 8 peach halves and working quickly. Sprinkle the almonds on top, pushing them gently into the cheese. Bake until the cheese starts to melt, about 4 minutes or less. Serve with the remaining raspberry sauce.

Nectarine and Almond Casserole

This luscious casserole disappears very quickly as people just can't stop helping themselves. I say it yields six servings, but if those last two people aren't fast enough it will feed four. This dessert can also be made with peaches. In either case, the fruits should be ripe, but not over-ripe. A lot of the lusciousness comes from the interaction of the amaretti cookies with the sweet juice of the nectarines, so make sure you use good-quality amaretti cookies that are usually found in Italian markets. • **Makes 4 to 6 servings**

9 to 10 ripe nectarines (about 2½ pounds)
1 cup crushed amaretti cookies
½ cup sugar
3 tablespoons apricot brandy
½ cup sliced almonds
4 tablespoons (½ stick) unsalted butter
¼ cup heavy cream
¼ cup water
¼ pound mascarpone cheese

1. Preheat the oven to 350°F. Lightly butter a 12 x 9 x 2-inch baking casserole.

2. Cut the nectarines in half from the stem end. Twist slightly so they separate, and remove the pit. Arrange the nectarine halves, cut side up, in the baking casserole, then sprinkle the crushed amaretti cookies over each half. Sprinkle the sugar over the fruit. Drizzle the apricot brandy over the fruit, and finally sprinkle the sliced almonds over. Dot each nectarine half with a very thin slice of butter. Drizzle the cream over everything. Pour the water into the baking casserole in between the fruit but not on them. Bake until bubbling and slightly crispy and the fruit is soft, about 40 minutes.

3. Remove the baking casserole from the oven. Tilt the baking casserole slightly and remove ¼ cup of the juice and stir it into the mascarpone cheese, mixing well. Serve the nectarine casserole hot or warm with the mascarpone sauce.

Blackberry and Cream Cheese Crêpes Casserole

This berry crêpe is a wonderful dessert casserole for a dinner party because nearly everything can be made a head of time, and then you just stuff, roll, and bake at the last minute. It works well with any kind of berry too. • **Makes twelve 7-inch crêpes to serve 6**

For the crêpes

2 large eggs
1 cup whole milk
1 cup all-purpose flour
2 tablespoons granulated sugar
2 tablespoons unsalted butter, melted
1 tablespoon rum
½ teaspoon salt
Vegetable oil or butter

For the stuffing

1 pound fresh or frozen blackberries (defrosted)
½ cup granulated sugar
¼ pound cream cheese, cut into 12 pieces
Confectioners' sugar

1 To make the crêpes, in a blender, blend the eggs for a few seconds, then add the milk, flour, sugar, butter, rum, and salt and blend until frothy. You can also blend in a bowl using a hand whisk if you don't have a blender. Cover and let stand at room temperature for 30 minutes.

2 To make the stuffing, in another medium bowl, crush the blackberries. If using fresh berries, toss the berries with the granulated sugar; if using frozen, let the berries drain a bit in a strainer before tossing them in a bowl with the sugar. Let the blackberries rest with the sugar for 30 minutes.

③ Brush some oil over a 7-inch crêpe pan or any non-stick skillet to coat lightly, or use a buttered folded paper towel to lightly coat the pan. Heat the pan over medium-high heat for a few minutes until very hot. Pour in a scant ¼ cup of batter and swirl the pan as you do so the batter spreads quickly to all surfaces of the pan. If necessary, spread further with a spatula, carefully drawing the edge of the spatula over the loose batter until it coats the whole surface and forms a very thin layer. Cook until the bottom is golden brown. Check by lifting up the edge of the crêpe with a spatula to look at the bottom, and then flip it if it is ready. Cook the second side until brown dots appear everywhere. The first side will be evenly brown and the second side will be spotted brown. The inside of the crêpe will be the spotted side. Transfer the crêpe to a plate, coat the pan with oil or butter as needed, and continue cooking all the crêpes. Let each crêpe cool down quite a bit before you stack them, otherwise they might stick together. (If you're not using the crêpes right away, stack them on a sheet of aluminum foil then cover with another sheet of aluminum foil and seal the edges well. Freeze until needed and defrost at room temperature before separating them.)

④ Meanwhile, preheat the oven to 350°F. Lightly butter a 12 × 9 × 2-inch baking casserole.

⑤ Place a crêpe in front of you on a work surface. Spoon about 2 table-spoons of the blackberry mixture and a piece of cream cheese on the crêpe. Fold the crêpe twice to form a triangle, or roll them up. Arrange the crêpe in the buttered baking casserole. Continue in this manner with the remaining crêpes, using about three-fourths of the blackberry mixture and all of the cream cheese, and arranging them attractively in the baking casserole.

⑥ Bake until heated through, about 25 minutes. Pour and spoon the re-maining blackberry mixture over the casserole and return to the oven for 5 minutes. Remove from the oven, sprinkle with confectioners' sugar, and serve hot.

Wild Strawberry and Cream Cheese Crêpe Casserole with Vanilla Sauce

Wild strawberries are usually available at farmers markets. They look like miniature elongated raspberries. In fact, raspberries are what you should use if you can't find wild strawberries. • **Makes 4 servings**

½ cup whipped cream cheese
6 tablespoons sugar
½ teaspoon almond extract
8 Crêpes (page 392)
2 cups wild strawberries or raspberries

For the sauce
½ cup crème fraîche
¼ cup sugar
½ teaspoon vanilla extract

1. Preheat the oven to 350°F. Butter a 12 × 9 × 2-inch baking casserole.

2. In a bowl, stir together the cream cheese, sugar, and almond extract. Arrange a crêpe in front of you on a work surface. Spread 2 or 3 tablespoons of the cream cheese mixture over the crêpe, then sprinkle some wild strawberries over. Fold the crêpe twice to form a triangle. Arrange the crêpe in the buttered baking casserole. Continue with the remaining crêpes, cream cheese mixture, and strawberries, arranging them attractively in the baking casserole.

3. Prepare the sauce by blending the crème fraîche, sugar, and vanilla in a bowl with a fork until the sugar has dissolved.

4. Bake the crêpes until the cream cheese starts to ooze from the sides, about 10 minutes. Spoon the vanilla sauce over the crêpes, bake another 5 minutes, then serve hot.

Almond and Cheese Crêpes

When you cut this crêpe with your fork, the sugary cheese oozes out invitingly. It's very simple to assemble and guests will enjoy it. The easiest way to roast almonds is by shaking them in a small cast-iron skillet over medium-high heat until they turn golden, which takes about 3 minutes, or you can place them on a tray in a toaster oven using high heat for a few minutes. • **Makes 4 servings**

½ cup whipped cream cheese
½ cup mascarpone cheese
10 tablespoons sugar
½ cup slivered or sliced almonds, toasted (see Note on page 000)
1 teaspoon almond extract
8 Crêpes (page 392)

1. Preheat the oven to 350°F. Butter a 12 x 9 x 2-inch baking casserole.

2. In a bowl, stir together the cream cheese, mascarpone cheese, 8 tablespoons (½ cup) of sugar, half of the almonds, and the almond extract. Arrange a crêpe in front of you on a work surface. Spread 2 or 3 tablespoons of the cheese mixture over the surface of the crêpe, and then roll it up and place it in the baking casserole. Continue with the remaining crêpes and cheese mixture.

3. Sprinkle the remaining 2 tablespoons of sugar and ¼ cup of almonds over the crêpes and bake until the cheese is oozing, about 12 minutes. Serve hot.

Cherry Clafoutis

A clafoutis is a cross between a thick pancake and a pudding. In any case, this recipe is the famous clafoutis of black cherries as they make it in the Limousin region of central France. One can make clafoutis with prunes or apricots too, but cherries are traditional. In southern California, cherries have a short season, coming to the farmers markets beginning in early May. Although the cherries should be tart, use whatever cherries you have available, including canned cherries or jarred morello cherries, if need be. Now the question: to pit or not to pit? French cooks leave the pits in because there's more flavor but they can be removed to make eating easier. The clafoutis can be eaten hot, warm, or at room temperature. This recipe is adapted from Robert J. Courtine's *La cuisine des terroirs: Traditions et recettes culinaires de nos provinces*. • **Makes 4 to 6 servings**

1 pound fresh cherries, stems removed
3 tablespoons all-purpose flour
¼ cup granulated sugar
⅛ teaspoon salt
4 large eggs
2 cups whole milk
2 large egg yolks
3 tablespoons kirsch
¼ cup confectioners' sugar

1. Preheat the oven to 375°F. Butter a glass or ceramic 9-inch baking casserole or pie pan.

2. Spread the cherries in the buttered baking dish. Sift the flour into a bowl and stir in the sugar and salt. Beat in the eggs, one at a time, adding some of the milk with each egg. Beat until all of the eggs and milk are well blended. Beat in the egg yolks. Pour the batter through a strainer and over the cherries. Sprinkle the kirsch over the batter. Bake until puffed up and dappled brown, 45 minutes to 1 hour (check after 45 minutes). Sprinkle the confectioners' sugar through a fine mesh strainer and over the clafouti, and serve hot.

Baked Figs

This is an extraordinary dessert, not just because it tastes so great, but also because it's so simple. I usually serve the figs with some room-temperature robiola cheese along with a few green grapes per person. The robiola cheese is a soft cow and sheep's milk cheese that can be found in fine Italian markets or cheese stores. You can also buy robiola cheese at igourmet.com and sometimes at Whole Food stores. You can replace it with any mild soft goat cheese. • **Makes 8 to 10 servings**

30 fresh figs, cut in half
¾ cup sugar
2 cups heavy cream, whipped until very thick
    but not forming peaks

1 Preheat the oven to 350°F.

2 Arrange the figs in a 10-inch round baking casserole, flesh side up. Sprinkle each fig half with about ½ teaspoon of sugar, but using all ¾ cup of sugar. Bake until the figs caramelize, about 25 minutes. Set the figs aside to cool, then place them in the refrigerator until cold. Place a dollop of whipped cream on each fig half and serve cold.

Rice Pudding Casserole

This deliciously sweet New England rice pudding comes out of the oven a golden brown color from the caramelized sugar. It's baked slowly, allowing the crust that forms to be stirred back into the pudding, giving it both a delicious taste and pleasing texture. It's gooey, studded with raisins, and utterly irresistible with whipped cream. • **Makes 8 servings**

3 cups whole milk

1 cup heavy cream

¼ cup uncooked short- or medium-grain rice

1 cup sugar

½ cup golden raisins

½ teaspoon freshly grated nutmeg

¼ teaspoon salt

2 cups heavy cream, whipped until very thick but not forming peaks

1 Preheat the oven to 250°F.

2 Mix together all of the ingredients, except for 2 cups of whipped cream, in a 12 x 9 x 2-inch baking casserole. Bake slowly, stirring carefully and often so that the brown crust that forms is folded back into the entire pudding, for 3½ hours; do not stir during the last 30 minutes of baking. Let cool to room temperature and serve with the whipped cream. You can reheat it just slightly if making it ahead.

Sicilian Rice Pudding

This pudding is a favorite of Sicilian children and will become a favorite of yours too. It's called *risu ammanticatu* which means whipped rice. Although you don't whip it at all, the finished pudding will look whipped. The almonds, cinnamon, candied fruit, and the rice itself are all a reminder of how significant the Arab influence was on Sicilian cooking. The cocoa is a Spanish influence. You can serve the pudding cold or at room temperature.

• **Makes 6 servings**

3 cups whole milk

1⅓ cups sugar

1 cup uncooked short-grain rice, such as Vialone or
    Arborio rice, rinsed well or soaked in tepid water for
    30 minutes, drained

1 tablespoon unsalted butter

Pinch of salt

1 tablespoon unsweetened cocoa powder

2 cups blanched whole almonds, toasted until light brown
    (page 295), finely chopped

⅓ cup chopped candied fruit

1½ teaspoons grated lemon zest

⅛ teaspoon ground cinnamon

① Preheat the oven to 450°F.

② In a saucepan, combine the milk, sugar, rice, butter, and salt, and bring to a boil over high heat. Reduce the heat to low and simmer, covered, until the rice has absorbed the liquid and is fluffy when pushed with a fork, 30 minutes to 1¼ hours, depending on the rice you use. Let cool.

③ Stir in the cocoa, half of the almonds, half of the candied fruit, the lemon zest, and cinnamon. Mix thoroughly. Transfer to a 12 × 9 × 2-inch baking casserole (or 6 individual ramekins) and place in the oven until the top turns very light brown, about 10 minutes. Remove from the oven, let cool again, then garnish with the remaining almonds and candied fruit. Serve at room temperature or cold.

Cranberry Crisp with Orange Flower Water Cream

This crisp is an old favorite at Thanksgiving, especially if you're like my family and feel that pecan pie or pumpkin pie is too filling after the feast. The original recipe, I believe, comes from a *Gourmet* magazine from the 1940s or 1950s. Orange flower water is sold in many supermarkets and definitely in Middle Eastern markets—just ask for it, as it may be shelved in a hard to find place in the supermarket. • **Makes 6 servings**

For the crisp

1 cup sugar
½ cup fresh orange juice
½ teaspoon ground cinnamon
2 cups fresh or frozen cranberries (defrosted)
8 tablespoons (1 stick) unsalted butter, melted
3 cups fresh bread crumbs (see Note)

For the sauce

1 large egg yolk
2 tablespoons sugar
1 cup heavy cream, whipped until very thick but
    not forming peaks
1 teaspoon orange flower water

1. Preheat the oven to 375°F. Lightly butter a 12 × 9 × 2-inch baking casserole.

2. To prepare the crisp, in a saucepan, bring the sugar, orange juice, and cinnamon to a boil. Add the cranberries and cook at a boil, stirring constantly, for 2 minutes.

3. In a bowl, pour the melted butter over the bread crumbs and toss well. Arrange a layer of buttered bread crumbs on the bottom of the buttered baking casserole, then spoon the cranberry mixture over the bread crumbs. Cover the cranberries with the remaining bread crumbs. Cover with aluminum foil and bake for 20 minutes. Uncover and continue baking until golden brown and crisp, about 15 minutes.

4. Meanwhile, to prepare the sauce, in a bowl, beat the egg yolk with the sugar until pale yellow, then fold in the whipped cream and orange flower water. Refrigerate until needed. Serve the hot cranberry crisp with the cold orange cream sauce.

Note: This amount can be made from crumbling six ½-inch-thick slices of 5¼ × 3-inch French or Italian bread in a food processor.

Blueberry Flummery

This New England dessert was made in colonial times and might also be called grunt, slump, fool, or buckle. Although *flummery* comes from a Welsh word meaning a soft oatmeal or mumbo jumbo, many early New England cooks just made up goofy names for dishes, so they have no real meaning. For example, in New England blueberries were once called whortleberries. Another suggestion for these strange names of soft-textured desserts places their origins among the Shakers who made them for their toothless elders. There are many recipes, and variations set each apart—for example, slump and grunt are often steamed rather than baked like this flummery. In any case, the dessert is related to the dessert puddings or porridge of seventeenth-century Wales. • **Makes 6 servings**

1 quart fresh or frozen blueberries, defrosted (about 1¼ pounds)
1 cup sugar
3 tablespoons unsalted butter, at room temperature
8 slices dense white loaf bread, trimmed of crusts
1 cup heavy cream, whipped with ¼ teaspoon freshly grated
    nutmeg until very thick but not forming peaks

1. Preheat the oven to 350°F. Generously butter a 9 x 9 x 2-inch baking casserole.

2. Place the blueberries in a colander and rinse them (you do not need to rinse the frozen ones). Transfer to a saucepan with the sugar and cook over low heat, stirring, until the sugar melts, about 5 minutes, then cook until bubbling and liquidy but the berries are still whole, 8 to 10 minutes.

3. Butter the bread and arrange half of the slices in the buttered baking casserole, fitting the slices snugly. Pour half of the blueberries and their sugar syrup over the bread, then cover with another layer of bread, and finish topping with the remaining blueberries and syrup.

4. Bake the casserole until mushy-looking on top, about 20 minutes. Remove from the oven and cool. Once it is at room temperature, chill in the refrigerator for at least 2 hours. Serve with the nutmeg-flavored whipped cream.

Sarah Pillsbury's Blueberry Cobbler with Raspberry Thumbprints

When I lived in New England, a blueberry cobbler could always be found on a diner's menu. It's also made a lot at home simply because it's so easy. The cobbles of a cobbler should be the flattened balls of short dough put on top of the blueberries. They should look like cobblestones, and if you lay them in an offset fashion they're quite attractive and appetizing too. The blueberries give off a lot of liquid and you'll need to add cornstarch to thicken the juices. This recipe is made for July 4th by my friend Sarah Pillsbury, who is the best pie maker I know. Serve with whipped cream or vanilla ice cream, or both. • **Makes 4 to 6 servings**

For the blueberries

2 pounds fresh blueberries
¼ cup sugar
2 tablespoons cornstarch
1 tablespoon freshly squeezed lemon juice

For the dough

1½ cups all-purpose flour
1 tablespoon sugar
1½ teaspoons baking powder
1/2 teaspoon salt
8 tablespoons (1 stick) cold unsalted butter, diced
1 cup whole milk
¼ cup raspberry preserves

1. Preheat the oven to 375°F.

2. Rinse the blueberries. In a bowl, toss the blueberries with the sugar, cornstarch, and lemon juice and let sit until needed.

3. In a bowl, mix together the flour, sugar, baking powder, and salt. Cut in the butter using two knives or a pastry cutter until the mixture looks like coarse oatmeal. Stir in the milk, form the dough into a ball, and knead a few times.

4. Pour the blueberries into an 11-inch pie pan and level them off to form an even top. Grease your hands with butter in order to form the dough without sticking. Form the dough into ³/₈-inch-thick, rough-edged patties 2¹/₂ inches in diameter (in other words when you pull the dough apart don't round them out, just plop them in your hand) and with your thumb form an indentation in the middle. Place the dough patties on top of the blueberries. You will have 9 or 10 biscuits. Spoon about a teaspoon or a little more raspberry preserves in the center of the indentation. Bake until the dough patties are golden brown and the blueberries are bubbling, 20 to 25 minutes. Serve hot.

Cottage Pudding

This old New England dessert comes from a recipe published in the *Hartford Times* of Connecticut in the 1850s. It has a pleasant light taste that is not too sweet. • **Makes 4 to 6 servings**

For the lemon sauce

½ cup sugar

1 tablespoon cornstarch

1 teaspoon grated lemon zest

1 cup cold water

2 tablespoons freshly squeezed lemon juice

2 tablespoons unsalted butter

Pinch of freshly grated nutmeg

¼ cup raisins

For the pudding

8 tablespoons (1 stick) unsalted butter, at room temperature

½ cup sugar

½ cup heavy cream

1 large egg, beaten to blend

1½ cups all-purpose flour

1½ teaspoons baking powder

½ teaspoon salt

½ cup milk

1 teaspoon vanilla extract

1. Preheat the oven to 350°F. Butter a 9-inch square baking casserole or cake pan.

2. To prepare the lemon sauce, in a saucepan, mix the sugar with the cornstarch and lemon zest. Add the water and bring to a gentle boil over medium-high heat. Reduce the heat to medium-low and cook, stirring constantly, until thickened, about 5 minutes. Remove from the heat. Add the lemon juice and butter, and stir until the butter melts. Stir in the nutmeg. Add the raisins and keep warm while you prepare the pudding.

3. To prepare the pudding, in a bowl, beat the butter until light and fluffy. Add the sugar and cream and continue beating until the mixture is lighter in color, about 2 minutes. Mix in the beaten egg.

4. In another bowl, sift the flour with the baking powder and salt. Stir the flour mixture and milk into the sugar mixture until well blended. Add the vanilla and blend it into the pudding mixture.

5. Pour the pudding mixture into the buttered baking casserole and bake until firm, very light yellow, and very slightly cracked on top, about 30 minutes. Serve hot with the lemon sauce.

Cherry Cottage Pudding
with Cherry Sauce

Many old-time New England puddings are disappearing, as warm desserts seem to become evermore old-fashioned. One bite of this delicious pudding and you'll see why "old-fashioned" is sometimes a good thing. This is the dessert to make in May and June when cherries are in season. If you can't get fresh cherries you can use frozen, jarred, or canned.

• **Makes 6 servings**

1 quart fresh cherries, pitted

3 cups water

8 tablespoons (1 stick) unsalted butter, at room temperature

⅔ cup plus ½ cup sugar

1 large egg, beaten to blend

½ teaspoon almond extract

1¾ cups all-purpose flour

1 teaspoon baking powder

½ teaspoon baking soda

¼ teaspoon salt

1 cup buttermilk

2 tablespoons cornstarch

1. Preheat the oven to 350°F. Butter a 12 × 9 × 2-inch baking casserole.

2. Place the pitted cherries in a large saucepan with the water and bring to a boil over high heat. Reduce the heat to low and simmer, stirring gently and occasionally, until the cherries are stewed and ready to burst, about 8 minutes. Drain the cherries, saving the juice for the sauce.

3. In a bowl, beat the butter and ⅔ cup of sugar together with an electric mixer or a fork until fluffy and light colored. Add the beaten egg and almond extract and beat well until smooth. Sift the flour, baking powder, baking soda, and salt into another bowl. Add the flour mixture to the creamed butter mixture alternately with the buttermilk, beating well after each addition. Fold in the stewed cherries.

4. Pour the pudding mixture into the buttered baking casserole. Bake until light brown on top, about 45 minutes.

5. Meanwhile, mix the cornstarch with the remaining ½ cup of the sugar in a saucepan. Add 3 cups of the reserved cherry juice and cook over low heat, stirring constantly, until slightly thickened, but a bit thinner than a syrup, about 10 minutes.

6. Remove the casserole from the oven, cut into squares, and serve hot with the cherry sauce.

Harwich Hermits

This sweet ancestor of the popular chocolate brownie (and blondie) is rich with the spices of the Indies, brought back by the Cape Cod sea captains of the early nineteenth century. It is said that Harwich hermits were packed away in tole canisters (sort of an old-fashioned cookie tin) by the sailors leaving on those long journeys. It is easiest to make this using an electric mixer, but you can use a wooden spoon too. This recipe is adapted from Eleanor Early's *New England Cookbook* published in 1954.

> • Makes about 50 hermits

8 tablespoons (1 stick) unsalted butter, at room temperature
½ cup sugar
2 large eggs, beaten to blend
½ cup molasses
2 cups all-purpose flour
1 teaspoon ground cinnamon
¾ teaspoon baking soda
¾ teaspoon cream of tartar
½ teaspoon freshly grated mace or nutmeg
½ teaspoon ground cloves
½ teaspoon salt
⅛ teaspoon ground allspice
½ cup currants, chopped
¼ cup raisins, chopped
¼ cup chopped walnuts
3 tablespoons chopped lemon zest

1. Preheat the oven to 350°F. Butter a 14 x 8-inch baking casserole or two smaller baking casseroles.

2. In a bowl, beat the butter and sugar together with an electric mixer until light. Add the eggs and molasses, beating to blend well.

3. In another bowl, sift the flour with the cinnamon, baking soda, cream of tartar, mace, cloves, salt, and allspice. Remove ¼ cup of the flour mixture and place it in a third bowl with the currants, raisins, walnuts, and lemon zest. Toss well so that the fruits don't stick to each other.

4. Add the remaining flour mixture and the flour-coated fruit mixture to the molasses mixture and stir to blend well. Spread evenly in the buttered baking casserole. The dough should only be about ½ inch thick. Bake until a knife comes out clean when stuck in the center, about 15 minutes. Cut into squares while it is still warm. Serve hot, warm, or room temperature.

Brownies

Given how simple brownies are it's amazing how varied they can be. Several times I've eaten what I considered to be the best brownies in the world at some potluck supper or another, where one never does find out who made them. And we have all eaten those horrible dry brownies that crumble. A brownie should be chocolatey and moist and hold together well. My kids and I give credit to their mother, my ex-wife Najwa al-Qattan, as a maker of the best brownies in the world. Her lentil soup had been chosen for *The 150 Best American Recipes: Indispensable Dishes from Legendary Chefs and Undiscovered Cooks* (Houghton Mifflin, 2006), so we're not surprised. She's been making them for thirty years but surprised me when she said the original recipe is from the Colby Hill Inn in Henniker, New Hampshire. Over the years, my son Seri has become a very good brownie maker. When the kids were little we would fight over whether to put the walnuts in or not (the kids didn't want nuts). The hardest part of making these brownies is obeying the last instruction in Step 2! • **Makes 30 brownies**

½ pound (2 sticks) unsalted butter
8 squares (½ pound) Baker's unsweetened chocolate
3½ cups sugar
4 large eggs
2 cups all-purpose flour
2 cups chopped walnuts
2 teaspoons salt
1 teaspoon vanilla extract

① Preheat the oven to 350°F. Butter a 15 × 11-inch cookie sheet with low sides.

② In a large saucepan, melt the butter and chocolate together over medium-low heat, stirring occasionally. Remove from the heat, add the sugar, and mix well. Add the eggs, one at a time, mixing well after each egg is added. Stir in the flour, nuts, salt, and vanilla, mixing well. Pour the mixture into the buttered cookie sheet. Bake until a knife inserted into the center comes out clean, 20 to 25 minutes. Let rest for 3 hours before cutting and serving.

Banana Casserole

This is my adaptation of the dessert I once had in a Cuban restaurant in Miami. The restaurant made it in individual ramekins, but it's called banana casserole. Serve it with vanilla ice cream. • **Makes 4 to 6 servings**

6 firm bananas, peeled and split lengthwise
½ cup packed brown sugar
8 tablespoons (1 stick) unsalted butter
½ cup raisins
½ cup chopped pecans
1 tablespoon brandy

1. Preheat the oven to 350°F. Lightly butter a 2-quart baking casserole.

2. Arrange half of the banana halves in the buttered baking casserole. Sprinkle half of the brown sugar on top and dot with the butter. Sprinkle with half of the raisins and all of the pecans. Repeat the layering with the remaining ingredients, except for the brandy. Bake until bubbling, about 30 minutes. Sprinkle with brandy, let rest 5 minutes, then serve hot.

Index